THE CRUCIBLE
OF PUBLIC POLICY

THE CRUCIBLE
OF PUBLIC POLICY

NEW YORK COURTS IN THE PROGRESSIVE ERA

BRUCE W. DEARSTYNE

excelsior editions

AN IMPRINT OF STATE UNIVERSITY OF NEW YORK PRESS

Published by State University of New York Press, Albany

Excelsior Editions is an imprint of State University of New York Press

For information, contact State University of New York Press, Albany, NY
www.sunypress.edu

Library of Congress Cataloging-in-Publication Data

Name: Dearstyne, Bruce W. (Bruce William), 1944– author.
Title: The crucible of public policy : New York courts in the progressive era /
    Bruce W. Dearstyne.
Description: Albany : State University of New York Press, [2022] | Series:
    Excelsior editions | Includes bibliographical references and index.
Identifiers: LCCN 2021044223 | ISBN 9781438488578 (hardcover : alk. paper) |
    ISBN 9781438488592 (ebook)
Subjects: LCSH: Political questions and judicial power—New York (State)—
    History—20th century. | New York (State). Court of Appeals—History—20th
    century.
Classification: LCC KFN5748 .D43 2022 | DDC 347.747/012—dc23/eng/20211015
LC record available at https://lccn.loc.gov/2021044223

10 9 8 7 6 5 4 3 2 1

CONTENTS

ACKNOWLEDGMENTS

The superb services of the New York State Archives were essential to completion of this book. Staff there made available the *Cases and Briefs on Appeal* from the New York Court of Appeals records held by the Archives. I am particularly indebted to James Folts, Head, Researcher Services, and William Gorman, Archivist, Researcher Services, for their assistance. These records include plaintiffs' and defendants' briefs and legal arguments for and against issues in cases before the court, cited in this book. Most had not been used by scholars before. They form an essential foundation for the book. I am very grateful for the Archives' assistance and support.

The Guilderland Public Library secured many books I needed through interlibrary loan. Personnel there were uniformly helpful. The library's services are always outstanding.

Cyra Nealon, my sister-in-law, and Mary Foglia, my niece, read the draft chapters of the book and identified changes and corrections that significantly improved the final product.

I am also very grateful to everyone at SUNY Press for their dedication and work that makes books like this possible. Editor Richard Carlin deserves special thanks for advising on the book in its initial stages. Jenn Bennett-Genthner, Production Editor, managed it through the production process. Michael Campochiaro, Senior Marketing Manager, led in marketing the book. Everyone at SUNY Press made the process easy. Thank you all!

My family has been a constant source of support as I worked on this book. My four grandchildren are always a source of inspiration. I hope this book will deepen their appreciation of the history of their state. Thank you for everything.

Stella Roberts

Maddie Roberts

Jack Gregory

Abbie Gregory

Finally, I dedicate this book to my wife, **Susan V. Dearstyne**. She read it all in draft, made many helpful recommendations, and also indexed it. Her patience, wisdom, insights, and encouragement have sustained my life and work for five decades. She has been essential to all my books including this one. Her love of New York history has been a constant incentive to push my research and writing into new areas. Without Susan's constant help, I could not have undertaken and completed the book.

INTRODUCTION

The Crucible of Public Policy: New York Courts in the Progressive Era discusses critical public policy issues that were thrashed out in the state's court system, mainly in the New York Court of Appeals, the state's highest court, during the Progressive Era, approximately 1900 to 1920.

Crucible in this context connotes a place of test or trial where forces interact to cause or influence change. The forces were usually private lawyers (representing individuals or corporations) and public lawyers—state attorneys general, district attorneys, and counsel for state agencies (representing the public). The issues at stake involved the force and interpretation of the law, the role of state government, and the liberties of individuals and organizations. The contests were important, some precedent setting, but fought with decorum in quiet courthouses, between lawyers with briefs brimming with legal arguments, appeals to precedents, and exhortations for judges to confirm or knock down state laws and regulations. The court of appeals was often the forum of last resort, the place where issues were finally hashed out and settled.

The stakes were high, for New York and beyond its borders. New York's highest court was arguably the second-most important in the nation, after only the United States Supreme Court. The legal scholar Stewart Sterk contends that during its first 150 years (beginning in 1847), the court of appeals had more impact in more areas of law than even the nation's highest court. "No federal court has exerted influence comparable to the Court of Appeals over the wide range of problems that confront most Americans in their everyday lives: contracts, torts, property trusts, wills, divorce law (to name a few)," he explains. "The leading law school casebooks—the sources that introduce law students into the profession—are

1

filled with Court of Appeals opinions, most of them chosen because they serve as the best exposition of important legal principles."[1] New York was the state that other states, and sometimes the US Supreme Court, watched to discern which way the judicial winds were blowing.

The Progressive Era was a time for reckoning with social and economic issues that had accumulated in the late nineteenth century as the state (and the nation) grew in population, cities came to dominate society, and complex industries rose to dominate the economy. Progressives went about the business of promoting integrity in politics, subordinating partisan and local interests to the general welfare, and making government more responsive to the people (e.g., fighting political bosses and pushing for direct primaries and other reforms to foster popular control). They were also proponents of using government to reconcile, rationalize, and improve people's lot and at the same time protect their liberty. President (and former New York governor) Theodore Roosevelt said in 1906 that "so far as this movement of agitation throughout the country takes the form of a fierce discontent with evil, of a firm determination to punish the authors of evil, whether in industry or politics, the feeling is to be heartily welcomed as a sign of healthy life."[2] Charles Evans Hughes, New York's great progressive Republican governor, in his 1907 inaugural address, endorsed forward-looking legislative action and "sympathy with every aspiration for the betterment of conditions and a sincere and patient effort to understand every need and to ascertain in the hard light of experience the means best adapted to meet it."[3]

New York was a pioneer in progressive legislation to regulate public health, safety, morals, and welfare. In dealing with businesses, progressives struck a middle course between laissez-faire (leave them undisturbed; they will treat the public and their workers fairly, and the state's economy will prosper) and socialism (government operating some enterprises). The middle course "accepted the existence of threatening businesses but tried to control their behavior. Corporations would be allowed to continue only under the watchful eye of government."[4] How companies treated their employees, e.g., maximum hours, working conditions, and safety measures, became a central governmental concern. The nineteenth century's pattern of industries concerned almost solely with production and profits gave way to a new twentieth-century paradigm of government setting parameters and limits in critical areas. The reformers were committed to addressing social issues and promoting the values of "commitment to community" and "mutualism and compromise" between labor and industry.[5]

New York was one of the first states to approach these issues through legislation. It tried to address the tension between too little state control and too much, the latter of which would contravene personal liberty and corporate autonomy. Therefore, the Empire State was also the place where some of the toughest regulatory and legal issues surfaced first in the courts and where regulatory laws were explored, endorsed, challenged, or bounced back to the legislature because they were deemed to be government overreach or unconstitutional. That stew of New York court cases, public policy, and politics makes the story particularly interesting.

Courts were often the final arbiters of difficult, portentous issues. The legal historian G. Edward White has called this time period "the era of guardian review" by the courts. White's focus is mostly on the US Supreme Court, but his characterization fits the New York Court of Appeals as well. The courts saw their mission as that of constitutional watchdogs, "guardians" of "timeless, foundational principles." This role was a "blend of traditional American conceptions of the functions of judges as interpreters of authoritative legal sources." But this was mixed with a "heightened sense" of the social context in this era of industry, class conflict, and the clash of interest groups. Judges determined the constitutional "right" and "justice" of laws. Guardian review thus projected a "role for judges as savants."[6]

The most contentious disputes about public policy issues in the courts were traceable to "the new conditions incident to the extraordinary industrial development" of modern times, the New York statesman Elihu Root noted in his address as president of the New York State Bar Association in 1912. These conditions "are continuously and progressively demanding the readjustment of the relations between great bodies of men and the establishment of new legal rights and obligations not contemplated when existing laws were passed or existing limitations upon the powers of government were prescribed in our Constitution." Individuals were caught up in vast, complex enterprises: "In place of the old individual independence of life, in which every intelligent and healthy citizen was competent to take care of himself and his family, we have come to a high degree of interdependence, in which the greater part of our people have to rely for all the necessities of life upon the systematized co-operation of a vast number of other men working through complicated industrial and commercial machinery."[7]

Many people were working for industrial companies, "great aggregations of capital in enormous industrial establishments working through vast agencies of commerce and employing great masses of men in movements of production and transportation and trade so great in the mass that each individual concerned in them is quite helpless by himself."[8]

This, in turn, necessitated the intervention of government with new laws to rebalance the rights of individuals with the power of the new organizations: "The relations between the employer and the employed, between owners of aggregated capital and the units of organized labor, between the small producer, the small trader, the consumer and the great transporting and manufacturing and distributing agencies, all present new questions for the solution of which the old reliance upon the free action of individual wills appears quite inadequate."[9]

It was up to legislators to make these new laws, but it fell to the courts to interpret and enforce them. Courtrooms became forums of last resort for contending parties thrashing out profound public issues, Root explained. He maintained that "it is because in the course of this process of readjustment occasionally a court finds that some new experiments in legislation or in administration contravene some long established limitation upon legislative or executive power, or finds that some crudely drawn statute is inadequate to produce the effect that was expected of it, or enforces some law which has unexpected results, that the present irritation and impatience toward the courts has been created." Courts had a special obligation to protect individual rights and enforce constitutional limits on governors and legislatures. They needed to validate laws that impinged on individual liberty or imposed "occasional inconvenience through their restraint upon our freedom of action." On the other hand, they needed to declare laws invalid when they exceeded those limits.[10]

New York Court of Appeals chief judge Alton B. Parker (1897–1904) understood the court's guardian/savant/arbiter status and what was expected of it. He projected an air of judicial objectivity and wisdom in the courtroom and expected his colleagues on the court to do the same. Parker used his court's visibility and stature to launch a campaign for the presidency on the Democratic ticket in 1904. That could not have happened from any other state's top court.

But Parker, as we shall see in several chapters in this book, also reflected the challenges, tensions, and inconsistencies of the court as it earnestly grappled with thorny issues. He characterized what the courts did as a stressful, high-stakes judicial balancing act. Courts were bound to support valid new laws and regulations approved by the people's elected legislators. "The courts are frequently confronted with the temptation to substitute their judgment for that of the legislature," Parker wrote in a 1904 court opinion, *People v. Lochner*. "A given statute, though plainly within the legislative power, seems so repugnant to a sound public policy as to strongly tempt the court to set aside the statute, instead of waiting, as the spirit of our institutions require, until the people can compel their representatives to repeal the obnoxious statute."[11]

But they also needed to hold up the state and federal constitutions as buttresses against legislation amounting to "the breaking down of the safeguards [on liberty and property rights] which the people secured by their constitutions." The courts are there to say to governors and legislatures " 'thus far and no farther can you go.' "[12] "We cannot leave our government to the professional politician," Parker explained, though not until several years after he had left the chief judge's post and his own failed presidential campaign was long past. We need "more wise deliberation and less hasty action" in legislatures and "eternal vigilance" to ward off "every assault upon the constitutional foundation of our liberty, prosperity and happiness."[13]

Sometimes, that meant approving a law that aligned with the state and federal constitutions but was obviously imperfect in practice. Other times, it meant declaring a popular law unconstitutional. The role of judicial umpire or traffic cop was essential but also uncomfortable.

It is glaringly apparent in retrospect that the judicial system whose operation this book discusses was a man's world. In fact, it was a white man's world, since attorneys of color were few in number and legislators and judges of color practically nonexistent until years later. There were few women attorneys and no women judges yet in the state court system. Women could not vote until 1917, so they were governed by laws made by men, even when those laws were ostensibly for their protection, such as limited working hours in factories. When they were involved in courts, the cases were defended or prosecuted by men and decided by men judges. But women played major roles in a number of the issues in the book as organizers for change, shapers of legislation, and, particularly in critical labor-reform areas, champions and advocates.

The structure of the state court system in this period had roots in the state's earliest years. It had evolved over the years and was embodied in the most recent version of the New York State Constitution, approved by voters in 1894, and then refined by subsequent amendments and legislative enactments.[14]

The first level, the Supreme Court of the State of New York, was vested with "general jurisdiction in law and equity."[15] Its title implies it was a single entity, but actually there was generally one state supreme court in each county. *Supreme Court* sounds like the top court, but these were (and still are) the state courts of original jurisdiction for most of the constitutionally significant cases of the sort covered in this book.

There were four regional appellate divisions of the supreme court, whose members were designated by the governor from justices of the supreme court, creating an intermediate appellate court system. The appellate divisions became the courts of final review on appeals on the basis of fact. (The judges on the supreme court and appellate division were officially titled *justices*, but they were commonly referred to as *judges*.)

The role of the court of appeals at the top of the structure was defined in the state constitution:

> The jurisdiction of the Court of Appeals, except where the judgment is of death, shall be limited to the review of questions of law. No unanimous decision of the Appellate Division of the Supreme Court that there is evidence supporting or tending to sustain a finding of fact or a verdict not directed by the court, shall be reviewed by the Court of Appeals. Except where the judgment is of death, appeals may be taken, as of right, to said court only from judgments or orders entered upon decisions of the Appellate Division of the Supreme Court, finally determining actions or special proceedings, and from orders granting new trials on exceptions, where the appellants stipulate that upon affirmance judgment absolute shall be rendered against them. The Appellate Division in any department may however, allow an appeal upon any question of law which, in its opinion, ought to be reviewed by the Court of Appeals.[16]

That court consisted of a chief judge and six associate judges (usually just referred to as *judges*), seven in all. Its jurisdiction was refined over subsequent years by constitutional amendment or legislative enactment, mainly to stem the flow of appeals to the highest court, which gave it a chronic backlog. Cases could be appealed to the court of appeals that involved questions of law, where the appellate division had reversed the original court or was itself divided in its decision, where the appellate division felt that the legal issues were so profound or unprecedented that the determination and guidance of the court of appeals were needed, or that were capital cases. The court of appeals could decline to hear an appeal but rarely did so. The court's jurisdiction was refined over the years through constitutional amendments and legislative enactments, but it remained the pinnacle of the crucible, the place where the most challenging issues were resolved.

The three-tiered structure worked tolerably well. Judges were elected, but the governor filled vacancies, and often the appointees ran for their positions at elections and thereby retained them. But appeals were common, and work piled up toward the top of the structure. Amendments to the constitution in 1899 permitted the governor, on appeal from an appellate division that help was needed, to make temporary additional appointments there and, on appeal from the chief judge of the court of appeals, to temporarily assign additional judges to that court until the calendar was reduced. A 1905 amendment authorized the legislature to increase the number of supreme court judges for any judicial district. It was common for a judge assigned temporarily to the court to later run for and be elected to that court when a vacancy occurred.

That all helped expedite things, but the court of appeals often had a chronic backlog, a reflection of the novelty and number of issues that were being considered in the court system.

Listed below are the chief judges and associate judges who served on the court of appeals in the 1890–1920 era. Party designations are noted, but their significance is limited since judges often ran unopposed, were affiliated with one party but endorsed by the other party (hence the note *Democrat/Republican* or *Republican/Democrat*), or changed political affiliation before joining the court. *Age limited* means they left when they met the mandatory retirement age—at that time, seventy years old (see tables I.1 and I.2).[17]

Table I.1. Chief Judges

Chief Judge	Years Served	Political Party	Notes
Charles Andrews	1881–82 and 1893–97	Republican	Age limited
Alton B. Parker	1898–1904	Democrat	Resigned to run for president
Edgar M. Cullen	1904–13	Democrat/ Republican	Appointed to fill vacancy, then elected, then age limited
Willard Bartlett	1914–16	Democrat	Age limited
Frank H. Hiscock	1917–26	Democrat/ Progressive	Age limited

Table I.2. Associate Judges

Judge	Years Served	Political Party	Comments
William S. Andrews	1917–28	Republican	Son of Chief Judge Charles Andrews
Edward T. Bartlett	1894–1910	Republican	
Willard Bartlett	1906–16	Democrat	Also served as chief judge
Benjamin N. Cardozo	1914–33	Democrat/ Republican	Also served as associate justice of the US Supreme Court
Emory A. Chase	1906–21	Republican	
Frederick Colin	1910–20	Republican	
William H. Cuddeback	1913–19	Democrat/ Independence League	
Edgar M. Cullen	1900–1913	Democrat/ Republican	Also served as chief judge
Robert Earl	1868–94	Democrat	
Abraham Elkus	1919–20	Democrat	
John Clinton Gray	1888–1913	Democrat	
Albert Haight	1895–1912	Republican	
Frank H. Hiscock	1906–26	Democrat/ Progressive	Also served as chief judge
John W. Hogan	1913–23	Democrat	
William B. Hornblower	1914	Democrat	
Celora E. Martin	1896–1904	Republican	

Name	Years	Party	Notes
Nathan L. Miller	1913–15	Republican	Also served as governor
Denis O'Brien	1889–1913	Democrat	Also served as New York attorney general
Rufus W. Peckham Jr.	1886–95	Democrat	Also served as associate justice of the US Supreme Court
Cuthbert W. Pound	1915–34	Republican/ Democrat	Also served as chief judge
Samuel Seabury	1914–16	Citizens' Union/ Municipal Ownership League/ Progressive/Democrat	
Irving G. Vann	1895–1912	Republican/Democrat	
William E. Werner	1900–16	Republican/Democrat	

Nice
mix.
Dems/ Repubs.

There are many issues and cases of importance in the court of appeals' work in the Progressive Era. This book is necessarily highly selective. The case selection follows these criteria:

- Deals with a key public issue of the era

- Explores important, complex issues of constitutional law

- Recognized as important at the time by the news media and the legal community

- Decision is illustrative of the view of the courts in assessing the validity of public policy and the degree to which policy may affect or restrict the rights and liberty of individuals or corporations

- Sets precedents

- Not explored in depth in historical accounts

Much of the discussion in the book is based on the extensive *Cases and Briefs* filed with the court of appeals by contending attorneys that explore policy and constitutional issues. They are preserved in the Court Records in the State Archives in Albany. Most have not been used by researchers before.

This book has twelve chapters and a conclusion:

Chapter 1, "Monitoring the Expansive State," introduces the role of the court of appeals as arbiter and mediator among the competing rights of the legislature to pass regulatory legislation, of individuals to personal liberty, and of business owners to manage their businesses without government interference.

Chapter 2, "The Right to Privacy," discusses the case of a young woman whose photo was used for advertising without her consent, which the court of appeals approved but the legislature the next year prohibited.

Chapter 3, "The Case That Helped Change Constitutional History and Launch a Quest for the Presidency," describes the 1904 case of *People v. Lochner*, where the court of appeals affirmed state regulatory authority, only to be overturned the next year by the US Supreme Court in the famous case of *Lochner v. New York*. The case brought national prominence to New York's chief judge, Alton B. Parker, helping him launch a presidential campaign in 1904.

Chapter 4, "The Chief Judge Runs for President," covers Chief Judge Alton B. Parker's unsuccessful run for the presidency in 1904.

Chapter 5, "Public Health and Individual Rights," analyzes how the courts handled the contentious issue of compulsory smallpox vaccinations for school students.

Chapter 6, "The Insanity Defense on Trial," analyzes how New York's legal community, its medical jurisprudence community, and its court system wrestled with the plea of insanity as a defense in a famous case and then contended with the claim that the insanity had been cured as a basis for seeking release from state custody.

Chapter 7, "The Debut of the Administrative State," explores the work of the New York State Commission on Gas and Electricity, the prototype of what would come to be called the administrative state, and the challenge to its constitutionality.

Chapter 8, "The Administrative State in Action," analyzes the early years of the state Public Service Commission, successor to the Commission on Gas and Electricity with much broader regulatory powers, created in 1907, and the role of the court in supporting its authority and work but occasionally limiting its power.

Chapter 9, "State Protection Denied for Women Workers," tells the story of New York's first attempt to restrict women from working nights in factories and the court's decision that it was unconstitutional.

Chapter 10, "State Protection Affirmed for Women Workers," is the next part of the story of the state's determination to restrict women's working hours, this time ending with the court approving the restriction.

Chapter 11, "Workers' Compensation Denied," is the story of New York's first law to protect workers injured or killed in workplace accidents, struck down by the court of appeals in 1911.

Chapter 12, "Workers' Compensation Affirmed," is the next part of the story, covering a state constitutional amendment to authorize workers' compensation, a new law, and validation of that law by both the New York Court of Appeals and the US Supreme Court.

The final section closes the story by noting the public's satisfaction with its state's highest court.

Many of the issues in this book reverberate today. The role of New York's highest court is still a challenging one. As Chief Judge Judith Kaye (1993–2008) wrote, "issues . . . that reach a state appeals court cannot be resolved simply by consulting a good dictionary or communing with the statutory text." Those courts decide difficult cases: "state court dockets comprise the battlefields of first resort in social revolutions." Courts exercise discretionary judgment: "state courts have openly and explicitly balanced considerations of social welfare and have fashioned new causes and action where common sense justice required." They may interpret the meaning of statutes broadly but, in the absence of a statute, courts should not "make law." On the other hand, "given the enormous volume of state court litigation, the unending array of novel fact patterns pushing the law to progress, and the inability of legislatures to react immediately to the many changes in society . . . courts interpreting statutes and filling the gaps have no choice but to 'make law' in circumstances where neither the statutory text nor the 'legislative will' provides a single clear answer."[18] The role of the courts is one of judgment and balance, says Kaye. That was also the case in the Progressive Era.

Chapter 1
MONITORING THE EXPANSIVE STATE

Figures 1.1–1.4. Four outstanding chief judges, pictured here from left to right, led the New York Court of Appeals in the Progressive Era: Alton B. Parker (1898–1904), Edgar M. Cullen (1904–13), Willard Bartlett (1914–16), and Frank H. Hiscock (1917–26). The court made landmark decisions on several public policy issues and was recognized as one of the most important in the nation. *Source:* Library of Congress Prints & Photographs Collection.

How far should the state go in regulating business and the economy for the benefit of the people? What happens when those regulations contravene personal liberties or interfere with the operation of business? These are the issues that New York courts, particularly the court of appeals, wrestled with in the late nineteenth and early twentieth centuries.

COURT OF APPEALS AS RUDDER, ARBITER, AND BUFFER

As the nineteenth century drew to a close, New York was growing robustly, its population increasing rapidly (particularly in New York City), and large-scale banks, businesses, and other commercial enterprises dominated the economy. State government was still a small-scale affair that had not caught up with the state's social and economic changes. That began to change in the last decades of the century with sporadic regulatory legislation.

The pace of new and expanded state programs and regulatory legislation accelerated markedly after 1900. This was the period of the Progressive movement. Progressives believed in using the government to advance social welfare, protect and improve people's lives, and rein in big business. The Republican governor Charles Evans Hughes (1907–10) led the enactment of a battery of reform laws. Democrats under the leadership of a new generation of urban-based reformers, such as Assemblyman (later governor) Alfred E. Smith and State Senator (later US senator) Robert Wagner, focused on labor and welfare legislation in the years after that.

 The state legislature passed laws to regulate business (e.g., supervising public utilities such as railroads and gas and electricity companies, regulating business transactions, taxing business franchises), labor (working hours, working conditions, workplace safety, workers' compensation, a ban on child labor in factories), education (New York's first state education department, compulsory student attendance), housing (minimum standards for tenements), and professions (licensing requirements for teachers, doctors, lawyers, and other fields). Other statutes strengthened the state's public health program and expanded its regulation of banking and insurance companies. New York built a new cross-state canal, launched a state highway program, and began construction of subways in New York City. Perhaps most important, women won the long-overdue right to vote by constitutional amendment.[1]

It was an exciting, bracing time of political change. But the validity and constitutionality of many of the new laws would be challenged in courts. The courts, whether they liked it or not, would be drawn into many of the most politically charged issues of the era.[2] The courts would mediate between contending interests, set limits on government initiatives, and decide on how far the law could go in protecting the rights of New Yorkers as a whole even when that meant constricting the rights of some. For several issues, it would be the court of appeals, rather than the governor or legislature, that provided a final reckoning. In other cases, court decisions would provoke the legislature into action.

Laws enlarging state authority were based on the legislature's implied and assumed "police power," the fundamental responsibility to act in the public interest. A popular 1904 legal text defined that as legislation that "aims directly to secure the public welfare and it does so by restraint and compulsion."[3] It explained that police power should be understood not as "a fixed quantity but as the expression of social, economic, and political traditions. As long as these conditions vary, the police power must continue to be elastic, i.e., capable of development."[4] There is a tension here that is at the heart of much of the court of appeals' travail during the era: advancing the "public welfare" via regulatory statutes meant "restraint and compulsion" that traversed someone's rights. That meant constant debate about how "elastic" the concept should be. At the beginning of the Progressive Era, the notion of police power as it applied to state regulatory legislation was still limited. By the end of the Progressive Era, though, the court had evolved a robust, assertive concept of police power, summed up in a decision upholding a law to protect tenants from eviction during the housing shortage after World War I:

> The state may establish regulations reasonably necessary to secure the general welfare of the community by the exercise of its police power although the rights of private property are thereby curtailed and freedom of contract is abridged. . . . The legislative or police power is a dynamic agency, vague and undefined in its scope, which takes private property or limits its use when great public needs require. . . . Either the rights of property and contract must when necessary yield to the public convenience, advantage and welfare, or it must be found that the state has surrendered one of the attributes of sovereignty for which governments are founded and made itself powerless to secure to its citizens the blessings of freedom and to promote the general welfare.[5]

But, in deciding on the validity of legislation, the court of appeals also looked to the past. Precedents in previous court of appeals decisions and US Supreme Court decisions were particularly important. For some issues, the court of appeals cited the decisions of other state courts. Occasionally, the court cited the decisions of English courts. Judges searched in previous decisions for precedent, what the legal community calls *stare decisis*, a Latin term for "to stand by things decided" when an issue has been previously brought before the court and a ruling issued. In fact, there was something approaching a "worship of precedent" at the end of the nineteenth century, as Judge Cuthbert Pound, who joined the court of appeals in 1915, later recalled:

> Ours [was] not to reason why but to find a case in point. The digests and text-books were sedulously thumbed with that end in view. . . . The worship of precedent, the recognition of *stare decisis* as an absolute dogma, went on with scarcely a voice of dissent or protest. The decision may have been wrong but we were never to doubt it. It may have been beside the point. Still, we would cite it especially if it were well known.[6]

Stare decisis was closely related to another concept, *common law*, a body of unwritten law based on judicial decisions and legal precedents established by the courts. That was sometimes called *case law* (in contrast to statutory law) or *judge-made law*. In extending and applying what it perceived as a common law principle, a court might cite common law in validating or striking down a statute. Other times, though, courts might use their own power to extend the common law to cover new circumstances, in effect making their own bit of judge-made law.[7]

Reform legislation also bumped up against constitutional limitations on state power. Opponents of the expansive state often cited a concept called *due process* or *substantive due process*. The US Constitution's Fifth Amendment, adopted in 1791, says that no person shall be "deprived of life, liberty or property without due process of law." The New York State Constitution has a similar phrase, in place since the state's origins. The US Constitution's Fourteenth Amendment, adopted in 1868, uses the same wording, called the due process clause, to describe state governments' obligations. That amendment was adopted in 1868 to help protect the rights of newly liberated Black Americans. As the wave of new progressive regulations began to rise in the late nineteenth century, corporate attorneys began to argue that the Fourteenth Amendment also protected the rights of *companies* to conduct their businesses as they saw fit and to contract with workers to work as they pleased. These lawyers said the amendment was a brake on state restrictions. One of the sources for this claim was New York's Roscoe Conkling, who had been a US senator when the amendment was composed and who asserted it was meant to apply to states regulating companies as well as people. Conkling's claim was misleading, but attorneys took up the cause, and the Fourteenth Amendment became a credible limit on government regulations. Lawyers sometimes cited the comparable provision in the state constitution, too, particularly when they were asserting the right of an individual to enter into contracts that might contravene state regulations, but most of their reliance was on the Fourteenth Amendment.[8]

Court review of laws for constitutionality was rare in 1850 but common by the end of the century. Counsel defending a client who had violated a law were more likely to invoke it as justification. Courts were amenable to mulling over these appeals—judges' assertiveness in interpreting and ruling on constitutionality enhanced their own authority and status. "Due process" and "equal protection of the law" cases became more numerous. When a state passed a law to regulate or prohibit some activity that could be viewed as taking away liberty or property from some people, if the court could say it was done in an unreasonable way, the law would be struck down as unconstitutional. The Fourteenth Amendment became a major factor in cases of the sort decided by the New York State Court of Appeals discussed in this book.[9]

In the closing years of the nineteenth century, the court of appeals had a conservative bent. It was inclined to display a solicitude for the rights of individuals and businesses using the Fourteenth Amendment as a shield against the intrusion of government.

For example, the state passed an act in 1884 to outlaw manufacture of cigars in tenement houses, deeming the practice a health hazard. The court unanimously struck it down in *Matter of Jacobs* in 1885, arguing the law "interferes with the profitable and free use of his property by the owner or lessee of a tenement-house who is a cigarmaker" and "trammels him in the application of his industry and the disposition of his labor, and thus . . . it deprives him of his property and of some portion of his personal liberty."[10] The justification that the act protected workers' health was dismissed by the court, who determined the law in fact had "no relation whatever to the public health." Tobacco-product manufacturing in crowded tenement house rooms was not the state's business.

The state banned manufacture of oleomargarine in 1884 on the stated justification that it could be mistaken for or misrepresented to customers as butter. Critics said the real motivation was to protect the state's dairy farmers from competition. The motivation did not really matter, said the unanimous decision of the court of appeals in 1885 in *People v. Marx*; the law was unconstitutional: "it is one of the fundamental rights and privileges of every American citizen to adopt and follow such lawful industrial pursuits, not injurious to the community, as he may see fit." Rejecting a "cramped" interpretation of the term *liberty*, the court said it meant "the right of a man to be free in the enjoyment of the faculties with which he has been endowed by his Creator, subject only to such restraints as are necessary for the common welfare."[11]

The Fourteenth Amendment was a hovering presence in the court of appeals from then on. The *Jacobs* decision was particularly influential. In the two decades after *Jacobs* and *Marx*, the court of appeals overturned forty-seven lower-court decisions and several laws on the basis of "due process."[12] Some statutes were reenacted with different wording to pass judicial muster next time around. But uncertainty about the courts' potential reaction made legislators wary when considering reform legislation. That uncertainty gave encouragement to business interests that wanted to deter what they regarded as intrusive regulations.

Sometimes, statutes were approved by the court of appeals, but barely. In 1892, the state authorized cities to create boards for examination and licensing of plumbers. A New York City plumber violated it by plying his trade without being certified by the city board, alleging the law was unconstitutional under the Fourteenth Amendment. A majority of the court of appeals, four judges, upheld the law in 1895. "The natural right to life, liberty and the pursuit of happiness is not an absolute right. It must yield whenever the concession is demanded by the welfare, health, or prosperity of the state," wrote Judge John C. Gray for the court. "If legislation is calculated, intended, convenient or appropriate to accomplish the good of protecting the public health and serving public comfort and safety, the exercise of the legislative discretion is not the subject of judicial review."[13]

Judge Rufus W. Peckham wrote a strong dissent, and two of his colleagues agreed: "the statute has no legitimate tendency to preserve, protect or defend the public health."[14] Its real purpose, according to Peckham, was "to enable the employing plumbers to create a sort of guild or body," with passing the examination as a ticket to admission. In a rare display of judicial pique with his colleagues in the majority, he added that "it seems to me most unfortunate that this court should by a constrained construction of this act as a health law, give its sanction to this kind of pernicious legislation."

The legislature passed a law forbidding barbers from working on Sundays. Barbers' health required that they get a day of rest, and working on Sunday violated the Sabbath. The law had some peculiarities; it made exceptions for barbers in New York City and Saratoga Springs, who could work for a half day on Sundays. A barber arrested for violating the law appealed on the grounds that the law was unconstitutional. In *People v. Havnor* (1896), Judge Irving Vann, speaking for the court, conceded that the law might be an example of one that trammeled an individual's rights. "The sanction for these apparent trespasses upon private rights is found in the principle that every man's liberty and property is, to some extent, subject to the general welfare, as each person's interest is presumed to be promoted by that which promotes the interest of all," he wrote. "Dependent upon this principle is the great police power, so universally recognized, but so difficult to define, which guards the health, the welfare and the safety of the public."[15] Three judges concurred, sanctioning the law with a majority of four.

But three judges dissented, and two wrote strong dissenting opinions. Judge John C. Gray asserted that the court "has overstepped the limits and has infringed upon the constitutional guarantees, which, in effect, assure to us the enjoyment of our liberty and of our property in all reasonable ways."[16] He continued that "under the constitutional guaranty, everyone is at liberty to follow any lawful avocation, which is not injurious to the community, and to enjoy its fruits and any interference by the legislature, under the guise of a police regulation, must be seen by the court to have some real reference to the common good." Judge Willard Bartlett called it "vicious class legislation" singling out one profession for intrusive restriction.

Other decisions in the same vein followed. Some reform legislation barely got through, but a lot of it was dispatched by the court. Critics called the courts obstructionist, stuck in time, blocking needed reforms.

NEW IDEAS FOR A NEW CENTURY

Progressive reforms were enacted at a rapid clip in the new century. At the same time, new judicial concepts were emerging that would make the judicial gauntlet many of the laws were destined to run less daunting.

Massachusetts judge Oliver Wendell Holmes's influential writings, particularly his book *The Common Law* (1882) and the widely read and cited essay "The Path of the Law" in *Harvard Law Review* (1897), helped shape a new view of the courts' roles.[17] Holmes argued that the law evolved from experience rather than logic. Legal rules are not deduced from logic or lockstep adherence to precedence but emerge case-by-case according to judges' backgrounds, perceptions, and judgments. They should be concerned with facts and consequences as much as with precedent. The Constitution itself contained principles embodied in the late-eighteenth-century version of the common law, but it was an organic, living document, and those principles should continue to evolve in courts. Judges understand the origins of legal principles but should be wary of letting historical distinctions affect the rights and obligations of businesses. Judges must recognize their obligation of weighing social advantage against tradition. In Holmes's view, *stare decisis* was upstaged by judicial flexibility and judgment. His influence grew when he was appointed to the US Supreme Court in 1902. He was a leader in the movement to make the law more flexible and applicable to modern conditions, sometimes called "the revolt against formalism."[18]

Roscoe Pound, dean of the University of Nebraska College of Law from 1903 to 1911 and after that a professor at Harvard Law School and dean there from 1916 to 1936, set forth the notion of "sociological jurisprudence" in a series of influential writings and lectures.[19] Pound urged judges to examine the actual effects of law within society. Law represents the principal means by which divergent interests are reconciled and brought into alignment with each other. "The right of the individual to contact as he pleases is upheld by our legal system at the expense of the right of society to stand between a portion of our population and oppression," Pound wrote in 1906. The "exaggerated respect" for individual rights based on common-law precedents should slowly give way to new statutes and court decisions, building on the common law but "pruned of its archaisms and antinomies" and attuned to modern needs. According to Pound, we can judge the "true value" of laws by studying "the scientific apprehension of the relations of law to society and of the needs and interests and opinions of society today."[20] Roscoe Pound's distant cousin, judge Cuthbert Pound, who joined the court of appeals in 1915 and was later chief judge, was one of the many New York jurists influenced by Roscoe Pound's ideas.

Another very influential new voice was Louis D. Brandeis, a Massachusetts workers' rights activist and social reformer (where he got the informal title of "people's attorney") and, later (1916), US Supreme Court justice. Brandeis appears again, in chapter 2 for his views on privacy and in chapter 10 for his writings on women's working conditions. Brandeis asserted that lawyers and judges must make the public interest paramount and protect the interests of the people. Courts needed to be sensitive to social needs, consider facts and conditions of contemporary life, and study politics and sociology as well as jurisprudence.[21] "The law has everywhere a tendency to lag behind the facts of life," Brandeis wrote in a widely read essay entitled "Living Law."[22] Judges needed to consider "arisen social need"; the law was meant to serve the public and had to keep up with the times.

Judges needed to keep the law up to the task, said an influential leader of the New York State Bar Association: "Rules or principles of law embodied in statutory form may be clear and sharply cut like the crystals of a rock but they lack the element of vitality of the growing organisms."[23] Judges needed to apply "judicial construction and interpretation" and, when that fell short, to prudently create and apply new common-law principles.[24] The common law should not be regarded as "a mere congeries of cases . . . a collection of cases to be memorized and blindly followed."[25] Judge-made law was beneficial because judges called on precedent and their own understanding of the law. They followed "principles of law" that were "based upon certain ideas of right and wrong and certain notions of good sense which, when declared by the Judge, appeal to the conscience and sense of the individual."[26]

Court of appeals judge Benjamin Cardozo, in a series of lectures at Yale Law School in 1921, described progressive-minded judges' perspective. He rejected the notion that judges needed to rely only on "found" law (mechanical interpretation of what the legislature enacts) or "made" law (the common-law concept elevated to the notion that judges should assertively carry out a "policy-making, quasi-legislative role").[27] That dichotomy was too simplistic. The courts' legal work was more complex and pragmatic than that. Instead, judges needed to extract principles and precedents, particularly in cases "where a decision one way or the other, will count in the future, will advance or retard . . . the development of the law."[28] They should investigate the origins and history of the issues before them. They "must let the welfare of society fix the path, its direction and its distance" in particularly important cases.[29]

The law needed to be flexible and adapt with the times. The power of interpretation might lapse over into judicial lawmaking for the good of society. Customs and viewpoints change. There was bound to be a mixture of judicial subjectivity and objectivity. "Judge-made law," Cardozo said, is one of the conditions of modern life.[30] But judges had a high duty to base their decisions on experience, study, and reflection. Occasionally they would be criticized, but, in the long run, they were justified in keeping the law current, fresh, and relevant.

THE COURT'S MIDDLE COURSE FOR A NEW CENTURY

The court of appeals slowly shifted its outlook in the years after 1900, influenced by the Progressive movement and the new judicial ideas summarized above. It gradually became more attuned to the tenor of the times, open to new ideas and tolerant of progressive laws. In the new century, judges "developed a new cult which exhorts and sometimes influences the court to cast off the iron bonds of precedent as a senseless impediment to free action and to make a fresh start," recalled Judge Cuthbert Pound, writing in 1932. "Law based on a traditionary [sic] line of decisions has become an impractical and antiquated method of doing justice . . ."[31] Precedent counted for less; evidence of changing needs, for more. The court became wary of following precedents too lockstep or setting restrictive new precedents of its own that later courts would, in turn, be bound to follow.

The court was still, deliberately, a low-profile branch of government in comparison to the governor and legislature. Judges were determined to "avoid controversy": "A proper sense of decorum leads a judge to stand aloof from the questions of the day until they come before him for judicial determination and then to approach them as if they had for the first time addressed themselves to his consciousness," said Judge Cuthbert Pound. "The judicial function is to hear and decide, not to engage in debate."[32]

Judges of the New York State Supreme Court, Appellate Division, and Court of Appeals were elected, but most of the contests were mostly low key, with both parties endorsing a candidate or candidates running with only token opposition. Judges were often selected by party leaders but were not strong partisans or wheelhorses for their political parties. The State of New York passed a direct primary law in 1911 that gave candidates more independence but still did not give voters much of a choice since many primary elections were uncontested. Governors made appointments when vacancies occurred, and often the appointees continued in office by election.

Judges on the court of appeals mostly got along well. Many lived in the same hotel in Albany and ate meals together while court was in session. When a case came in, the chief judge would usually assign it to one of the associate judges, based on rotation, judges' interests, or which associate judge the chief judge thought best to manage it through the review process. The judges on the court of appeals and the attorneys who appeared before them often knew each other. In many cases, a county district attorney or an assistant state attorney general represented the state and argued for the constitutional validity of the law in question. The attorneys for each side made oral presentations before the court, usually limited to one hour. Judges might ask questions but usually kept them short because the court was often pressed for time and behind in its work. The attorneys submitted detailed legal briefs (which are now preserved in the State Archives and form the research basis for much of this book). The briefs advanced legal positions and included multiple citations to previous court decisions in support of their case.[33]

By the time the court of appeals judges considered the cases, the issues and legal precedents had been laid out in detail by appellate division decisions and counsel's briefs. After the presentations, the judge assigned to manage the case made an oral report at a postargument conference and sometimes wrote a summary of opposing presentations. The court's deliberations took place in chambers, away from the public, and left no record.

The chief judge might try to convince everyone to agree or to change their minds. The discussions were frank, but the tone was respectful. Chief Judge Alton B. Parker (1898–1904) was likely to urge respect for legislative prerogative. Chief Judge Edgar M. Cullen (1904–13) might urge attention to precedent ("Get out the books!" and check precedents, he would sometimes tell his colleagues on the court) and personal liberty.[34] The chief judge then either decided to write the court's opinion himself or assigned a colleague to write it. He tried for unanimity but did not try to head off dissent or shape dissenters' opinions.

Opinions in key cases were reported in the press but usually did not attract much public attention. The opinions were likely to be long; studded with citations to previous cases, legal texts, and other sources; and conclusive. They are dense legal documents and unlikely to be mistaken for literary masterpieces, except for the opinions of Benjamin Cardozo, which are models of literary clarity. Judges did not give media interviews and seldom wrote about their opinions (a few made retrospective comments after retirement).

The court of appeals endorsed the incipient "administrative state" with strong regulatory oversight delegated to commissions and boards (chap. 7). It invalidated regulation of women's working hours in 1907 but approved it eight years later when more extensive evidence of need was presented (chaps. 9–10). It struck down a workers' compensation law in 1911 but approved another in 1915 after the state constitution had been amended to sanction it (chaps. 11–12).

But its course was uncertain and inconsistent.

Chief Judge Alton B. Parker pushed the court to support legislation unless it was clearly constitutionally defective. In a 1900 opinion approving a statute governing railroads that was admittedly dated and arcane, he explained that the courts nevertheless should not second-guess the legislature:

> Whether the legislation was wise is not for us to consider. The motives actuating and the inducements held out to the legislature are not the subject of inquiry by the courts, which are bound to assume that the law-making body acted with a desire to promote the public good. Its enactments must stand, provided always that they do not contravene the Constitution, and the test of constitutionality is always one of power—nothing else. But in applying the test the courts must bear in mind that it is their duty to give the force of law to an act of the legislature whenever it can be fairly so construed and applied as to avoid conflict with the Constitution.[35]

Parker nudged his colleagues on the court to a 4–3 decision affirming regulation of the hours of bakers in the case of *People v. Lochner* (chap. 3) in 1904. But that decision was reversed by their more conservative brethren on the US Supreme Court in the famous decision of *Lochner v. New York* in 1905.

That year, after Parker had left the court, it went against the grain of *People v. Lochner* and aligned more with the spirit of *Lochner v. New York* in considering a law regulating bulk sale of goods. In *Wright v. Hart*, Judge William Werner, writing the court's decision, said the legislature has "overstepped the limits of its power" with this "drastic and cumbersome" law.[36] The "shibboleth of legislatures and courts known as the police power . . . begins where the Constitution ends" and can't be used to trample on constitutionally guaranteed rights.[37] The law was deemed unconstitutional.

But the issue was close, as it often was in courts in the Progressive Era. The vote was four to three; in effect, the law went down by one vote. Judge Irving G. Vann wrote a spirited opinion chastising his colleagues for invalidating the law. Lots of laws infringe on personal liberty, Judge Vann pointed out, including laws governing contracts, limitations on the heights of buildings, requirements that tenements be furnished with water, and laws restricting professions. "The question before us is one of power, not policy. Courts may pass upon the power of the legislature, but not its policy. Statutes, whether wise or unwise, are equally binding upon us, provided no provision of either [the state or federal] Constitution is molested." The law was a proper exercise of police power that "aims to promote the public welfare by compulsion and restraint and it is under the exclusive control of the legislature."[38] Chief Judge Edgar M. Cullen, Parker's successor, added his own dissent, concurring with Vann.

In 1916, the court reversed itself. It considered a bulk-goods regulatory law, enacted by the legislature in 1914, similar to the one it had invalidated in *Wright v. Hart* back in 1905. In the intervening years, the US Supreme Court and several state courts had swung toward tolerating such regulations. This time, Judge Benjamin Cardozo, a proponent of flexibility and pragmatism who had joined the court in 1914, wrote the decision, for a unanimous court. In light of the court decisions in the years since *Wright v. Hart*, as well as changing economic conditions and shifting public views, the court of appeals had changed its mind:

> We think it is our duty to hold that the decision in *Wright* v. *Hart* is wrong. The unanimous or all but unanimous voice of the judges of the land, in federal and state courts alike, has upheld the constitutionality of these laws. At the time of our decision in *Wright* v. *Hart*, such laws were new and strange. They were thought in the prevailing opinion to represent the fitful prejudices of the hour. . . . The fact is that they have come to stay, and like laws may be found on the statute books of every state. . . . In such circumstances we can no longer say, whatever past views may have been, that the prohibitions of this statute are arbitrary and purposeless restrictions upon liberty of contract. . . . The needs of successive generations

may make restrictions imperative to-day which were vain and capricious to the vision of times past. . . . Our past decision ought not to stand. . . . We should adopt the argument and the conclusion of the dissenting judges in *Wright* v. *Hart*, and affirm the validity of the statute on which the plaintiff builds his rights.[39]

In a 1905 decision, the court approved a 1904 law requiring real estate agents to be registered with city authorities in first- and second-class cities (New York City and the state's other large cities). An agent who operated without a license in New York City was fined and jailed. He appealed on the basis that the law did not apply throughout the state and violated his constitutional rights without due process. Wrong on both counts, said a unanimous court. The legislature has a right to restrict regulatory laws to specified geographical areas. People have a right to carry on legitimate businesses, but the state has a right to regulate:

If the statute comes fairly within the scope of the police power it is a valid law, although it may interfere, in some respects, with the liberty of the citizen, which of course includes his right to follow any lawful employment. A statute to promote the public health, the public safety or to secure public order or for the prevention or suppression of fraud is a valid law, although it may, in some respects, interfere with individual freedom. All business and occupations are conducted subject to the exercise of the police power. Individual freedom must yield to regulations for the public good. . . . Legislation is valid which has for its object the promotion of the public health, safety, morals, convenience and general welfare or the prevention of fraud or immorality.[40]

In a 1907 case involving the constitutionality of a law governing sale of real estate, Judge Albert Haight, for a unanimous court, focusing on limits on state power rather than reach, struck down the law as an arbitrary infringement on rights and liberties:

To justify the state in interposing its authority in behalf of the public, it must appear that the interest of the public generally, as distinguished from those of a particular class, require such interference and that the means are reasonably necessary for the accomplishment of the purpose and not unduly oppressive upon individuals. The legislature may not, under the guise of protecting the public interest, arbitrarily interfere with private business or impose unusual and unnecessary restrictions upon lawful occupations. . . . Liberty, in its broad sense, means the right not only of freedom from servitude, imprisonment or restraint, but the right of one to use his faculties in all lawful ways; to live and work where he will, to earn his livelihood in any lawful calling and to pursue any lawful trade or avocation.[41]

In a 1909 case, a New York City advertising company proposed to erect a sign atop an office building. A City ordinance set the limits on height of such signs at 9 feet. The company wanted a higher sign. The court of appeals seemed to side with the City on principle. "The police power, so difficult to define, but so frequently invoked, is confined to such reasonable restrictions and prohibitions as are necessary to guard public health, morals and safety, and to conserve public peace, order and the general welfare. Regulations and ordinances within such general definition are valid," said the court in what had by then become a familiar litany for the police power. "The city may make and enforce such regulations and ordinances, although they interfere with and restrict the use of private property."[42]

In this case, though, the court questioned the rationale for the ordinance and the City's claim that it protected public safety (from large signs falling on people from rooftops): "It appears from the ordinance in question that it was not enacted in the interest of public health, morals or safety or to conserve public peace, order and general welfare, and the ordinance so far as it relates to sky signs is arbitrary and unauthorized." Citing a number of decisions in other states as further justification, the court found the ordinance invalid.[43]

Sometimes, it was something of a split decision—asserting the court's authority but deferring to the legislature. In *People v. Klinck Packing Co.* (1915), the court confirmed a 1913 law requiring twenty-four consecutive hours of rest in every seven days—what came to be called the "one day's rest in seven" rule—in "factory or mercantile establishments." The law was fine, said the court. "It is of course very familiar law that the legislature under its so-called police power may by enactments which really tend to accomplish such beneficial public purposes interfere in many and substantial ways with individual rights without being considered as in conflict with the constitutional safeguards which surround such individual."[44] *Lochner v. New York* was not a deterrent; that pertained only to hours of people in bakeries, said the court, construing that far-reaching decision in a narrow way. "Nowhere . . . is anything said which condemns the principle that occasionally a day of rest may be secured to employees if the legislature deem it wise so to do, and in the absence of express declaration to that effect it would not be reasonable to believe that the court intended to overthrow everything that had been stated and decided by the courts of various jurisdictions on that subject."[45] The law exempted some employees, such as janitors and watchmen; that was acceptable, too.

But the provision that exempted "employees, if the commissioner of labor in his discretion approves, engaged in the work of any industrial or manufacturing process necessarily continuous, in which no employee is permitted to work more than eight hours in any calendar day" presents "greater difficulties," said the court.[46] That gave the commissioner too much authority, despite the wide latitude of legislative delegation that the court had approved in the *Saratoga Springs* case (chap. 7) in 1907. "This particular provision is not immediately involved in the cases before us and it is not so connected with the general scope and purpose of the legislation that its imperfections totally destroy the latter."[47] The legislature is still in session, and, said the court deferentially, "we have thought it our duty to call to the attention of that body while it is in session the doubts which have arisen in our minds, in order that the subject may receive such consideration as seems appropriate." The court stopped short of saying the provision was actually unconstitutional. The legislature seems to have ignored the hint and left the law intact.

JUDGES EXPLAIN AND DEFEND THE COURTS

As the new century wore on, labor unions, whose strength was growing, complained that the courts issued too many injunctions against strikes. The courts took too long to decide cases. Legal proceedings cost too much. Wealthy defendants and corporations hired politically connected attorneys who were well known to the judges and, in part because of that, effective in swaying them.

Some reforms were easy. The constitution permitted the governor to temporarily appoint additional judges to the court of appeals to relieve backlogs. Another law permitted retired court of appeals judges to act as referees in lieu of court proceedings if both parties agreed. The legislature passed new laws consolidating old ones. Rules of evidence and proceedings were streamlined and tightened to speed cases. Judges toned up their opinions to make them more understandable and convincing to a broader public. Judge Cuthbert Pound explained that "expense and delay have caused prospective litigants to turn from the courts to adjust their differences through settlements or arbitrations without regard for legal liability."[48] That lightened the caseload on the court.

Public criticism of controversial court decisions was practically unheard of before the turn of the century but increased after that. The US Supreme Court was panned for striking down state regulatory laws. The New York Court of Appeals was criticized for several opinions in cases covered in this book, both for what it *did* (e.g., invalidating a law banning night work by women in factories in 1907 [*People v. Williams*] and the workers' compensation law in 1911 [*Ives v. South Buffalo Railway Co.*]) and for what it *did not* do (e.g., not asserting a common-law right of privacy in 1902 [*Roberson v. Rochester Folding Box Co.*]). Former president (and New York governor) Theodore Roosevelt, seeking another term as president in 1912, criticized several courts for their "foolish and iniquitous decisions" and called the workers' compensation decision "repugnant . . . to every believer in justice and righteousness."[49] He proposed giving voters the right to recall and override state court decisions that declared laws unconstitutional. Roosevelt's harsh attacks brought rebukes from Alton B. Parker and other leading jurists. Some critics went even further, advocating letting voters recall erring judges as well as their decisions. The recall proposal went nowhere in this state, though it did advance elsewhere. But the ex-president's hammering the issue of courts obstructing social reform sanctioned criticism by others. New York City mayor (and former judge) William Gaynor, in a speech in May 1912, criticized the court of appeals for its *Jacobs* decision back in 1885. Courts seemed to be striking down good laws right and left, he asserted: "they are declaring unconstitutional and void the statutes passed for social and economic welfare all over the country."[50]

The New York Court of Appeals could not with propriety and decorum publicly defend itself. But the state bar association could. It appointed a committee, headed by Alton Parker, which reported in 1913 that the courts were sound, their decisions well considered and well documented. The basic problems were "misstatements and misrepresentations of the decisions and attitudes of the Courts," "misapprehension of the powers and duties of Courts and Judges," and "the fault finding of defeated litigants and their attorneys." Most of the criticism in the press was "simply abuse and misrepresentation." Some critics said the courts stopped short; others that they went too far. The committee argued that "the United States Supreme Court is criticized for legislating, and on the other hand, our Court of Appeals is criticized because it does not legislate, and change the law as they understand it to be, in order that they may thus keep abreast of the times and facilitate progress in accordance with a supposed preponderating public sentiment."[51]

Recall of judges or decisions "would destroy the independence of the judiciary and the impartial administration of justice and deprive all classes of the community of the protection now afforded to individual rights, by substituting for the training, intelligence and conscience of the judiciary, and settled rules of law, public clamor, agitation and constantly varying opinions of voters overruling the judgments of the courts and punishing judges for unpopular decisions."[52] The committee recommended that attorneys undertake to explain the courts' functions, and the limitations imposed by the federal and state constitutions, to the public. The proposal for recall of judges or decisions found little support in New York, though it did advance elsewhere.

Some of the leading judges of the state set forth explanations in the ensuing years, and elaborated on them later, of how the courts handled profound constitutional issues:

JUDGES NEED TO BE INDEPENDENT

Judges need to be insulated from recall and unfair political criticism so they can maintain their independence and objectivity. "Our common law system of jurisprudence is founded upon the courts. The courts not only administer the law, but declare the law," a leading New York attorney explained. Going further, and putting things more directly than most judges did, he continued, "Indeed it may be said that the law is what the courts declare it to be."[53] The real problem is that the public misperceives the courts as favoring vested interests over popular needs. But the system was actually fair and balanced. "Weaken the power of the courts to protect 'property' and you necessarily weaken the power to protect life and 'liberty' against unconstitutional encroachments."[54]

COURTS DO NOT REACH OUT FOR POWER

Judge Cuthbert Pound explained that courts invalidated laws only after careful consideration and that "this power rests for its security on a practical working theory rather than an unquestioned, ultimate, exclusive prerogative." Courts feel their way along. *"The term 'constitutional right'* as applied, in the first instance, to a new problem, is often of a vague and unsubstantial nature, dependent upon the proper balancing of many conflicting interests, social, public and private." Courts did not go looking for things to review: *"executive and legislative power and justice, properly exercised, are not proper subjects of judicial review;* . . . administrative orders should be reviewed only when a justiciable question is presented and the courts should consider only such matters as come within the scope of judicial power."[55]

COURTS JUST FOLLOW THE CONSTITUTION

Chief Judge Emeritus Edgar Cullen, writing in 1914, a year after his retirement, criticized those who "indulge in aspersions on the State judiciary" as uninformed or politically motivated and ambitious. Some criticize the court for usurping power, but others insist that "it is reactionary and does not respond to the present change of thought and to the growing demand for social justice." Actually, Cullen writes, the court is "stationary," following the true path of the constitution. The public, if dissatisfied with a decision, should change the constitution, not blame the courts.[56]

COURTS ARE BOUND BY TRADITION BUT OPEN TO NEW IDEAS

"Judges often look backward rather than forward," Judge Cuthbert Pound wrote in 1922, but decisions are not "wholly bound by the rules of past generations." The court changes its mind as new evidence is presented: "case law is not wholly a matter of precedent"; it is "a progressive science." The judge continued, "The opportunity still exists for great lawyers to make great arguments in the face of obsolescent decisions and for judges not only to 'hold fast to that which is good,' as they must in all decency and respect for their place, but [also] 'to prove,—i.e. establish the validity of,—all things.' "[57] Elsewhere, he wrote that "what is antiquated today was once modern and practical. Call it sociological justice or any other hard name from the vocabulary of technical philosophy as you will, the courts have always in a greater or less degree given ear to those who contend for a modification of the old rule to conform to modem conditions."[58]

COURTS PROTECT INDIVIDUAL LIBERTY

Former chief judge Cullen decried the trend toward "collectivism" and "paternal or socialistic government" based on the principle that "liberty is the right of part of the people to compel the other part to do what the first part thinks the latter ought to do for its own benefit."[59] There were simply too many laws being passed that intruded on people's lives and businesses, favored labor over business, and regulated business in the guise of new taxes. The direct primary, recently adopted in New York, was inferior to the traditional convention system where party activists could hammer out platforms and select qualified candidates. It all came down to protecting individual liberty, said the retired chief judge, in terms stronger than he had used on the bench: "I protest against being compelled to surrender my liberty at all."[60]

THE COURT OF APPEALS IS ACTUALLY PROGRESSIVE

Some of the judges and leaders of the legal profession insisted that the court was actually quite progressive. Judge Frank Hiscock, who joined the court in 1906 and served as chief judge in 1917–26, later said the court espoused "a liberal, but justifiable and faithful, interpretation of the constitutional provisions in the direction of upholding the legislative function to adopt enactments for the public protection and welfare of the public." Sometimes, the court is locked into invalidating laws that just do not align with the constitution. But in other cases, "it is permissible to give to the law that flexibility which it must have if it is to keep pace with the changes in social and industrial life and by modifying or extending some rule of yesterday to make it more applicable to the modern conditions of today or by formulation of some new principle." The court had resisted a "clamor for paternalism and regulation" and struck down the defective 1910 employers' liability act but approved the new act after it was sanctioned by constitutional amendment. It had upheld housing laws, consumer protection laws, and laws regulating commercial transactions. The court had changed its mind about regulation of women's working hours after being presented with "a large amount of new and cogent knowledge and testimony."[61]

THERE ARE TOO MANY DEFECTIVE LAWS

One contributory factor to the courts' backlog and their reputation for striking down legislation was the fact that legislatures passed too many laws. Just about any "agitation of a public or moral question" leads to "popular clamor" for a new law, former chief judge Alton B. Parker wrote in 1906, even though existing laws may be more than up to the task if they were really enforced. The "misdirected or ignorant zeal" of governors and presidents in pushing for new laws was a substantial factor. Congress and state legislatures turned out new laws at the rate of 15,000 per year. This "over legislation" or "legislative waste" provided opportunities for political maneuvering and corruption. Too many recent laws were intruding on personal freedom and right of contract. Many were crudely and hastily drafted and defective and were inevitably challenged in courts, which unsurprisingly found them unconstitutional.[62]

JUDGES ADVANCE JUSTICE THROUGH COMMON LAW

Alton B. Parker, during his tenure as chief judge, had been a champion of validating regulatory legislation and a skeptic of carrying the common law into new areas. In retirement, though, he believed state police power was galloping unrestrained across the political landscape. Legislatures were acting in haste, passing too many ill-advised laws in a "reckless groping for remedies" to complicated problems.[63] Many cases involving the constitutionality of such laws presented an opportunity for the court "to work out justice" and "establish a sound rule," Parker said in his presidential address to the American Bar Association in 1907.[64] He asserted that judges should be trusted to apply "knowledge of principles established by prior decisions. In this way our unwritten law, better known as the common law, has been so developed as to meet the exigencies of our wonderful growth and expansion, and of our complicated business and social conditions."

Chapter 2

THE RIGHT TO PRIVACY

Figure 2.1. Eastman Kodak Company used this image of the "Kodak Girl" to market its cameras to the broad public. The cameras were easy to use and took good-quality photos. Their availability and widespread use raised legal personal privacy issues in the Progressive Era. *Source:* Eastman Kodak Company, "No. 28. The Kodak Girl." 1909. Library of Congress Prints & Photographs Collection.

Do New Yorkers have a legal right to privacy? The court of appeals said no in a landmark decision in 1902. The decision was unpopular, public opinion demanded state protection, and the legislature enacted a privacy law in 1903, but it defined the right narrowly. That limited statutory protection is still the main basis of privacy law in New York today.

This privacy story began in the spring of 1900 when seventeen-year-old Rochester resident Abigail Roberson was teased by her friends about advertising flyers from Franklin Mills Flour Company adorned with her image under the company's trademark caption, "Flour of the Family." Nothing identified it as Abigail Roberson, and only people who knew her recognized her image.

The Franklin Mills company, located in nearby Lockport, and the Rochester Folding-Box Company, which supplied its boxes and advertising flyers, hoped the image would attract attention and get people to buy Franklin Mills flour. Young women were sometimes likened to delicate flowers in popular conversation and literature in those days, and presumably the advertiser hoped people would link the image of this "flower" of some family to the "flour of the family." The image and advertising theme suited Franklin Mills' advertising pitch as a healthful flour for everyone in the family. "The fine flour of the entire wheat . . . containing as it does all the phosphates, mineral salts, and gluten of the entire wheat, is recommended by many physicians for use in the preparation of food for those suffering from weak stomach, because it is easily digestible," said one of its ads. "Nourishing as it does every part of the body, it is . . . especially valuable in the diet of children."[1]

In the subsequent litigation, the source of the photo and whether it was taken with or without Abigail Roberson's consent were never disclosed. The companies later denied that they knew who was pictured in the image on their flyers. They felt no obligation to check or to get anyone's permission. After all, using photos or images of people to advertise commercial products without their consent was common. Occasionally, men's images were appropriated to sell products like cigars and whisky. Usually, though, it was attractive young women. In the dawning age of mass consumption, "youth, beauty, innocence, or sophistication" got attention and sold things.[2]

What could Margaret Bell, Abigail's aunt and guardian, do to shield her niece from this commercial exploitation and humiliation? Calling the police was not an option—there was no explicit state law guaranteeing right to privacy or forbidding unauthorized use of a photo for commercial purposes. Bell decided to engage a prominent local attorney, Milton E. Gibbs, to file a lawsuit in her niece's name. Gibbs pursued the case with ardor. He abhorred the exploitation of women in commercial advertising and would later emerge as a local leader in the campaign for women's voting rights.

Gibbs's lawsuit on behalf of Abigail Roberson acknowledged the absence of specific statutory law. Instead, it asserted that what the two companies had done was invasion of personal privacy and that the courts actually had three bases for ordering it to cease. One, the notion of "torts"—some acts that cause harm are wrongful and intolerable even if not explicitly forbidden in the law. Two, the notion of "common law"— legal doctrine, sometimes popularly called judge-made law, derived from judicial precedent rather than from statute. Three, "equity"—gaps in the law where courts could provide solutions based on fairness.

Gibbs's complaint claimed that Abigail Roberson had been humiliated by "scoffs and jeers" of people who recognized her image, that "her good name has been attacked, causing her great distress and suffering both in body and mind," and that she suffered "mental pain and distress" so severe that it required the care of a physician and bed rest. The harm to Abigail Roberson was similar to libel, slander, breach of promise, and "all actions of tort where the wrongful act of another causes an injury, a recovery is allowed for mental pain and distress and grace caused by such wrongful act."[3]

The complaint asked for damages of $15,000 and an injunction against further unauthorized use of the photo.

TECHNOLOGY AND MEDIA OUTDISTANCE THE LAW

The issues that played out in Abigail Roberson's case had two roots.

The first was rising public concern about popular photography. Like the Roberson case itself, this story began in Rochester, where, in 1888, the inventor George Eastman marketed his new "Kodak" camera, which was simple, light, relatively inexpensive, and easy to use. Amateur photography burgeoned. Thousands of cameras were sold and used by average individuals and families. Hundreds of photo studios opened. Photos proliferated. But the Kodak, as the company advertised, could be used for taking surreptitious photos of unsuspecting people. To many people, cameras seemed intrusive. People feared being photographed when they were off guard.

Ads for cameras highlighted cameras' ability to capture people's likenesses without their consent or knowledge. Photographers began selling photos, mostly of young women. Newspapers began using more photos; one newspaper hired a photographer to take photos of people in the street. Businesses began using more photos in ads and on packages, even using images of First Lady Frances Folsom Cleveland (1886–89 and 1893–97) in ads for pianos, soap, cigarettes, and patent medicines.[4]

People liked the convenience of the innovative cameras but became increasingly wary about their potential use for surreptitious photography. Women's rights advocates, particularly those pushing for woman suffrage, took up the cause of protecting women from use of photos taken without their consent or in ways that they had not approved. Using women's photos to sell commercial products was unfair and exploitative. This dimension of the argument became part of women's struggle for full citizenship rights. It strengthened the call for legal intervention and protection.[5]

The second driving factor was rising concern about the intrusive press. Newspapers at the end of the century were becoming bolder and more impertinent in reporting on people's personal lives, particularly the doings of the rich and famous. In New York City, Joseph Pulitzer's *New York World* competed with William Randolph Hearst's *New York Journal* in the arena of "yellow journalism," with eye-catching headlines, reports of scandals and corruption, gossip, human-interest stories that often featured bizarre or tragic incidents in people's lives, and splashy photos.[6]

More responsible, constrained editors urged their sensationalistic colleagues to rein things in. Edwin L. Godkin, longtime editor of the *New York Evening Post*, in an influential article in *Scribner's Magazine* in 1890 entitled "The Rights of the Citizen to His Own Reputation," asserted an individual's right to draw "the line between his life as an individual and his life as a citizen . . . the power of deciding how much or how little the community shall see of him, or know of him." But "the chief enemy of privacy in modern life is that interest in other people and their affairs known as curiosity." In the old days, it was village gossip. Now "a particular class of newspapers" has "converted . . . gossip into a marketable commodity."[7]

Godkin offered no solution other than journalistic self-restraint and chastisement and shunning of offending publications. New York legislators were not up to the task of confronting the issue, either. In the 1890s, a bill making it illegal to print a photo of a person without their consent failed in the state legislature. A similar measure failed in Congress, mostly due to opposition from newspaper publishers.

THE COURTS' AMBIVALENCE

The issue then began playing out in the courts, including in New York, but the results at the time of *Roberson v. Rochester Folding Box Co.* were inconclusive.

The actress and singer Marion Manola appeared in a Broadway comic opera, *Castles in the Air*, in 1890. The stage manager hired a photographer to surreptitiously photograph her in a revealing costume from one of the theater boxes, intending to use the images to promote his production and boost attendance. Manola objected and secured a court order to restrain the manager from using the photos. The court decision got lots of press attention, but it really did not spell out legal limits on the use of photos or right of privacy.[8]

Another newsworthy case arose when a woman's group announced plans to erect a bust honoring Mary Hamilton Schuyler at the Chicago World's Fair in 1893. Schuyler, the granddaughter of the first secretary of the treasury, Alexander Hamilton, and the great-granddaughter of New York revolutionary general Philip Schuyler, had been a prominent socialite and philanthropist before her death fourteen years earlier. But her nephew and other family members sued to stop the action, arguing that it would violate her privacy, contradict her sense of modesty, and offend their own sensibilities. They also objected that Schuyler's bust would be displayed at the fair near one of woman suffrage leader Susan B. Anthony, since Schuyler was not a fan of the right to vote for women. It made for an odd, distended privacy case at best. The New York Supreme Court and Appellate Division sided with the family in shielding Mary Schuyler's privacy.

The case reached the New York Court of Appeals in 1895. By then, it was in effect moot because the fair had closed. The court took it up anyway. Judge Rufus Peckham, writing for the court, reversed the lower courts, holding that the family did not present sufficient evidence to void the creation of the bust. Mrs. Schuyler's privacy died with her, the judge explained. But Peckham wrote that "courts have the power in some cases to enjoin the doing of an act where the nature and character of the act itself is well calculated to wound the sensibilities of an individual, and where the doing of the act is wholly unjustifiable, and is, in legal contemplation, a wrong, even though the existence of no property, as that term is usually used, is involved in the subject."[9] Peckham's ambivalent opinion was less than a model of clarity. But his assertion of courts' powers seemed to open the door to courts defending the right to privacy in cases where the issue was more clearly joined. Milton Gibbs cited Peckham's opinion in his brief for Abigail Roberson.

RETROFITTING THE LAW

The law and the legal right to privacy obviously did not dovetail very well. But the connection was redefined, clarified, and reasserted in an influential 1890 article entitled "The Right to Privacy" in the *Harvard Law Review*.[10] It was signed by two young Boston attorneys, Samuel D. Warren and Louis D. Brandeis, who were partners in a law firm. Warren had been annoyed by the newspaper publicity surrounding his wedding to Mabel Bayard, socially prominent daughter of US Senator Thomas Bayard; intrusive investigative reporting about his family; and gossip about friends' personal lives in the society columns of newspapers. Mabel Bayard was a friend of Frances Cleveland and understood the exposure that public figures had to contend with. Warren was the instigator, but Brandeis was a facile writer, and the article was mostly his work. It was one of the first stellar documents that would earn him the informal title of "the people's lawyer" for his legal briefs in favor of individual rights and labor legislation and would eventually propel him to the US Supreme Court in 1916.

The article explained the existence of what the authors called "the right to be let alone." It drew that catchy phrase from legal scholar Thomas M. Cooley, who had brought it to life in his authoritative 1888 work *A Treatise on the Law of Torts*.[11] It was rooted in the common law's long-standing protection of "the right to life" and property. But now that protection needed refreshing and expanding because of cameras and newspapers: "Instantaneous photographs and newspaper enterprise have invaded the sacred precincts of private and domestic life. . . . The press is overstepping in every direction the obvious bounds of propriety and of decency. . . . Solitude and privacy have become more essential to the individual. . . . [But the press] both belittles and perverts" through spreading gossip and untrue stories.[12]

The authors acknowledged that express statutes were absent and case law was scanty. But they insisted that the common law secures to individuals the right to determine whether their thoughts, sentiments, emotions, and likenesses could be made public. As society becomes more complex, the common law's protections need to be stretched and interpreted in new ways. That implied a right to one's "inviolate personality" and "a general right to privacy for thoughts, emotions, and sensations," according to Warren and Brandeis.[13] In turn, there is an implied contract between a photographer and a person being photographed. The person's image is a representation of the person. The image belonged to the person photographed; reproducing and disseminating it was tantamount to stealing it.

Warren and Brandeis conceded that the right to privacy could not be invoked to prohibit publication of something that is "of public or general interest"; documents in the public domain (e.g., evidence in court); "oral publication," that is, spoken words; or a photograph or document where the person has given consent to dissemination.[14] But people whose privacy had been invaded had a right to bring an action of tort for damages or an injunction.

"The Right to Privacy" article became influential soon after its publication. It was controversial but also persuasive in part because it eloquently summed up and presented what most people instinctively felt: people had a right to privacy even if statutes did not spell it out. Using someone's photo without permission was just plain wrong. It was the most cited article in American legal scholarship until 1947. Harvard Law School dean Roscoe Pound claimed that in effect it added a new chapter to American law. Plaintiffs seeking damages for invasion of privacy began citing it; judges began acknowledging it in their decisions.[15] The Warren/ Brandeis article was a subtext in the legal discussions in the *Roberson* case.

TWO NEW YORK COURTS SAY YES TO THE RIGHT TO PRIVACY

Roberson's counsel, Milton Gibbs, drew heavily on the Warren/Brandeis article in his brief. The supreme court in Monroe County found in Abigail Roberson's favor in July 1900. Justice John M. Davy, relying heavily on Gibbs's brief, ruled the use of the photo had inflicted "mental pain" and "anguish."[16] Abigail Roberson was "a young woman of rare beauty," but "this she enjoys as a private citizen."[17] Privacy is "a product of civilization." People have a right to keep to themselves. "Her face is her own private property," a right that cannot be taken from her "without her consent."[18] Davy cited several decisions from English courts and other state courts, concluding that these legal precedents were inconclusive or did not go far enough. But, he continued, "the rule that an individual shall have full protection in person and property is as old as the common law." Davy referenced Thomas Cooley's assertion of "the right to be let alone" and interpreted previous court decisions as indicating an implicit right to privacy. He ruled in Abigail Roberson's favor.

The two companies appealed.

A year later, in July 1901, the appellate division affirmed the supreme court's decision. Justice William Rumsey, writing for the court, acknowledged that "the theory upon which this action is predicated is new" but that judges had an obligation to dispense justice in line with the common law even when an issue had not been precisely addressed in the past—"every person has a complete and perfect right of indemnity from all interference with himself or, as it is succinctly stated by Judge Cooley, he has the absolute right to be let alone."[19] The defendant violated the right of personal immunity, the right not to be interfered with, and "injures the plaintiff's reputation by words spoken in respect of it and the like act which injures her feelings and diminishes the respect with which she is held in the community by saying or doing something in regard to her which tends to bring her into unnecessary and unwarrantable notice."[20] They had violated "the right of property which everyone has in his own body."[21]

MARSHALING THE ARGUMENTS FOR THE COURT OF APPEALS

The companies appealed to the court of appeals. By that time, the case had attracted a good deal of media attention, with most editorials commending the state supreme court and the appellate division court for protecting an innocent young lady's rights.

Opposing counsel made their cases in their briefs, which rummaged through the precedents and literature and marshaled arguments.

Milton Gibbs's brief cited previous court decisions but denied the proposition that courts must be bound only by precedents of fact and not principles: "To protect rights and address wrongs, such as are under consideration in this case, has always been and now is the special and peculiar province of the Equity side of the Common Law." He praised the "careful and learned" Warren/Brandeis article, asserted that no opinions in New York courts really contradicted it, and said it led to the conclusion that "the person aggrieved . . . shall be adequately and properly protected." "The court is asked to enjoin the defendants from continually and willfully wounding the sensibilities of a young woman in her lifetime and especially as the acts of the defendants are for the one and only purpose of selfish and private gain." It really wasn't a question of whether a property right per se exists. The court had "full and complete jurisdiction to grant the relief asked for by this plaintiff" given her "touching appeal." Fundamentally, everyone has a right to their own photograph. "The fact that this case may be new . . . is not a sufficient reason for turning the plaintiff out of court." The defendant has suffered "mental pain and anguish and . . . personal annoyance and inconvenience." The brief's concluding sentence summed up the case: "Defendants have no right in morals, in conscience, in law or in equity, for the sole purpose of selfish gain, to harass and cheapen a beautiful young woman by circulating her photograph without her consent."[22]

The companies' counsel, Rochester attorney Elbridge Adams, began his brief by asserting that the companies did not know whose image they were using. In fact, "the 'likeness' may be only a fanciful resemblance" to Abigail Roberson. It might be the image of some other woman who looked like her. In any case, the defendants did not know they did not have permission to use the image. Moreover, "there is no law on the statute books of the state which gives the right of action upon the facts alleged by the complainant." Equity could not be stretched to cover it. The appellate court's decision "is not based upon legal principles clearly applicable to the state of facts. . . . The 'right of privacy' is not a legal actionable right." The Warren/Brandeis article "is undeniably clever and ingenious but the argument is based wholly upon analogy—a dangerous form of reasoning—and is the product of a theoretical and visionary jurisprudence, scheming for an ideal humanity, rather than that of a practical and scientific jurisprudence based on settled principles of law." Adams discussed previous decisions but focused on Judge Peckham's opinion in *Schuyler v. Curtis*, quoting him to the effect that "the mere fact that a person's feeling may be injured" is not enough to forbid legal action. He conveniently left out Peckham's comments about courts' potential power to render justice in situations like this. Pushing the privacy argument too far risks trampling on the Constitution's guarantees of freedom of speech and press, said Adams. "There is no law against impertinence," and "outraged sensitivities" are not enough. Supporting Roberson's claim would result in a flood of litigation. "Sorrow sometimes comes to jurisprudence when the 'hard case' is permitted to make bad law," he admonished the court.[23]

THE CHIEF JUDGE SAYS NO TO THE RIGHT TO PRIVACY

Chief Judge Alton B. Parker wrote the decision for the court of appeals on June 27, 1902, reversing the lower courts and ruling against Roberson.[24]

Parker, a Democrat, elected chief judge in 1897, was already one of the nation's most prominent judges just by his virtue of his position as head of the nation's most important state court. The introduction to this book and chapters 3 and 4 delve further into his judicial philosophy. Parker could have assigned another judge to write the *Roberson* opinion but decided to do it himself, for at least three reasons. One, he was concerned with the creeping tendency of the courts to overreach and address questions that should be left to legislatures. Two, privacy was an unsettled area of the law and one where more and more people seemed to be looking to the courts for guidance. Three, though personally modest and judicious in manner, Parker was also politically ambitious. He was positioning himself to secure the Democratic nomination for president in 1904, a seemingly unlikely prospect in 1902 but one that, against the odds, he would achieve two years later, as related in chapter 4. A strong, decisive opinion in the *Roberson* case could boost his reputation as a leader. The chief judge set out to write an opinion that the legal community, political leaders in New York and elsewhere in the nation, the media, and the public would find persuasive.

The chief judge wrote the court's decision, which denied Roberson's claim. Parker had hoped for a united court behind his decision. But only three of his colleagues concurred, giving him a majority of four, and three dissented.

Like his colleagues in the lower courts, the chief judge in his opinion ranged authoritatively through English and US legal precedents before setting forth the decision. His opinion included several contentions.

WARREN AND BRANDEIS ORIGINATED THE CONCEPT OF RIGHT TO PRIVACY

Parker noted that the appellate court admitted there was no definite legal precedent for their decision in favor of Roberson and that the concept of right to privacy did not appear explicitly in any court decision. For a precedent-oriented judge like Parker, that was a definitive argument. The so-called right to privacy originated when "it was presented with attractiveness and no inconsiderable ability" in the "clever" Warren/Brandeis article, Parker insisted. He paraphrased from the article that "a man has the right to pass through this world, if he wills, without having his picture published, his business enterprises discussed, his successful experiments written up for the benefit of others, or his eccentricities commented upon either in handbills, circulars, catalogues, periodicals or newspapers, and, necessarily, that the things which may not be written and published of him must not be spoken of him by his neighbors, whether the comment be favorable or otherwise."[25] That was actually a good summary of what Warren and Brandeis had been getting at. Referring to masculine terms, which was standard in legal opinions in those days, might seem to confine it to men only. Such privacy was a state of affairs that all people might reasonably desire, Parker conceded, but he found no legal protection for it.

THE CONCEPT OF RIGHT TO PRIVACY HAS NO PRECEDENT IN LAW OR COURT DECISIONS

Much of Parker's opinion consisted of his selective interpretation of English and American cases and precedents cited by Warren and Brandeis and the appellate division court. Most of the decisions really pertained to property rights, not to the right to privacy, the chief judge insisted. For instance, English courts had enjoined a craftsman from selling copies of an etching he had made of Queen Victoria's husband Prince Albert at the prince's request, but on the grounds that the prince's property rights, not his privacy rights, had been infringed. The judge explained that a decision in favor of a woman who sued a photographer whom she had hired to take photos of her, who then used them to illustrate Christmas cards, was based on an implied contract that the photos were only for the woman's own use, not on a violation of her privacy. Publishing a private letter without the writer's permission was not legal because the writer owned the letter, not because of any violation of privacy. Judge Parker concluded that "each decision was rested either upon the ground of breach of trust or that plaintiff had a property right in the subject of litigation which the court could protect."[26]

The judge could find no US decisions that supported Roberson, either. One decision approved use of a photo of a "public character." The *Schuyler* case was ambivalent and inconclusive, Parker explained. In any event, "it is not authority for the existence of a right of privacy which entitles a party to restrain another from doing an act which, though not actionable at common law, occasions plaintiff mental distress."[27]

HURTING SOMEONE'S FEELINGS IS NOT A CRIME

The chief judge struck what seems to modern readers a patronizing, condescending note in implying that Roberson's attractiveness reflected in the image should be a source of pride for her: "The likeness is said to be a very good one, and one that her friends and acquaintances were able to recognize; indeed, her grievance is that a good portrait of her, and, therefore, one easily recognized, has been used to attract attention toward the paper upon which defendant mill company's advertisements appear." Such publicity, which some people might find "agreeable," he continued, "is to plaintiff very distasteful, and thus, because of defendants' impertinence in using her picture without her consent for their own business purposes, she has been caused to suffer mental distress where others would have appreciated the compliment to their beauty implied in the selection of the picture for such purposes." His use of the phrases "distasteful to her" and "damages to her feelings" framed the issue as one of personal hurt feelings rather than a legal offense against her.[28]

SUPPORTING ABIGAIL ROBERSON'S CLAIM WOULD OPEN THE FLOODGATES TO PRIVACY LITIGATION

Echoing another of company counsel Elbridge Adams's warnings, Parker insisted that

> the attempts to logically apply the [privacy] principle will necessarily result, not only in a vast amount of litigation, but in litigation bordering upon the absurd. . . . The right of privacy, once established as a legal doctrine, cannot be confined to the restraint of the publication of a likeness but must necessarily embrace as well the publication of a word-picture, a comment upon one's looks, conduct, domestic relations or habits. And were the right of privacy once legally asserted it would necessarily be held to include the same things if spoken instead of printed, for one, as well as the other, invades the right to be absolutely let alone.

Going further, Parker added that "the mischief which will finally result may be almost incalculable under our system which makes a decision in one case a precedent for decisions in all future cases which are akin to it in the essential facts."[29]

THIS IS BEYOND THE COURTS' AUTHORITY; IT IS UP TO THE LEGISLATURE

"The so-called right of privacy has not as yet found an abiding place in our jurisprudence, and, as we view it, the doctrine cannot now be incorporated without doing violence to settled principles of law by which the profession and the public have long been guided," said the judge. It is up to the legislature because of "the absolute impossibility of dealing with this subject save by legislative enactment, by which may be drawn arbitrary distinctions which no court should promulgate."[30]

DISSENTING JUDGES ASSERT THE RIGHT TO PRIVACY

One of the three dissenters, Judge John C. Gray, wrote a powerful opinion in which the other two dissenters concurred. " 'The law' is made up largely of judge-made law," Gray had insisted in a legal journal article a decade earlier.[31] Judges adhere to the law and the opinions of other courts; they read the law journals; but their responsibility in jurisprudence is broader than that. When the issue is unprecedented and the way forward is not clear, judges give weight to people's customs and their own ethical viewpoints: "a great part of the law of this century is due to the opinions of individual judges on ethical questions."[32] This case warranted explicitly expanding the judge-made law's protection of privacy, according to the dissenters.

PREVIOUS COURT DECISIONS IMPLICITLY RECOGNIZE THE RIGHT TO PRIVACY

Gray's dissent conceded that no court had specifically and unequivocally acknowledged a right to privacy. But, echoing Warren and Brandeis, he argued that such a right "is a proposition which is not opposed by any decision in this court and which, in my opinion, is within the field of accepted legal principles." He claimed that in Peckham's *Schuyler* decision, the right to privacy "if not actually affirmed in the opinion, was, very certainly, far from being denied."[33]

THIS IS AN ASSAULT ON ABIGAIL ROBERSON, NOT JUST HURT FEELINGS

Parting sharply with Parker, Gray explained that Roberson's "objection to the defendants' acts is not one born of caprice; nor is it based upon the defendants' act being merely 'distasteful' to her. We are bound to assume . . . that the conspicuous display of her likeness, in various public places, has so humiliated her by the notoriety and by the public comments it has provoked, as to cause her distress and suffering, in body and in mind, and to confine her to her bed with illness." The decision should not depend upon "the complainant's ability to prove substantial pecuniary damages." It is enough to "wound the feelings and to subject the plaintiff to the ridicule, or to the contempt of others."[34]

THE LAW NEEDS TO CATCH UP WITH SOCIAL CHANGES

"The right of privacy, or the right of the individual to be let alone, is a personal right. . . . It is the complement of the right to the immunity of one's person. The individual has always been entitled to be protected in the exclusive use and enjoyment of that which is his own. The common law regarded his person and property as inviolate, and he has the absolute right to be let alone," said Gray. He continued,

> That the exercise of the preventive power of a court of equity is demanded in a novel case, is not a fatal objection. . . . In the social evolution, with the march of the arts and sciences and in the resultant effects upon organized society, it is quite intelligible that new conditions must arise in personal relations, which the rules of the common law, cast in the rigid mould of an earlier social status, were not designed to meet. It would be a reproach to equitable jurisprudence, if equity were powerless to extend the application of the principles of common law, or of natural justice, in remedying a wrong, which, in the progress of civilization, has been made possible as the result of new social, or commercial conditions.[35]

UNAUTHORIZED USE OF A PHOTOGRAPH IS HARMFUL

"Instantaneous photography is a modern invention and affords the means of securing a portraiture of an individual's face and form," Judge Gray noted. That alone would make it "a species of aggression."[36] This plaintiff has the same right to be protected against the use of her face for defendant's commercial purposes as she would have if they were publishing her literary compositions. The right would be conceded, if she had sat for her photograph; but if her face, or her portraiture, has a value, the value is hers exclusively; until the use be granted away to the public." Gray concluded that "the injury to the plaintiff is irreparable; because she cannot be wholly compensated in damages for the various consequences entailed by defendants' acts. The only complete relief is an injunction restraining their continuance."[37]

A RARE RESPONSE TO PUBLIC CRITICISM

Court of appeals decisions usually did not garner much public attention, but the *Roberson* case touched a public nerve and generated lots of press attention in New York and elsewhere, almost all critical. Roberson, an innocent young victim protected by the rulings of New York's supreme court and appellate division, had been abandoned by the court of appeals by a vote of four to three. She became the object of lots of public sympathy. Some commentators criticized the court's timidity in not adjusting the law to keep up with the times. Others said it would encourage more invasive stealth photography. The usually restrained *New York Times* declared in a strident editorial on August 23 that the "amazing opinion" meant that "the right to privacy is not a right which in the State of New York anybody is bound to respect or which the courts will lend their aid to enforce."[38] If it were Chief Judge Parker's daughter rather than Abigail Roberson in the flour ads, the *Times* uncharitably suggested, the opinion would have been different.

Judges almost never responded to public criticism. But the crescendo of negative reaction over the *Roberson* decision prompted an unprecedented response from the court. Chief Judge Parker was appalled but judiciously kept silent. But his colleague, Judge Denis O'Brien, who had concurred in the majority opinion, wrote an article defending the decision and refuting its critics. The article paraphrased and endorsed Parker and summarized his key points; it may well have been a joint effort. It was published in a law journal rather than as an op-ed or in a popular magazine, giving it a penumbra of legal provenance, but it was intended for a popular audience and garnered lots of attention.

O'Brien began by quoting the August 23 editorial in the *New York Times* condemning the decision. The *Times* was usually "well-informed and conservative," but this piece, and others like it, were "inaccurate and misleading." The defendants' use of Roberson's photo may have been "impertinent and disagreeable," but it was not illegal. "A woman's beauty, next to her virtues, is her earthly crown," Judge O'Brien explained, "but it would be a degradation to hedge it about by rules and principles applicable to property in lands or chattels." The court did not decide that there was no right to privacy in New York, he explained, but merely that this plaintiff had not made the case for "interference by a court of equity by the writ or process of injunction." The courts were on solid ground when they "have simply applied settled principles to new facts and conditions," but there were not relevant, legally recognized principles here. The right of privacy was a concept "quite too fanciful for judicial recognition as a legal principle." Judges had to be conservative and tied to law and precedent and can't bend for every new idea that comes floating in on "the popular breeze." O'Brien continued that "the right of privacy . . . if it exists at all," must be regulated by "the courtesies and proprieties of life" and not the courts.[39]

Courts do not make laws but rather enforce those that exist, the judge lectured his readers. The legislature should act, as Chief Judge Parker had recommended. But Judge O'Brien was not optimistic about the prospect. "The right of privacy, so called, represents an attractive idea to the moralist and social reformer," but reducing it to a statute would be beset by "serious difficulties." It would be "quite impossible" to define the term and concept of *privacy* with precision. The "right of privacy," as bandied about by the decision's critics, "is such an intangible thing and conveys such a vague idea that it is very doubtful if the law can ever deal with it in any reasonable or practical way."[40] Having set up the case for how difficult writing privacy legislation would be, O'Brien concluded that the way was clear for the legislature to take up the work if it felt up to the challenge.

THE LIMITS OF THE LAW

The 1903 legislature took up Chief Judge Parker's and Judge O'Brien's challenge to enact a privacy law. It used Judge Gray's dissent for guidance. But Judge O'Brien's prediction proved correct—writing legislation was a challenge. *Privacy* turned out to be next to impossible for the lawmakers to define. The press, which had criticized the court's *Roberson* decision, now pulled back and opposed legislation that might have restricted newspapers' rights to publish private information and photographs. The result was a short piece of legislation that provided that "a person, firm or corporation that uses for advertising purposes, or for the purposes of trade, the name, portrait or picture of any living person without having first obtained the written consent of such person, or if a minor of his or her parent or guardian, is guilty of a misdemeanor."[41] People who felt these rights had been violated could apply for a restraining order and sue for recovery of damages.

The law, one of the first of its kind in the nation, was a compromise between people who wanted a right to privacy and the marketing and media sectors and others who wanted the right to publish photos. Freedom of speech and the right of publicity had confronted the right to privacy. The law was called a privacy law but was in reality was something much more modest, a personal image protection law.[42] Elbridge Adams, the attorney for Franklin Mills and Rochester Folding-Box Companies, called it "a short step in the direction of protecting the right of privacy." Adams found it ironic that some of the newspapers that had criticized his clients for their use of Abigail Roberson's photo and then chastised Judge Parker for not backing her had opposed a stronger statute out of apprehension that "press-stranglers" might use it to stifle freedom of the press.[43] But Adams cautioned that the law could be misused. For instance, if an artist made a sketch of a woman and it happened to resemble the likeness of someone else, that person might sue under the law.

Advertisers pulled back on unauthorized use of photos but challenged the law's constitutionality in court. In 1908 the court of appeals affirmed its constitutionality. The Sperry & Hutchinson company issued "trading stamps," which stores purchased and gave out as bonuses to shoppers. The shoppers could then redeem the accumulated stamps for housewares and other items. A woman sued Sperry & Hutchinson for use of her photograph without her consent in an ad for their stamps. The state supreme court and the appellate division ruled in her favor, citing the act as a violation of the 1903 privacy law. The company appealed, asserting the law was unconstitutional on the grounds that it deprived people of liberty and property without due process of law. It also argued that it was ex post facto in restricting use of photos that the company had obtained before the law went into effect.

Judge Willard Bartlett wrote an opinion for the unanimous court of appeals: "Unless we are bound to assume that there is an inherent right in the public at large to use the names and portraits of others for advertising or trade purposes without their consent, the legislative restrictions of their liberty imposed by this act is not an exercise of power which affords the basis of any legal objection in a court of justice." The judge also easily disposed of the objection that the law covered photos taken before the law was passed. Even for those photos, "written consent of the person represented" would be needed for their use. Sperry & Hutchinson's counsel's objection that the law would cause inconveniences for photographers seemed "quite fanciful and hardly likely to arise."[44] The company appealed to the US Supreme Court, which endorsed the court of appeals decision and upheld the constitutionality of the law.[45]

In the meantime, other states began passing privacy laws. Some followed New York, but others constructed their own, reflecting their view of common-law protections and the appropriate reach and constraints of the law. Courts in other states, which often looked to New York for wisdom and precedent, often referred to *Roberson* but usually to Judge Gray's dissent rather than Chief Judge Parker's majority opinion.

PRIVACY AND POLITICS

Alton Parker resigned as chief judge in 1904 and ran for president on the Democratic ticket. During the campaign, the candidate objected to photographers intruding on his privacy—for instance, trying to get a photo of him emerging from the Hudson River after an early morning swim near his estate in Esopus and annoying his wife by hanging around the porch of their house. "I reserve the right to put my hands in my pockets and assume comfortable attitudes without being everlastingly afraid that I shall be snapped by some fellow with a camera," he complained to the press. Abigail Roberson wrote a letter to the editor of the *New York Times* telling Parker that she had it "on very high authority" that "you have no such right." She recalled his opinion stating that the "so-called right to privacy" did not exist and that Parker was now asserting a right for himself and his family that he had denied to her in his court. Going further, she called herself "a poor girl making my living by my daily efforts," while he was a candidate for the nation's highest office. "The right which you denied me, but which you now assert for yourself, was stronger in my case than in yours."[46]

Roberson was a bit off the mark. Her situation and Parker's were dissimilar. Her image had been used for advertising purposes, legal when it was done but illegal since the 1903 law (at least in New York State).

Parker was a prominent news maker, and the New York statute (and federal statutes) did not preclude the use of his photo in newspapers.

Parker lost the election to the incumbent president and Republican nominee, Theodore Roosevelt.

The legislature took up the issue of privacy a number of times in the ensuing decades. But what was worked out and put onto the statute books in 1903 endures. New York's privacy law, now section 50 of the state Civil Rights Law, uses almost the same wording as the 1903 privacy law. Section 51, added later and updated in 2014, added "voice" to what is protected and spells out actions for injunctions and damages. New York did not develop a common-law right to privacy, and in fact privacy has continued to be an elusive concept. In 1960, legal scholar William Prosser parsed the "privacy tort" into four segments: (1) intrusion upon someone's seclusion, (2) unreasonable publicity given to someone's private life, (3) appropriation of someone's name or likeness, and (4) publicity that unreasonably places someone in a false light before the public.[47] New York had at least partially addressed (3) in its 1903 privacy law and the subsequent law still on the books. But the other three remain ambiguous, not fully resolved, still under discussion, and often judgment calls for the courts.[48]

Chapter 3

THE CASE THAT HELPED CHANGE CONSTITUTIONAL HISTORY AND LAUNCH A QUEST FOR THE PRESIDENCY

Figures 3.1 and 3.2. New York Court of Appeals chief judge Alton Parker, left, wrote the decision in *People v. Lochner* (1904) affirming the state's authority to regulate working hours and conditions for bakers. Fellow New Yorker Rufus Peckham, right, US Supreme Court associate justice, wrote the decision in *Lochner v. New York* in 1905 overruling Parker and restricting that authority. *Source:* Library of Congress Prints & Photographs Collection.

Does New York State have the right to regulate bakers' hours and working conditions? The New York State Court of Appeals said yes in 1904 in an opinion that helped launch Chief Judge Alton Parker's quest for the presidency. The United States Supreme Court said no in 1905 in one of the most important, influential, and controversial court decisions in US history. The Supreme Court effectively reversed itself in a key decision in 1937. New York judges wrote all three opinions.

On January 12, 1904, New York State Court of Appeals chief judge Alton B. Parker delivered the court's decision in the case of *People v. Lochner*. The court affirmed an 1895 state law limiting the hours of work in bakeries to ten hours per day or sixty per week and imposing sanitary regulations. The US Supreme Court overturned that decision the next year in a landmark opinion written by another New Yorker, Associate Justice Rufus Peckham. Parker's *Lochner* opinion, that the state's police power may trump an individual's liberty of contract, and Peckham's *Lochner* opinion, that liberty of contract should usually outweigh the state's regulatory authority, defined opposing judicial doctrines that have continued ever since that time.

Former US Supreme Court chief justice William Rehnquist called Peckham's opinion "one of the most ill-starred decisions that [the court] ever rendered."[1] Justice John Roberts, in his confirmation hearing to be chief justice of the Supreme Court in 2005, said that in the *Lochner* case the Supreme Court was "not interpreting the law, they're making the law. . . . Substituting their judgment on a policy matter for what the legislature had said."[2] Historians have mostly agreed with those critical assessments. But they have neglected the history of the case as it moved through New York state courts and the decisive court of appeals decision.

NEW YORK'S ENTRY INTO REGULATING BUSINESS

New York's industrial code at the end of the nineteenth century was scant; most businesses and industries were unregulated. One of the state's first forays into the regulating arena came in a somewhat surprising place, bakeries. By the end of the century, there were small bakeries in basement locations in every city, hundreds in New York City alone, to meet the needs of the state's growing urban population. Bread and pastries were baked on site and sold locally, while they were fresh (plastic wrapping, preservatives, and refrigeration were lacking in those days), often to the tenants of the buildings in whose basements the bakeries were located and residents of nearby homes. Bakers worked long hours and were exposed to flour dust, gas fumes, dampness, and extremes of heat and cold. The small bakeries were owner/proprietor operated, with a limited number of employees, usually paid by the hour or by the day.

But both political parties came to favor regulating bakeries after newspaper exposés of unsanitary working conditions and contaminated baked goods were published. Most bakery proprietors were independent owners and had no organization to lobby against regulatory legislation. Unions favored the legislation as something that they hoped would benefit their members. Republicans held the majority in both houses of the legislature, and two of their members, Assemblyman Arthur Audett from Brooklyn and Senator Cornelius Parsons from Rochester, drafted a bill. The proposed law's sections regulating the workplace seemed fairly innocuous. For instance, one section required that "all buildings or rooms occupied as biscuit, bread, pie, or cake bakeries shall be drained and plumbed in a manner conducive to the proper and healthful sanitary condition thereof, and shall be constructed with air shafts, windows or ventilating pipes, sufficient to ensure ventilation."[3] The restrictions on working hours—workers could be "permitted or required" to work no more than ten hours per day and sixty hours per week—were more concrete and would prove more contentious and harder to enforce. But the bill was not controversial. It passed the legislature unanimously, Democrats joining their Republican colleagues, with little fanfare. Republican governor Levi Morton signed it on May 2, 1895.[4]

The law, inconsistently enforced because the state had only a handful of inspectors, soon met opposition. It thwarted overtime work, essential for a business that responded to daily fluctuations in demand. Critics charged selective enforcement and targeting of nonunion shops. Unions shifted to skepticism and opposition because it made overtime work for their members more problematic. Workers grumbled that working hours should be a matter for them and their employers, not the state.

The law also ran against the tradition that the state should not interfere with employee-employer relations or place unnecessary limits on individual freedom. Opponents rallied behind the concept of substantive due process. The US Constitution's Fourteenth Amendment proscribed state laws abridging "life, liberty, or property, without due process of law."

It had been adopted in 1868 to help protect the rights of Black Americans, former slaves in the South, after the Civil War. The New York State Constitution had a similar, but briefer, provision. Years later, business attorneys began to argue that it also applied to the rights of employers to run their businesses without state interference and to employees' rights to contract to work as they pleased. They contended it trumped the state's police power—the power to regulate social and economic affairs for the general welfare, health, and safety of the people. In the closing years of the nineteenth century and the opening years of the twentieth, the "substantive due process" shield was pressed into service by the business community to forestall or overturn incipient state regulatory intervention. Usually, lawyers attacking regulatory laws cited the Fourteenth Amendment, and occasionally the state constitution provision as well.[5]

Joseph Lochner, a Utica bakery owner, believed that New York State could not tell him how to operate his business. He deliberately employed a baker for a more-than-sixty-hour week. The baker, a young German immigrant named Aman Schmitter, was also a friend of Lochner's and sometimes boarded with him. Lochner and Schmitter may have cooked up the lawsuit together to test the constitutionality of the law. Lochner was arrested and fined $20 in the state supreme court in Oneida County in April 1899. He continued openly employing Schmitter above the legal limit and was fined again, $50 for a second offense.

He refused to pay this time and appealed his conviction to the Appellate Division of the Supreme Court of the State of New York. His counsel sharpened the argument that Lochner's right to contract and his employees' right to work were guaranteed by the Fourteenth Amendment. Lochner lost again. The appellate decision noted that "courts cannot inquire whether the legislative enactments are unwise or expedient" and that "nothing but a clear usurpation of power prohibited by the Constitution" would justify overturning the law. Like any other business, Lochner was "subject to the police power of the State to regulate or control its use, so as to protect and preserve the public health, the public morals and the general safety and welfare of the public."[6] But the decision was divided: three were against Lochner and in support of the state law; two dissented in his favor.

Lochner appealed to the New York State Court of Appeals in a dispute that was attracting increasing public attention and was coming to be regarded as a constitutional test case. The court agreed to hear his case.

MARSHALING THE LEGAL ARGUMENTS

Opposing counsel developed briefs for consideration by the court of appeals that foreshadowed both the judges' majority opinions and the dissents.

Lochner's attorney, William S. Mackie of Utica, contended that the law violated the Constitution's provision that no one could be deprived of any right or privilege except through due process of law. Lochner was meeting all the sanitary conditions imposed by the law. In fact, Mackie claimed, the law coupled sanitary regulations with limitations of hours mostly to give the state the opportunity to regulate work time, and that went beyond the state's authority and was arbitrary. "The miller, the butcher, the sugar refiner, and the miner," and all other manufacturing and transportation companies, escaped similar regulation. Bakers need to vary their working schedules in order to meet fluctuating customer demand. The law makes authorizing and paying for overtime difficult. Bakers themselves could work more-than-ten-hour days; shouldn't their employees have the same right? Anyway, employees could evade it by working in more than one bakery. The brief argued that the court decisions cited by prosecutors and relied on by the two courts that had upheld the law were either mistaken or not appropriate here.[7]

Oneida County district attorney Timothy Curtin prepared the respondent's points since the case was first tried in county court there. His brief cited several legal cases, e.g., the 1898 US Supreme Court decision *Holden v. Hardy*, which upheld a Utah law limiting the number of hours of work for miners as a legitimate exercise of state police power. He argued that government can regulate its citizens and the legislature has broad discretionary powers. Baking work was exhausting, and working too many hours will cause workers to "become overworked, tired out and liable to become impaired in health." It really did not burden bakery owners; if they found it too restrictive, they could simply hire more employees.[8]

THE CHIEF JUDGE AS A JUDICIAL STATESMAN

The case reached the court of appeals in October 1903 and was decided in January 1904. It achieved high visibility for three reasons. One, it would be decided by the most important state court in the nation, second only to the US Supreme Court in visibility and influence. Two, it would test the validity of an important and possibly precedent-setting regulatory law at a time when the Progressive reform movement, whose hallmark was government regulation of business, was starting to gain traction in New York and elsewhere in the nation.

Three, Democrat Alton Parker (1852–1926), chief judge of the court of appeals since 1897, was a leading contender for his party's presidential nomination in 1904. Parker had won his position as chief judge decisively in the 1897 election after serving for several years on the state supreme court and the appellate division of the supreme court. Parker's judicial career had advanced through the help of his powerful mentor, David B. Hill, who served as lieutenant governor (1883–85), governor (1885–91), and US senator (1891–97).[9] Parker was modest and judicious but also politically shrewd and ambitious. He had the presidency in distant view in each of his highly visible opinions in the 1900–1904 period. He knew what cases were in queue for consideration by the court since he was responsible for selecting and scheduling them. *Lochner* would be his last high-visibility case before his presidential run. It would provide an opportunity for the judge to write an opinion that was not only judicially correct but also politically advantageous.

As chief judge, Alton Parker had been a cautious, judicious progressive. In a 1902 controversial and much-criticized decision discussed in chapter 2, he had written the majority opinion denying a woman the right under the common law to forbid a flour company from using her image in their advertising.[10] In another 1902 decision, he upheld the right of a union to threaten to strike to compel an employer to discharge nonunion workers.[11] He was wary of cases that threatened to draw the court into competitive business situations. In a 1903 decision, Judge Parker held that an association of wholesale druggists formed to secure lower prices from manufacturers was not a combination in restraint of trade or a violation of antitrust laws. "This is a controversy between opponents in business. . . . When one party finds himself overmatched by the strength of the position of the other . . . quite often he turns to the courts . . . and makes himself for the time being the pretended champion of the public welfare in the hope that the courts may be deceived into an adjudication that will prove helpful to him," wrote the judge. "[But the] real purpose is to strengthen the strategic position of one competitor in business as against another," and the courts should stay out of such contests.[12]

Parker believed that the courts usually needed to respect and defer to the legislature even when it passed poorly written statutes or seemingly faulty public policies. In a 1901 dissenting opinion that foreshadowed the philosophy behind his opinion in the *Lochner* case three years later, he argued that the majority of his court erred in siding with a contractor who had not paid a prevailing wage on a contract with New York City, as required by law. The majority criticized the law for being too vague, though it stopped short of declaring it unconstitutional. The chief judge called the majority's opinion "a judicial encroachment upon legislative prerogative." The language of the statute was "so carefully guarded as to leave no room for doubt that the legislature, appreciating the limits of its authority," had been well within its constitutional authority.[13] The law might be poorly drawn but "there is nothing in the Constitution to restrict the power of the legislature" to act as it did.[14] The law should stand.

Chief Judge Parker acknowledged the central importance of the by-then-famous phrase "due process of law" but thought courts were tempted to overuse it to invalidate state regulatory legislation. In a trip to Georgia on July 4, 1903, to test the political waters for his possible run for the presidency, he had addressed that state's bar association with a speech emphasizing that the Fourteenth Amendment should be interpreted conservatively because it was mainly adopted to protect newly liberated Black Americans from state coercion, not to protect businesses from state regulation. The speech caught the attention of New Yorkers. Paraphrasing the chief judge, a *New York Times* editorial said the amendment probably would not have been passed if voters had foreseen its unintended use to protect business interests. It reported that Parker did not expect the Supreme Court to use the amendment "to impose on state governments further restrictions than are absolutely necessary."[15]

The chief judge developed that view in a three-part article in the American Bar Association's journal, the *American Lawyer*, later that year. Parker traced the concept of due process of law back to English legal traditions and the Magna Carta and discussed how courts had viewed it over the years. The "sole purpose" of the phrase as used in the US Constitution's Fourteenth Amendment was to ensure the rights of formerly enslaved people. New York's Senator Roscoe Conkling, a member of the committee that drafted the amendment, later asserted that it was broader than that, intending to protect corporations as well as people. Parker reiterated that the amendment would not have been approved by the states with that interpretation attached to it. The courts, however, had adopted that broader interpretation of its coverage, and a good deal of case law had developed. Parker cited several Supreme Court decisions but emphasized those that upheld state regulatory laws. One example was *Holden v. Hardy*, where the court had followed the decision of Utah's highest court in validating a law regulating miners' working hours in 1898. Parker cited several other Supreme Court decisions where state taxation and regulatory laws "have been sustained as a valid exercise of the police power." The court clearly recognized that states had "the necessity of recognizing the change of conditions" in regulatory legislation. States' highest courts were in a good position of judging the validity of state legislation against the measure of the Fourteenth Amendment because they understood those conditions. The judge expressed hope that the Supreme Court would act "conservatively" when deciding cases involving the "restraining power" of the Fourteenth Amendment against the states, as it had in *Holden v. Hardy*.[16]

The chief judge of the nation's most important state court had made a high-profile plea (or prediction) in the journal of the nation's bar association for the Supreme Court to show lenience, forbearance, and light application of the Fourteenth Amendment. He had implied that the nation's highest court needed to consider deferring to the states' highest courts, which understood the context and purpose of regulatory laws in their states. The US Supreme Court's *Lochner* decision would contradict his views.

THE MAJORITY OF THE COURT ENDORSES THE LAW

It was no surprise when Judge Parker assigned himself to write the court's opinion in the *Lochner* case. His opinion forcefully upheld the bakeshop law's constitutionality.[17] The opinion is longer and in some ways more persuasive than the famous one that overturned it in the United States Supreme Court the next year. Parker made several points:

The Fourteenth Amendment and a Comparable Clause in the New York State Constitution Were Not Intended to Infringe the State's Police Power

He cited several Supreme Court decisions "sustaining statutes of different states which . . . seem repugnant to the 14th amendment, but which that court declares to be within the police power of the states." He followed the Oneida County district attorney and the appellate division court in emphasizing *Holden v. Hardy* (1898), which upheld a Utah law limiting the number of hours of work for miners as a legitimate exercise of state police power. New York State case law was "all in one direction," too, he said, in support of broad state intervention. Parker cited an 1895 opinion by then court of appeals judge Rufus Peckham, who had become a justice of the US Supreme Court the next year: " 'Laws and regulations of a police nature, though they may disturb the enjoyment of individual rights, are not unconstitutional. . . . They do not appropriate private property for public use, but simply regulate its use and enjoyment by the owner.' "[18] Citing Peckham's proregulation stance was good strategy. Peckham, on the US Supreme Court at the time of Parker's writing, usually went in the opposite direction, against state regulation. Parker may have been hedging his bets, recognizing that Peckham's views would be critical if the case were appealed to the US Supreme Court, which as it turned out is what happened.

Changing Conditions Warrant Changing Regulations

The Constitution must be read in light of changes in society and the economy, Parker said: "by the application of established legal principles the law has been, and will continue to be developed from time to time so as to meet the ever-changing conditions of our widely diversified and rapidly developing business interests."[19]

Courts Should Not Second-Guess the Legislature

"The courts are frequently confronted with the temptation to substitute their judgment for that of the legislature," the chief judge wrote.[20] But whether the legislation is wise "is not for us to consider. The motives actuating the legislature are not the subject of inquiry by the courts, which are bound to assume that the law making body acted with a desire to promote the public good." Where interpretation is needed, "the court is inclined to so construe the statute as to validate it."[21]

The Public Interest Is Served by Sanitary Bakeries

"That the public generally are interested in having bakers' and confectioners' establishments cleanly and wholesome in this day of appreciation of, and apprehension on account of, microbes, which cause disease and death, is beyond question," Parker asserted. The statute is designed "to protect the public from the use of the food made dangerous by the germs that thrive in darkness and uncleanness."[22]

The least strong part of the judge's opinion was the argument in favor of the regulation of working hours. In fact, he handed his critics the kernel of an argument by saying that if the regulation of hours stood alone, "I should incline to the view that the enactment was unconstitutional. . . . That would be to infringe upon the liberty of contract." But, in a tenuous connection, Parker asserted that "the legislature had in mind that the health and cleanliness of the workers, as well as the cleanliness of the work-rooms, was of the utmost importance, and that a man is more likely to be careful and cleanly when well, and not overworked, than when exhausted by fatigue, which makes for careless and slovenly habits, and tends to dirt and disease."[23]

Two of Parker's colleagues, Judge John C. Gray and Judge Irving G. Vann, wrote concurring opinions: courts should presume legislative competency, the US Supreme Court has validated similar statutes, and the law is based on legitimate concerns about the health of bakery workers and the general public. Judge Albert Haight concurred without an opinion. That gave Parker four votes, enough to prevail.

THREE JUDGES SAY NO

But three judges dissented from the chief judge, and two of them, Denis O'Brien and Edward Bartlett, wrote opinions that set forth many of the arguments that Lochner would use to appeal and the majority of the US Supreme Court would use to overturn the bakeshop law the next year.

Judge O'Brien usually agreed with Parker. In the controversial *Roberson* case two years earlier, he had taken the extraordinary step of publishing an article defending the chief judge's decision. But in his *Lochner* dissent, O'Brien assailed the law for permitting bakery *proprietors* to work as long as they wished but forbidding them from "permitting or requiring" *employees* to do the same. Overtime for extra pay beyond the law's restrictions was forbidden "no matter what may be the wants or necessities of the business, or the judgment or will of the [worker]. . . . It is obviously one of those paternal laws, enacted doubtless with the best intentions, but which in its operation must inevitably put enmity and strife between master and servant." Moreover, the judge asserted, "what possible relation or connection the number of hours that the workmen are permitted to work in the bakery has, or can have, to the healthful quality of the bread made there is quite impossible to conceive." It discriminates against one group of workers while leaving others—e.g., farm workers or domestic servants (who, the judge wryly observed, might bake bread and pies for more than ten hours per day in their employers' homes)—unregulated. The whole thing amounted to an "arbitrary and unnecessary restriction." "Mere legislation" cannot deny bakery workers or anyone else of life, liberty, or property, which are protected by the Constitution's Fourteenth Amendment.[24]

Judge Bartlett issued a short but incisive dissent. The claim that baking is unhealthy "will surprise the bakers and good housewives of this state" who do it every day. There really is no "risk of health and life" in the vocation of baking as there might be, for instance, in making steel and mining coal. New Yorkers had been baking for hundreds of years with no documented health problems. The law thrust state government into an area where it did not belong and where its intervention simply was not needed. It represented another example of "the full panoply of paternalism" and state regulatory overreach, which was becoming all too common, Bartlett concluded.[25]

The court had ruled, 4–3, in favor of the constitutionality of the law and against Lochner.

Judge Parker used the opinion to burnish his image as a progressive-minded leader. He secured the Democratic nomination for president and resigned from the court of appeals in August 1904. He ran a lackluster campaign, discussed in chapter 4. The Democrats circulated his *Lochner* opinion as one of their campaign documents. It showed, they explained, that Parker had workers' best interests at heart and would favor government regulations to improve their employment conditions. But Parker never really connected with the electorate. He lost the race decisively to another New Yorker, incumbent president (and former governor) Theodore Roosevelt.

NEW YORKERS SQUARE OFF IN WASHINGTON

In the meantime, Joseph Lochner appealed the court of appeals' decision to the US Supreme Court, which agreed to hear his case.

The case by then had attracted lots of attention. It originated in the nation's largest and most important state, the main opinion had been written by a presidential candidate, and it presented far-reaching constitutional issues. By this time, Lochner had engaged new attorneys, including the very capable Henry Weismann. He had been a bakery union official when the bill passed in 1895 and lobbied for it. But he later became a bakery owner himself and counsel for the union, went through "an intellectual revolution," and changed his mind, coming to regard the law as a vexatious interference with bakeshop business.[26] The brief he submitted to the court documented the law's disruptive impact on bakers. He also integrated two points that had surfaced in the New York Court of Appeals' O'Brien and Bartlett dissents: bakery work was not inherently unsafe, and the provision limiting hours was an unwarranted incursion on liberty of contract. New York attorney general Julius M. Mayer, elected for the first time in 1904 and charged with defending another important New York law (a franchise tax on public utilities) before the Supreme Court at about the same time, had limited time to prepare the state's *Lochner* defense. He may have been overconfident; Parker's opinion seemed solid. He relied mostly on that opinion in his brief to argue that the court should defer to the New York legislature, the law protects the health of workers and the public, and the burden is on Lochner to prove that the law is not warranted.[27]

The Supreme Court had been inconsistent in its view of state regulatory statutes, approving some and invalidating others for authorizing excessive state oversight. But Associate Justice Rufus W. Peckham (1838–1909) had emerged as a shrill and increasingly influential proponent of freedom to contract and an opponent of state regulatory enactments. Peckham had been Albany County district attorney and a judge on the New York State Supreme Court, 1883–85, and then the court of appeals, 1886–95. Peckham was elevated to the US Supreme Court in 1896 by another New Yorker, president (and former governor) Grover Cleveland. A dapper dresser with a long mustache and snow-white hair, he could be sociable and congenial. He was "sturdy, independent, kindly, modest, well poised. . . . He loved justice with all his heart," according to his colleague Alton B. Parker, praising Peckham at a memorial service after his death in 1909.[28]

But he had strong convictions, despised hypocrisy, disliked compromising, and sometimes tried to overawe his judicial colleagues with strongly expressed opinions. "Justice Peckham is regarded as the most outspoken man on the United States Supreme Court," a newspaper observed.[29]

Peckham had occasionally endorsed government regulations. In an 1897 opinion, he applied the federal Sherman Antitrust Act of 1890 to invalidate a traffic-pooling and price-fixing agreement among railroads.[30] But for the most part he distained government intrusion into business affairs and people's lives. If there was no clear-cut, overriding public purpose for a regulation, then it should not exist, Peckham felt. "More than any other judge, Peckham was the exemplar of the conservative jurist early in [the twentieth] century. His decisions were prime applications of the dominant legal thought of the day—using the law as the barrier against interferences with the operation of the economic system."[31] In 1889, while still on the New York State Court of Appeals, he delivered a vigorous dissent in a case involving a state law fixing the rates of grain storage elevators, calling it "paternal government," "wholly useless for any good effect, and only powerful for evil," "vicious in its nature, communistic in its tendency."[32]

In 1897, Justice Peckham wrote the majority opinion in *Allgeyer v. Louisiana*, striking down a statute forbidding citizens of that state from doing business with out-of-state insurance companies unless they registered with Louisiana authorities. The law contravened an individual's "liberty of contract," Peckham insisted. He wrote:

> The "liberty" mentioned in [the Fourteenth] amendment means not only the right of the citizen to be free from the mere physical restraint of his person, as by incarceration, but the term is deemed to embrace the right of the citizen to be free in the enjoyment of all his faculties, to be free to use them in all lawful ways, to live and work where he will, to earn his livelihood by any lawful calling, to pursue any livelihood or avocation, and for that purpose to enter into all contracts which may be proper, necessary, and essential to his carrying out to a successful conclusion the purposes above mentioned.[33]

When the Supreme Court majority, in *Holden v. Hardy*, upheld a Utah law limiting the number of work hours for miners and smelters as a legitimate exercise of the police power of the state, Peckham had written a vigorous dissent.[34] Peckham, who maintained a summer home in Altamont, New York, near Albany, undoubtedly followed the progress of the *Lochner* case through the New York courts. He knew and respected Alton Parker from their days serving on New York courts. Parker's opinion was powerful. On the other hand, the court of appeals decision had been four to three, with the dissenters presenting persuasive arguments against the law. State courts in some other states had struck down regulatory measures as contravening the Fourteenth Amendment, but before *Lochner* the US Supreme Court had been relatively lenient. *Allgeyer v. Louisiana*, Peckham's handiwork, had been an exception. Peckham saw a chance to drive his point home with a strong *Lochner* decision.[35]

Convinced he could get the majority of his colleagues on the court to see things his way, Peckham asked Chief Justice Melville Fuller for a chance to write the opinion in the case. The stage was set for a confrontation between Alton Parker's supportive view of the state's regulatory right and his fellow New Yorker Rufus Peckham's insistence on the paramount status of liberty of contract.

Lochner v. New York was decided on April 16, 1905, by a 5–4 vote, with Peckham writing the majority opinion. It became one of the most influential and famous decisions in American judicial history.

Peckham denied that bakers are "wards of the State" and ridiculed the assertion that their work was dangerous. He asserted that the law did not constitute a legitimate exercise of police power and contended that it contravened Joseph Lochner's and his employees' right of contract. "No State can deprive any person of life, liberty or property without due process of law," said the judge, conveniently citing his own opinion in Allgeyer v. Louisiana. "There is no reasonable ground for interfering with the liberty of person or the right of free contract by determining the hours of labor in the occupation of a baker. . . . Clean and wholesome bread does not depend upon whether the baker works but ten hours per day or only sixty hours a week."[36] Peckham was, in effect, ratifying the dissenting views of New York Court of Appeals judges O'Brien and Bartlett the previous year. Four other justices agreed with Peckham.

Four others, however, disagreed and dissented. Justice John Marshall Harlan, in a dissent endorsed by two other justices, contended that the liberty to contract is subject to reasonable regulation imposed by the State acting under its police power. Justice Harlan's dissent mirrored Judge Parker's opinion. Justice Oliver Wendell Holmes dissented in a witty opinion where he claimed that the majority followed "an economic theory which a large part of the country does not entertain."[37]

Lochner v. New York had wide influence, achieved fame, and went permanently into the history books. People v. Lochner, its immensely important New York predecessor, went into the footnotes. It is often not even mentioned in discussions of the federal version of the case.

PARKER VERSUS PECKHAM FOR MORE THAN A CENTURY

Peckham's Lochner opinion, and the judicial philosophy it embodied, had staying power for many years. In the ensuing three decades, the Supreme

Court used the Fourteenth Amendment's due process clause to strike down dozens of state and federal laws.[38] Many laws designed to regulate social and economic conditions of the industrial and urban eras—minimum wage laws; child labor laws; regulations of insurance, banking, transportation, and other companies—fell to Peckham's logic. In other cases, legislatures hesitated to enact reforms that might fall afoul of Peckham's dictum. The courts were more lenient toward laws regulating occupations that government prosecutors could prove to the court were inherently unhealthy or dangerous. In the years after the *Lochner* case, several states passed laws regulating work in mines and smelters and on railroads, which mostly withstood challenges in court.[39]

With a touch of New York defiance, the state Department of Labor made a point of saying the federal decision was reached "by the narrow majority of one" and that it pertained to the bakery law only and would not deter other state regulations. Holmes's dissent "sounds the key-note of the twentieth century" with its "trenchant declaration" in favor of state powers.[40] That was a bit of wishful thinking; the Supreme Court's *Lochner* opinion gave New York legislators pause as they considered regulatory measures after it. By 1912, though, New York's union bakers had gained the ten-hour day—not through legislation or court decisions but through union initiatives and collective bargaining.

New York State enacted multiple laws to regulate factory working conditions after the tragic Triangle Shirtwaist Factory fire of 1911, where many people died because of inadequate fire escapes. In 1907, as discussed in chapter 9, the New York State Court of Appeals invalidated a statute prohibiting night work in factories by women on the grounds that it was discriminatory and denied them equal rights with men. But eight years later, as discussed in chapter 10, it effectively reversed that ruling and sustained a similar night-work law, citing "new and additional knowledge," including reports of the New York State Factory Investigating Commission established after the Triangle fire and "scientific and medical opinion that night work by women in factories is generally injurious."[41]

The struggle over *Lochner* continued for years. Considering the US Supreme Court, New York Court of Appeals, and Appellate Division of the New York State Supreme Court, eleven thoughtful judges had come down in favor of the law, ten against. The Supreme Court's *Lochner* decision brought lots of criticism. One of the most strident critics was Theodore Roosevelt. He had been president when *People v. Lochner* was rendered in 1904 and when *Lochner v. New York* reversed it in 1905 but made no public statements at that time. Beginning in 1910, when he was seeking the presidency again, he began citing the decision as an example (among others) of the courts favoring business interests and ignoring the public welfare. He called for public referenda on court decisions that overturned legislative enactments as unconstitutional, a proposal that found little support.[42] Notably, Roosevelt did not publicly acknowledge that the court of appeals in his own state, in an opinion written by his 1904 rival for the presidency, had been on what he now said he regarded as the right side of the issue.

The kernel for a revival of Parker's proregulation reasoning was always present. A decisive case in the 1930s once again put two New Yorkers at center stage: Chief Justice Charles Evans Hughes, who had been a progressive Republican governor of New York (1907–10), and President Franklin D. Roosevelt, who had also served as governor, from 1929 to 1933.

As governor, Hughes pushed through the New York state legislature a number of regulatory measures similar to the Bakeshop Act that the Peckham court had invalidated. Hughes served as a justice of the US Supreme Court from 1910 to 1916 and had tended to favor regulations. He served as secretary of state from 1921 to 1925 and was appointed chief justice of the US Supreme Court in 1930. He was regarded as a senior judicial statesman. But as chief justice his position on government regulation was ambivalent, sometimes favoring reformist laws and other times voting to invalidate them. In the mid-1930s, the court heard constitutional challenges to several of Franklin D. Roosevelt's New Deal reform and regulatory laws. Four of Hughes's ultraconservative colleagues on the high court, who had views of FDR "ranging in charitableness from an image of villainy to one of idiocy," badgered government counsel and found one or two colleagues on the court to rule one New Deal measure after another unconstitutional.[43] For instance, they struck down the business-regulatory codes of the National Recovery Act in 1935 and the Agricultural Adjustment Act in 1936.

Several state laws, too, went down in the early 1930s. The court in effect seemed to have reverted to Peckham's laissez-faire reasoning. In 1933, New York State passed a law to set minimum wages for women. Joseph Tipaldo, manager of the Spotlight Laundry in Brooklyn, refused to pay his female employees the weekly minimum wages required by state law and falsified his employment and pay records. The state courts found him guilty and imposed a fine. He appealed his conviction up to the US

Supreme Court, which struck down the New York law in a 1936 ruling. "The right to make contracts about one's affairs is a part of the liberty protected by the due process clause," wrote Justice Pierce Butler, one of the court's most consistently conservative judges, in the majority opinion.[44]

Justice Butler's reasoning was lockstep with Justice Peckham's in *Lochner*: government should not go where the Constitution does not specifically authorize it to go. Hughes and three colleagues dissented in this case. Many of the negative decisions were 5–4. Hughes realized that the court's decisions were striking down useful legislation and stirring political criticism.

In 1937, President Roosevelt proposed to enlarge the Supreme Court, allegedly to promote efficiency and speed decisions, but really to give him a chance to name more supportive justices. "During the past half century, the balance of power between the three great branches of the Federal Government, has been tipped out of balance by the Courts in direct contradiction of the high purposes of the framers of the Constitution," said FDR in a speech that year.[45] Supporters described it as an antidote to obstructionism and "government by judiciary"; opponents called it "packing the court."

Many years earlier, as related in chapter 7, in a speech when he was governor, Hughes had said "We are under a Constitution, but the Constitution is what the judges say it is."[46] Critics of the court often cited Hughes's admission, but he recognized it still had some merit. The Constitution had to adapt to the times—for instance, the impact of urbanization and industrialization—and it was the responsibility of judges to make that happen. Hughes was alarmed at FDR's scheme, but he was sincerely changing his mind about government regulation.

Taking an opportunity to move the court in a new direction, Hughes wrote the court's opinion in the 1937 case of *West Coast Hotel Co. v. Parrish*.[47] The case concerned a Washington State minimum-wage law much like the New York law the court had struck down in 1936 in the *Tipaldo* case. But the court approved the Washington State law by a 5–4 vote. Hughes had helped convince a swing voter, Justice Owen Roberts, to side with him in upholding it. "Liberty implies the absence of arbitrary restraint," Hughes wrote, "not immunity from reasonable regulations and prohibitions imposed in the interests of the community."[48] The opinion reached back, at least in spirit, to the opinion of his fellow New Yorker Alton B. Parker to justify state regulation on two grounds: the public interest warrants it, and the Fourteenth Amendment tolerates it.

THE PUBLIC INTEREST IS SERVED BY THE REGULATION AT ISSUE

"What can be closer to the public interest than the health of women and their protection from unscrupulous and overreaching employers?" Hughes asked. "And if the protection of women is a legitimate end of the exercise of state power, how can it be said that the requirement of the payment of a minimum wage fairly fixed in order to meet the very necessities of existence is not an admissible means to that end?"[49]

THE FOURTEENTH AMENDMENT DOES NOT PROHIBIT REASONABLE REGULATION

The law's opponents allege violation of freedom of contract. "What is this freedom? The Constitution does not speak of freedom of contract," Hughes noted, building his case against overly restrictive judicial philosophy dating back to Peckham. "The Constitution does not recognize an absolute and uncontrollable liberty. . . . The liberty safeguarded is liberty in a social organization which requires the protection of law against the evils which menace the health, safety, morals and welfare of the people. . . . This power under the Constitution to restrict freedom of contract has had many illustrations. That it may be exercised in the public interest with respect to contracts between employer and employee is undeniable."[50]

Thirty-three years after his *Lochner* decision, Alton Parker had made something of a comeback in Charles Evans Hughes's words. Peckham's *Lochner* sway seemed to be finished with the *West Coast Hotel Co. v. Parrish* decision. The court that same year upheld the constitutionality of the Social Security Act and the National Labor Relations Act. Thereafter, it was decidedly supportive of government regulative initiatives. President Roosevelt's court-enlargement scheme sputtered out for lack of support.

Since that time, in general, the Supreme Court has mostly favored Parker's view over Peckham's.

THE DEBATE GOES ON

Legal scholars still debate the *Lochner* case, though few take cognizance of the New York Court of Appeals decision. Opinions over the years have varied.[51] As noted at the beginning of this chapter, Chief Justices Rehnquist and Roberts have both condemned the Supreme Court decision, and most legal scholars have agreed. Federal judge and legal scholar Ted Stewart called the Supreme Court decision "a great power play" by the court to run roughshod over legislatures and set itself up as "the ultimate decider" as to just what constituted "due process" and whether a particular piece of legislation unreasonably interferes with someone's liberty.[52]

Most commentators overlook Alton Parker and the New York Court of Appeals' strong affirmation of the state's regulatory powers. Parker's decision was in effect an affirmation and defense of Progressivism and later reform movements, e.g., the New Deal. In that sense, he was ahead of his time in this opinion.

But other scholars have sided with Peckham, interpreting his views as consistent with preceding Supreme Court decisions, supportive of government neutrality and constitutionally guaranteed liberties, and a bulwark against government regulatory overreach.[53]

The issue of how far government may go in restricting individual rights in order to protect individuals' well-being and the welfare of the people will continue to be a matter for judicial attention and public debate. Therefore, *Lochner* seems destined for continued discussion and debate, with the contending views of two New Yorkers, Alton B. Parker and Rufus W. Peckham, reverberating in the background.

Chapter 4

THE CHIEF JUDGE RUNS FOR PRESIDENT

Figure 4.1. Campaign poster for Alton B. Parker and Henry G. Davis, Democratic candidates for president and vice president, 1904. The Parker-Davis campaign foundered and went down to defeat that November. *Source:* Library of Congress Prints & Photographs Collection.

Alton B. Parker (1852–1926), elected chief judge of the New York Court of Appeals in 1897, secured the Democratic presidential nomination in 1904. He lost the election to incumbent president (and former New York governor) Theodore Roosevelt. Parker is the only chief judge to have sought the presidency, and his against-the-odds candidacy shows the strengths, but more prominently the limitations, of an outstanding judge seeking high elective office.

THE POLITICALLY ASTUTE CHIEF JUDGE

Alton B. Parker did not campaign directly for the 1904 presidential nomination. He believed that his Democratic party should seek out and select its nominee, reflecting the will of the people. But he was not a passive observer, either. He relied on a panoply of surrogates and advocates and his own sterling reputation as a chief judge of the top court in the nation's most populous and important state. The judge had no executive or legislative experience. He capitalized on fortunate circumstances (the Democrats were thin on presidential timber that year) to deliver the nomination.

Parker, who hailed from Esopus, a picturesque town on the Hudson River near Kingston, entered politics through election as Ulster County Surrogate Court judge in 1877. He gradually made his way up the state's Democratic power structure by supporting Democratic power brokers Grover Cleveland (governor 1883–85 and a two-term president after that) and David B. Hill (who served as Cleveland's lieutenant governor and then served as governor 1885–91 and US senator 1891–97). Parker campaigned for Cleveland and managed Hill's 1884 gubernatorial campaign. Hill embraced patronage in politics, opposed civil service, and was known for his sharp-elbowed partisan tactics. He occasionally bent ethical rules, such as serving as both governor and senator in 1891. Hill had presidential aspirations of his own in the 1880s and 1890s, but his arrogance and power grasping alienated too many party leaders. Hill would never be president, but along the way he had made many political allies in the Democratic party.[1] Hill saw his friend and protégé Alton Parker as a potential president. Parker, congenial and highly capable, had none of Hill's ethical flaws. He made political friends easily and never alienated political leaders. He was a model of judicial probity.

Parker stayed on good terms with both Cleveland and Hill (who occasionally competed with each other for state party leadership) and with Tammany Hall, New York City's powerful Democratic organization.

With Hill's strong support, Parker advanced to the state supreme court, then to the appellate division of that court. He distinguished himself as a judge though a record of independent jurisprudence, support for laws for the betterment of society, and an aversion to courts second-guessing the legislature. Nominated for chief judge by Democrats in 1897, he scored an upset victory over the Republican nominee, US Circuit Court judge William Wallace. The outcome was partly due to Parker's reputation for judicious independence and partly to Republicans feuding with independent and good-government groups in New York City.

Judge Parker's electoral triumph got lots of political attention. Winning New York State was essential to winning the presidency. New York in those days tended to go Republican—presidential candidate William McKinley won the state easily in 1896 (and would again in 1900), and Theodore Roosevelt won the governor's race in 1898. Alton Parker won in between, in 1897, the only Democrat elected to statewide office from 1893 to 1900. That made him a political star.[2]

"Mr. Parker was an able man, a lieutenant of Mr. Hill's, standing close to the conservative Democrats of the Wall Street type," Theodore Roosevelt (TR) wrote in his autobiography. "The Judge at once loomed up as a Presidential possibility, and was carefully groomed for the position by the New York Democratic machine, and its financial allies in the New York business world."[3] Roosevelt became friendly with the judge during the time they served together in Albany while TR was governor (1899–1901). Roosevelt had attended Columbia Law School but had not completed his law degree, and Parker gave him advice on studying the law. He predicted to TR's wife, Edith, that her husband would be nominated for vice president in 1900, which he was. TR was elected vice president and became president when William McKinley was assassinated in 1901. After that, Alton Parker and Theodore Roosevelt eyed each other as rivals for the presidency in 1904.[4]

JUDICIAL STATESMAN

As chief judge, Parker insisted judges should carry out their duties, keep a low profile, and stay out of the news. He rarely talked to the press. He was wary of cases that threatened to draw the courts into competitive business situations. In a 1903 decision, Parker held that an association of wholesale druggists formed to secure lower prices from manufacturers was not an illegal combination in restraint of trade or a violation of antitrust laws as the manufacturers claimed. "This is a controversy between opponents in business," the judge admonished. Courts should not be drawn into disputes where the "real purpose is to strengthen the strategic position of one competitor in business as against another."[5]

When the law clearly supported one party over another in a dispute, Judge Parker steadfastly followed the law. In a 1902 decision, he upheld the right of a union to strike to compel an employer to discharge non-union workers. "A labor organization is endowed with precisely the same legal right as an individual to threaten to do that which it may lawfully do," he wrote.[6]

Parker felt that courts should avoid making precedent-setting decisions on social issues where the legislature had not acted. In 1902, as discussed in chapter 2, he ruled against a plaintiff who asserted a common-law right to privacy, insisting that the legislature needed to address the issue. The legislature passed a privacy law the next year that did just that, confirming the wisdom of the judge's decision, his supporters said.[7]

But where legislators had acted, courts should be supportive. In the January 1904 opinion in *People v. Lochner* (see chap. 3), Parker upheld a state law regulating working hours and conditions for bakers.[8] That opinion was summarized in newspapers, quoted in political speeches in Congress, and incorporated into the *Congressional Record* for free circulation through the US mail. After he was nominated for president, Democrats occasionally circulated it as a campaign document. Parker's supporters used it to burnish their candidate's image as a judicious progressive. The decision was overturned by the US Supreme Court, but not until the next year.

Parker was a proven Democratic vote-getter in a predominantly Republican state. His judicial career had left him untainted by political dealmaking. He had made no political enemies. His solid, well-reasoned opinions gave him an aura of authority and reliability. His *Lochner* decision boosted his visibility. Democrats were looking for a nominee who would stand in contrast to William Jennings Bryan, their 1896 and 1900 candidate whose populist, antibusiness rhetoric had led him to defeat both times. Bryan pushed a policy of inflating the currency by minting and coining silver, a strategy favored by debtors and some other groups but anathema to business. Republicans had endorsed the monetary gold standard, which meant a stable monetary system. They asserted that silver coinage would inflate and destabilize the currency and the economy and cast Bryan as a dangerous radical. After going down to defeat with Bryan twice, Democratic leaders shied away from silver and began endorsing the traditional gold standard for currency, something they had favored before Bryan came on the scene.

Grover Cleveland, a Democrat who had served as president 1885–89 and 1893–97, would have made a strong candidate but declined to run. Privately, he lauded Alton Parker as a solid, reliable New Yorker who could beat Theodore Roosevelt. The Democrats needed a steadfast candidate. The other possible nominees in 1904 were lackluster or had alienated voting blocs over the years. For instance, one front-runner, Maryland senator Arthur P. Gorman, had a strong legislative record but had lost the support of a large bloc of potential voters by pushing for high tariffs. Former attorney general and secretary of state Richard Olney had antagonized labor interests by his use of injunctions to break up strikes. New York congressman William R. Hearst, the flamboyant publisher of the *New York Journal*, mounted a campaign based on attacking business, a tactic that scared or alienated most Democrats and would have limited appeal to the voters.

Alton Parker had not alienated anyone. David B. Hill quietly built support for him through his network of Democratic leaders in other states, emphasizing that Parker could carry New York, which was essential to winning the presidency. Parker journeyed by train between Rosemount, his Esopus estate on the Hudson River, and a hotel near the court of appeals building in Albany where he stayed during the week when court was in session. He presided quietly over his court, carrying out his duties, and seldom ventured out of state.

But he traveled to Tallulah Falls, Georgia, to address the Georgia Bar Association in July 1903 on the topic of "Due Process of Law" and to test the political waters for a presidential run. Parker told the Georgians that the due process clause of the US Constitution, and similar provisions in state constitutions, should not be used to thwart state regulatory legislation. His speech was widely reported in the press. He elaborated that theme in an erudite article later that year in the American Bar Association's journal and would return to it again in the next year in his *Lochner* opinion.[9] The Georgia audience cheered Judge Parker's message; one lawyer shouted, "Our next president!"[10]

Southern Democrats, disillusioned from losing twice with Bryan, silver, and an alliance with the West (Bryan hailed from Nebraska), began seeing an alliance with New York, Alton B. Parker, and sound money as the route to victory. After all, that had worked twice, with Cleveland's

1884 and 1892 victories; three times if you counted 1888, where Cleveland won a popular majority but lost in the electoral college. Hill and other supporters expanded on that receptiveness to assert that it showed Parker's progressive bent and his appeal in the "Solid South," reliably Democratic in elections since the Civil War and Reconstruction. Parker issued no policy statements—a frustrated William Jennings Bryan called him "an interrogation mark"—but his bandwagon steadily gained passengers.[11] A number of Midwest and Southern states endorsed him. Charles F. Murphy, head of Tammany Hall, coming round to agreement with his sometime political rival Hill, announced Parker would be New York's choice.

Parker seemed the antithesis of Republican president Theodore Roosevelt, who had become president only because William McKinley had been assassinated in 1901. TR had compiled a vigorous record, intervening to settle a nationwide coal strike, promoting conservation, and taking legal action under the antitrust law to dissolve a railroad consortium called the Northern Securities Company. TR had supported a revolution in Panama so it could achieve independence from Colombia and then negotiated with leaders of the new nation to build a canal to link the Atlantic and Pacific Oceans. The president was inclined to be bold and dramatic. He exercised power on the principle that he could take action unless the Constitution prohibited it. Parker, by contrast, projected an image of judicial restraint and placid predictability. Democrats hoped that was what the voters wanted after three years of TR's energetic and sometimes unpredictable actions.

THE CONVENTION'S CHOICE

In the spring of 1904, press portraits began to emerge of the judge as a man who relished hard work, had raised the court of appeals' efficiency, and wrote fair, well-reasoned opinions. "There is nothing judicial" about the man himself, explained a flattering feature article in the *New York Times*.[12] He was friendly and outgoing, an easy conversationalist, and a good neighbor. He raised prize pigs at Rosemount (and was fond of telling visitors that pigs were really intelligent animals). He swam in the Hudson River just off his dock every morning (weather permitting). The judge often rode his horse over the rolling Esopus hills as he pondered public issues. He and Mrs. Parker went by boat each Sunday to Kingston to worship at the Episcopal Church, where his son-in-law was the minister. A strong family man, Parker was pictured in photos holding his grandchildren on his lap. As a young teacher before becoming a lawyer, the story went, he had thrashed a school bully. His political courage, independence, rectitude, mature judgment, and adherence to principle were outstanding.

As the convention approached in July, newspapers reported that the judge was writing judicial opinions at Rosemount but taking time to pitch hay with his hired men. He had a phone connection to Kingston but spurned suggestions to install a special line so he could be instantly notified of his nomination. His attitude of casual nonchalance seemed to confirm his lack of political motivation.[13]

This was the era before presidential primaries, so the nomination depended solely on the will of the convention. Delegates began arriving at St. Louis early in July. The city was in a festive mode, hosting the Louisiana Purchase Exposition, informally and more grandly called the St. Louis World's Fair. David B. Hill regaled reporters with stories of one endorsement for his candidate after another. The convention keynote speaker, Mississippi's John Sharp Williams, the leader of the Democrats in the House of Representatives, lit into President Roosevelt's record. Hill and other gold-standard advocates tried for an endorsement of the gold standard in the platform. Bryan and his silver allies blocked that. Fighting Bryan on the convention floor over a monetary plank in the platform might spark Bryan's opposition to Parker and possibly split the party. The platform simply omitted any reference to the monetary issue, and delegates found an easy consensus on other topics.

The country called on New York to unite behind a candidate and present him to the convention, Martin W. Littleton, Brooklyn borough president and a budding orator, told the convention crowd in nominating Parker. New York responded with "a man who cut his way through poverty and toil until he found the highest peak of power and honor in the state . . . a man who puts against the strenuous sword play of a swaggering administration a simple faith in the perfect power of the constitution." His candidate had been silent on the issues because "he does not claim to be the master of the Democratic party but is content to be its servant." The party's platform would be the basis for Parker's winning campaign for a united Democratic Party.[14]

Littleton's speech and Hill's behind-the-scenes maneuvering helped cement an alliance of delegates for the consensus candidate, Parker. Eight candidates were nominated for the presidency at St. Louis. The result was never really in doubt. Parker easily triumphed on the first ballot.[15]

ENDORSING SOUND MONETARY POLICY

Judge Parker was informed of his nomination by a reporter who greeted him after his morning swim in the Hudson the next day. He said nothing to the press, but later that day he telegraphed the convention that he favored the gold standard for the nation's monetary system. If the convention did not agree, it should nominate someone else. The convention had sidestepped that touchy issue, as noted above. But, put on the spot by their nominee, the convention passed a resolution and embodied it in a response telegram: the platform was silent because the gold standard was "not regarded as a potential issue in this campaign" and therefore there was nothing expressed in the telegram that "would preclude a man entertaining them from accepting a nomination on said platform."[16] Parker pronounced that response good enough and indicated he would accept the nomination.

The dramatic telegram may have been Parker's own idea. But it may well have been something cooked up beforehand by the judge and his New York friends as a fallback if there were no gold plank in the platform. Parker sent his telegram to the New York delegation chair, his political friend William F. Sheehan, a former assemblyman and lieutenant governor, who also had political ties to Hill. Sheehan and Hill huddled with convention leaders before the telegram was read to the convention managers and helped draft the convention's response. The dramatic "gold telegram" buttressed Parker's image as a leader. It made headlines in newspapers across the nation and gave the press some cause for enthusiasm. Theodore Roosevelt told friends it had transformed the bland judge into a viable presidential contender. It was certainly good political theater.

The convention closed after nominating eighty-year-old Henry G. Davis, a former West Virginia senator, for the vice presidency. Davis was a millionaire through his coal and railroad holdings. Democratic leaders hoped he would financially support the campaign, but he disappointed them. He was too old to actively campaign. His presence on the ticket did not help Parker.

A MODEST CAMPAIGN KICKOFF

Alton Parker went by train from Kingston to Albany for one final meeting of the court of appeals early in August, avoiding reporters. He wrote a few final opinions, then resigned to begin his campaign. The election was only three months away, putting Parker at a disadvantage with TR, who was already well known throughout the country. He might have decided to undertake a national campaign, traveling around the country, as Bryan had in the 1896 and 1900 contests. Instead, Parker opted for a campaign that resembled what several earlier presidential candidates, including McKinley, had done, by receiving prearranged delegations of visitors and giving speeches from Rosemount's front porch, often called a "front porch" campaign. He ventured no further than New York City, Connecticut, and New Jersey for the few speeches he did give in other venues, all in the last days of the campaign. Staying at home had worked for McKinley, but he was a well-known political figure before the campaign began, while Parker was an obscure one. Parker's supporters gave speeches elsewhere in the country. Too often, though, it was apparent that the Democratic orators did not really know their candidate and lacked enthusiasm for him. The Republican campaign, by contrast, was better organized, better funded, and able to put more (and more enthusiastic) speakers on the road. TR stayed in the White House and did not campaign, but he got in the news anyway just through his actions as president.

Parker's positions on the issues of the day were not spelled out in detail in his speeches, and he referred reporters to the party platform, adopted at the St. Louis convention, and the party's *Campaign Text Book*, a longer advocacy document, for elaboration. The platform called for the "strictest economy and frugality" and reducing government expenditures. "Republican extravagance" under Roosevelt's incumbency was to result in the expenditure of $2,641,724,019 in four years, more than $211 million greater than in the four years of McKinley's presidency, although he conducted the Spanish-American War, and nearly $900 million greater than in the last four years of President Cleveland. The platform advocated evenhanded enforcement of the antitrust laws. It referred to federal departments "known to teem with corruption" without being specific and promised "honesty in the public service" under a new Democratic administration. The platform inveighed against President Roosevelt's "executive usurpation" under the guise of "executive construction of existing laws" with "the tyrant's pleas of necessity or superior wisdom." The Democrats called for eventual independence for the Philippines, where an insurrection had been raging for years against US occupation after the nation had taken the islands from Spain after the Spanish-American War in 1898.[17]

"The existing Republican administration," the platform declared, "has been spasmodic, erratic, sensational, spectacular and arbitrary. It has made itself a satire upon the Congress, courts, and upon the settled practices and usages of national and international law."[18] Democrats would bring respite, executive restraint, and a return to constitutional principles. To make sure that message got through, the party's *Campaign Text Book* included the full text of the US Constitution as well as the party platform and other material.

In those days, party leaders journeyed to the candidate's home to bring him official notification of his nomination. The candidate responded with a speech laying out his vision for the nation. Missouri's Democratic senator Champ Clark, who had chaired the St. Louis convention, led the official notification delegation on a chartered excursion boat up the Hudson from New York City to Rosemount on August 10. Intermittent showers threatened to disrupt the ceremony. August Belmont Jr., a wealthy New York City financier and horse-racing enthusiast who had become a Parker campaign advisor and contributor, slipped and fell in the mud as he made his way up the hill from Parker's dock to his house. Parker's local friends and supporters had to contend with mud-slicked roads to get to Rosemount for the event. Between showers, listeners sought refuge from the heat by crowding under the estate's shade trees.[19]

Senator Clark hailed Parker as the leader of "a reunited party that goes forth . . . to conquer."[20] The grateful nominee responded with a long speech from his front porch. He called for limited government; "conservative, instead of rash action"; and "strict observance of constitutional limitations, enforcement of law and order and rugged opposition to all encroachment upon the sovereignty of the people."[21] TR had gone too far with his attacks on the trusts. The solution to the issue of trusts and business concentration was application of existing laws and judicial precedents as interpreted and applied by judges, what was sometimes called case law or the common law. "The common law as developed affords a complete legal remedy against monopolies," said the ex-judge.[22] No new legislation or regulations were needed, Parker insisted. The high tariff enacted by the Republicans to protect business was hurting people and would be reduced.

The most spirited part of the candidate's acceptance speech condemned militarism and foreign adventuring:

The display of great military armaments may please the eye, and, for the moment, excite the pride of the citizen, but it cannot bring to the country the brains, brawn and muscle of a single immigrant, nor induce the investment here of a dollar of capital. . . . I protest . . . against the feeling, now far too prevalent, that by reason of the commanding position we have assumed in the world, we must take part in the disputes and broils of foreign countries. . . . We should confine our interventional activities solely to matters in which the rights of the country or of our citizens are directly involved.

Parker closed by promising not to run for a second term if elected this time.[23]

It was a measured, unexciting speech by an honorable, modest man. Its tenor was executive restraint, smaller government, and staying out of foreign quarrels and other nations' affairs. Its vision for the nation entering the twentieth century was more or less a nostalgic return to the predictability and calm of the closing years of the previous century. Its panacea for the trust problem, letting the courts deal with it, seemed meek, unequal to the task. Its concept of executive power and leadership was constrained. "It does not appear to me that Mr. Parker's speech has done much to animate the party," British ambassador Mortimer Durand confided to a friend.[24] That was an understatement. The campaign was off to a tepid start.

LOW-PROFILE CAMPAIGN

Parker expanded his views in a formal acceptance letter a few weeks later. The candidate promised "economical administration and honesty in the public service." He would promote "peace, prosperity and contentment" by following traditional ways rather than "new ideals" that could lead to "injury of our national character and institutions." He would oppose "the arrogation of unconstitutional powers" by the president. He would reduce the tariff and lower the cost of government through "economy of administration." The methods TR had used to acquire the Panama Canal route were "a source of regret," but, as president, Parker would go on with the canal. In foreign affairs, a Parker administration would pursue a policy of "minding our own business in lieu of spectacular intermeddling with the affairs of other nations."[25]

Beginning in early September, Democratic leaders chartered steamboats in New York City for groups of the party faithful who wished to see the candidate in person. A band on board kept the happy Democrats entertained. Boats left the city in the morning for the trip upriver to Parker's dock at Rosemount. When the boat reached "Parker Point" just below the estate, the crowd began chanting the campaign's informal campaign slogan, "WHAT'S THE MATTER WITH PARKER? HE'S OUR MAN!" The band struck up a lively tune and cheering began. The boats landed at Parker's private dock, and the people made their way up the hill to the house. Parker appeared on the veranda, was cheered, welcomed his guests, and then delivered a carefully prepared speech laden with generalities in his rather dry, formal manner. Neighbors sometimes showed up. Ulster County sheriff's deputies were on hand at the candidate's presentations just in case any rowdies showed up. But there was no trouble. The audiences were always respectful.

Parker's carefully prepared speeches elaborated on the themes of limited government, restrained executive power, and opposition to adventuring abroad. After the speeches, there might be picnics, but the candidate publicly objected to littering by his guests. He had restricted news photographers from taking pictures of him at home after an audacious photographer had tried to catch him on film emerging from one of his early morning Hudson River swims. Special Democrats might get a tour of the estate or a look at Parker's prize hogs, cattle, and sheep in the estate's barn or pasture. In the late afternoon or evening, the ship headed back to New York. The next day, the speech would be printed, or at least summarized, in the press.

The campaign did not seek out press coverage. Reporters sometimes dropped by Rosemount, but the candidate would only talk about his livestock, crops, or the weather. They sometimes observed political leaders going into Parker's house, but no one told them what was discussed.

Parker's speeches were laced with nostalgia for an earlier, simpler era. At a time of change, the nation needs to return to and adhere to first principles, he repeatedly insisted. "We should return to the principles and ideals which during the first century of our National existence have proved so just and beneficial," he said in one speech. Rather than meddling in distant lands, we should concentrate on "the building up of our great country" and solving "the political and social problems which surge upon us."[26]

The federal government's budget was constantly growing, due in part to alarming and unwarranted increases in the nation's armed forces. He condemned continued occupation of the Philippines, noted that people living there were naturally restive under American rule, and reiterated the Democratic platform's call for eventual independence. "The Republican Party stands for the subjection of defenseless foreign peoples. Democracy [the Democratic Party] stands for freedom," he said in one speech. "No government has the right to make one set of laws for those 'at home' and another and different set of laws, absolute in their character, for those in 'the colonies.' "[27] The Philippine issue had an ethical dimension, but it did not resonate with American voters in 1904.

Parker did not cite his judicial opinions, though some of his supporters touted his *Lochner* decision. Surprisingly, Republicans mostly avoided or downplayed them. They concentrated on Parker's lack of executive experience, the vagueness of his proposals, and his party's recent erratic history with Bryan. Some Republicans characterized him as being too cozy with Wall Street or too closely allied with Tammany Hall.

As the fall wore on, it was apparent that the Democrats lacked drama or momentum. The Democratic National Committee lacked a plan for reaching out to and tailoring a message for particular voting blocs. Democrats' main campaign strategy was to attack Roosevelt as dangerous. A popular magazine that favored Parker featured a cartoon of TR trampling on international law and the Constitution, bearing the labels *Extravagance, Personal Orders Substituted for Acts of Congress, Protection for Monopoly, Despotism, Militarism,* and *Imperialism.*[28] But the accusatory refrain wore thin with the public. Most Americans regarded TR as energetic and reflecting a feeling of optimism about the nation's future. They were satisfied and confident in his leadership. Parker seemed unable to define a decisive issue or to offer a compelling reason for the nation to change leaders. Democratic Party leaders in key states were supportive but not enthusiastic. Parker's campaign even failed to reach out to traditional Democratic voting blocs such as the Irish American community.[29]

Parker was respected but did not kindle excitement even among the Democratic political base. Former president Grover Cleveland, a strong Parker supporter after his nomination, commended the judge's "courage, fairness, and impartiality" and his "constant and unyielding devotion to duty" in an article in a popular magazine. But Cleveland's concluding endorsement was lukewarm: "the American people will make no mistake" if they elect the judge who has "safe and conservative conceptions of Presidential responsibilities."[30] Another laudatory magazine article conceded that Parker's personality was "less picturesque, less dashing, less original, and less brilliant" than Roosevelt's but countered that he was courageous and reliable. It concluded with a mild endorsement: "A great genius? Probably not. But a sane, courageous, unselfish patriot of the old, pure, Democratic type—that he is beyond all question."[31]

Such tepid support for the reticent candidate was sinking his campaign. Parker met with campaign leaders in New York in late September and learned that the campaign was running short on cash but apparently gave no direction for raising more funds. Early the next morning, he took a leisurely walk down Fifth Avenue, around Washington Square, and back to his hotel, apparently without even being recognized by citizens in the largest city in his home state. His campaign needed a boost. But he declined campaign advisors' recommendations to launch a speaking tour to raise his profile.[32]

Newspaper humor columnist Finley Peter Dunne claimed that President Parker would put the country to sleep.[33]

By contrast, Roosevelt's campaign organized committees to appeal specifically to demographic groups including Jewish, Irish American, and German American voters and other voting blocs. The president was said to favor a strong national defense. He wanted a positive climate for business and was determined to oppose trusts. He would mediate between labor and management, putting the public interest above all else. TR articulated the spirit and philosophy of the emerging Progressive movement. Democrats in effect positioned themselves as the more conservative of the two major parties, ceding the middle and the left of the political spectrum to Republicans without challenge.[34]

CONTROVERSY AT THE END OF THE CAMPAIGN

Late in the campaign, Democratic political leaders and newspapers, led by Joseph Pulitzer's *New York World*, shook things up. They asserted that the railroad magnate E. H. Harriman, the banker J. P. Morgan, and other monied interests were secretly contributing large sums to Roosevelt's campaign. There were no campaign finance laws in those days, so the contributions were legal and did not have to be disclosed.

A congressional investigation some years later would confirm the essential allegations in the newspapers' reports. Roosevelt *had* sought support from Harriman and others for the campaign in New York, where he feared Parker's vote-getting appeal and where the Republican nominee for governor, Frank Higgins, was running a listless campaign. TR's campaign managers had also sought funds from business leaders. Standard Oil Company, for instance, contributed $100,000, a very large sum in those days. In some cases, as Roosevelt later insisted, he had directed that the contributions be returned. Sometimes, they were. But in other cases, TR did not make his wishes entirely clear. In other instances, staff told him they returned the money but kept it in the campaign's coffers, and TR did not check to see if his wishes had actually been carried out. In addition, the Democrats' allegations had two inconsistent lines: business favored Roosevelt because he protected corporate interests versus business feared him and hoped campaign contributions would dissuade him from more anticorporate crusades like the Northern Securities suit. Moreover, Parker and the Democrats were receiving hefty contributions from the financier August Belmont and the railroad leader James J. Hill.[35]

But Parker suddenly seized on accusations in the press of big business support for his rival and, at the end of October, made a series of accusatory speeches in New York City, New Jersey, and Connecticut, the farthest he ventured from Esopus. He denounced TR as the candidate of big business and deception. Companies were contributing to his campaign to buy influence and benefits. George B. Cortelyou, who had been TR's secretary of commerce and labor before resigning earlier in 1904 to become chair of the Republican National Committee, was alleged to be using his business contacts to facilitate the payments. "This country shall not pass into the hands of the trusts!" Parker exhorted an audience in Hartford, Connecticut, which cheered him for several minutes. The ex-judge turned out to be a rousing speaker. TR quickly responded that the accusations were false. Parker, who had insisted on solid evidence in his courtroom, offered no real evidence to support his accusation. His last-minute lashing out seemed like an act of desperation.[36]

VOTERS ENDORSE THE PRESIDENT AND REJECT THE JUDGE

On election day, Parker lost by more than two million votes, carrying only the Solid South, consistently Democratic since Civil War days. He lost his native state, New York, to TR.

With prosperity at home and the nation at peace, it is unlikely that any Democrat, even one more colorful and assertive than Alton Parker, could have defeated Theodore Roosevelt in 1904. But Parker might have done better. His personal restraint, bland conservatism, and passive campaign tactics were out of sync with a nation yearning for dynamic leadership. He never made it clear just why he wanted to be president. The Republicans ran an effective campaign, pointing to their candidate's record of achievements and his opponent's lack of executive experience or vision for the future.

Parker did not accept responsibility for this defeat. He blamed "division and faction in our ranks over a period of eight years" prior to the contest, which had left the Democratic Party weak. "Demagogic appeals" by Roosevelt and the Republicans confused the electorate and siphoned off voters.[37] But corrupt corporate money was the main culprit, Parker maintained. Republican contributors' "acts were unlawful and their purposes corrupt. . . . They intended to have the money used, as it was, in corrupting the electorate. . . . Such men desire the triumph of that party which will better serve their personal financial interests and will—for contributions past, present, and future—continue to protect those interests by lenient legislation and by pretense at execution of a law which shall be tenderly blind to all their offenses."[38]

ALTON PARKER AS SENIOR STATESMAN

Alton Parker never again sought public office. He established a law firm in New York City and enjoyed a lucrative law practice for the rest of his life (he passed away in 1926). He rented a suite of rooms at the Ambassador Hotel in the city but spent much of his time at his beloved Rosemount.

As the former chief judge in the nation's largest and most important state, and the presidential nominee of one of the two great political parties, he naturally had stature and commanded attention and respect. He became a senior statesman in the Democratic Party, often quoted in the press on the political issues of the day. He helped organize Democrat John A. Dix's successful campaign for governor in 1910. He worked to derail William R. Hearst's bid for the gubernatorial nomination in 1918, throwing his support to former assemblyman Alfred E. Smith, who won. As evidence leaked out over the years about corporate contributions to Roosevelt in 1904, he continued his assertion that corrupt Republicans were adept at securing funds from people and companies interested in legislation or in lax enforcement of the law. Parker mostly avoided national politics, endorsing William Jennings Bryan, for the third time the Democratic nominee in 1908, but not actively campaigning for him.

In the fall of 1910, TR, seeking another presidential term, began condemning the courts for being too conservative in invalidating state regulations, citing the Supreme Court's 1905 *Lochner* decision as a prime example. As noted in chapter 1, Parker led the New York State legal community in rebuffing Roosevelt's criticism of the New York Court of Appeals. Addressing the *Lochner* case, Parker responded that both the court of appeals and the US Supreme Court had issued divided opinions on the case, a sign that "the case was a close one about which minds much differ," and all judges and courts merited respect. Parker spurned TR's "offensive criticism" of the nation's highest court, calling it evidence of the ex-president's desire to encroach on the court's authority.[39] Parker called TR a "usurper" for trying to dictate to the New York Republican Party who its gubernatorial nominee would be that year.[40]

Parker likened Theodore Roosevelt to a demagogue who would substitute strongman rule for a government of law. In a speech to the 1912 Democratic National Convention, Parker attacked Roosevelt (by then running for president on the new Progressive Party's ticket) as a threat to the nation motivated by a "lust for power." Republican president Taft, running for reelection, was taken to task for failing to reduce the tariff and curb the trusts. Democrats, by contrast, were men of high ideals who would enact legislation to help the people and wage war against corruption in politics.[41] Parker was no fan of New Jersey governor Woodrow Wilson, that year's nominee, but campaigned on his behalf.

Parker chaired the 1912 state Democratic convention that nominated New York City congressman William Sulzer for governor. He soon came to regret the choice. Sulzer was elected but, once in office, proved to be flamboyant and unpredictable, leveling sensational charges of corruption against legislative leaders (who also were fellow Democrats). The legislature turned the tables on the governor, investigated his campaign finances, and turned up evidence that he had diverted campaign contributions to personal use. The assembly impeached the governor in August 1913. The drama then moved to the New York Court for the Trial of Impeachments, under the state constitution consisting of the state senate and the court of appeals meeting jointly, with Parker's successor, Chief Judge Edgar Cullen, presiding. Assembly impeachment managers hired Alton Parker as their chief prosecutor. In uncharacteristically strong language, the ex-judge said that Sulzer's actions "constitute willful and criminal violations of public duty and personal dishonor; they defy the majesty of a sovereign State, insult the intelligence of a free people, and outrage every sense of honor."[42] The hapless Sulzer was convicted and removed from office.

In addition to serving as a senior statesman in the Democratic Party, Parker became something of an emeritus figure in the legal profession. He served as president of the American Bar Association (1906–7) and the New York State Bar Association (1913–14). In his speeches and writings, he sang the praises of the common (judge-made) legal doctrine, expanding on one of the themes of his 1904 presidential campaign. He decried the trend for state legislatures and Congress to pass thousands of new laws each year, far more than needed, in response to the popular clamor for government action.[43]

"Legislators crazed with ambition," groping for remedies to complex social and economic problems or driven by the press or popular clamor, passed a flood of laws, he said in his presidential address at the American Bar Association's annual convention in 1907. Often the laws were drafted in haste, amended on the fly as they went through the legislature, and were flawed by the time they reached the statute books. That put a burden on the courts to interpret and apply them and, sometimes, strike them down as unconstitutional. That, in turn, led to public impatience with the courts, which irresponsible politicians capitalized on to criticize the courts as obstructionist. Relying on judges thoughtfully and judiciously making common law is better: "The common law is expanded slowly and carefully by judicial decisions based on a standard of justice derived from the habits, customs and thoughts of a people. . . . [It is] an ideal method of building the law of a people."[44]

Parker railed against the drift toward consolidation of executive power, often using his nemesis Theodore Roosevelt as a prime example. The executive is "sufficiently dangerous to constitute a risk," he told the graduating class of Yale Law School in June 1914. "There is serious danger of usurpation."[45] He also warned against federal government overreach, the tendency of Washington to gather more and more power at the expense of the states, in contravention of the Constitution.

Alton Parker's views on international affairs evolved as World War I progressed. At first, he championed nonintervention and neutrality. At a July 1914 conference, he pointed to a century of Anglo-American friendship as proof that heavy armaments are not needed to maintain peace.[46] But as Germany stepped up its submarine warfare campaign against the United States, Parker shifted to advocating military preparedness and fully supported president Woodrow Wilson's decision to ask Congress for a declaration of war in April 1917.

Parker was friendly toward organized labor and represented the American Federation of Labor in the Danbury Hatters' case (1908), involving the application of antitrust laws against a union. The union had organized a boycott of the goods of a company that refused to unionize. Parker argued that the boycott was a legitimate tactic for the union to use. But the US Supreme Court disagreed, holding that the boycott constituted unlawful restraint of interstate commerce and was a violation of the federal antitrust law.[47]

Parker may have taken a liberal position regarding unions, but he aligned with Red Scare hysteria after the war. By then he was president of the National Civic Federation, an alliance of business, labor, and political leaders established back in 1900. It had promoted moderate Progressive reform and sought to resolve disputes between industry and organized labor. After the war, though, the organization turned its energies to fighting a perceived threat from communists and radicals. Parker appointed a committee to expose disloyalty, particularly in education and the churches. He supported immigration restriction and deportation of alleged radicals.[48]

When Alton Parker died in 1926, he was recalled as a Democratic presidential candidate who took his defeat gracefully and then became a citizen ready to give time and labor to worthy causes. His 1904 campaign themes—a return to a simpler time, less government spending, smaller government, circumscribed executive power, deference to judges to espouse the law—were out of sync with an energetic nation eager to get on with the twentieth century.

But Parker's espousal of the courts upholding the constitutionality of well-considered legislation reverberates to this day. His views on the common law, while not always consistent, are worth consideration. His caution against potential presidential overreach is definitely worth recalling. His call for economical government might give us pause in this era of high government spending. His warning about the corrosive role of money in political campaigns still rings true today.

Chapter 5

PUBLIC HEALTH AND INDIVIDUAL RIGHTS

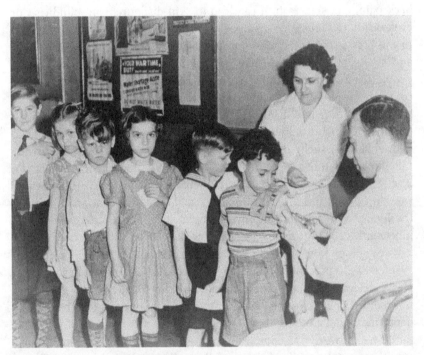

Figure 5.1. Students lining up for vaccination in New York City. State requirements for smallpox vaccinations for school students were confirmed by the courts three times in the Progressive Era. *Source:* George Graham Bain Collection, Library of Congress.

Can the state require a student to be vaccinated for smallpox as a condition for attending public school? Health officials asserted that was one of the state's public health responsibilities. Critics claimed such a requirement trammeled personal liberty and parental rights. The New York Court of Appeals confirmed the state's authority three times in the Progressive Era—in 1894, 1904, and 1914.

MEDICAL BREAKTHROUGH AND PUBLIC POLICY

Smallpox is a highly contagious viral disease spread by infected humans in close contact with each other. Its symptoms are fever, stomach and back pain, and skin rash. It can lead to skin disfigurement, blindness, or even death. Outbreaks of smallpox date from the time of New Netherland in the 1600s, and the disease ravaged New York cities in the eighteenth and nineteenth centuries. There is no cure for smallpox. For many years, people tried a process called variolation: material from smallpox sores (pustules) was given to people who had never been afflicted, either by scratching the material into the arm or having them inhale it through the nose. People usually went on to develop minor symptoms associated with smallpox, such as fever and a rash, but were then immune to the full impact of the disease. In 1796, an English doctor, Edward Jenner, discovered that vaccinations of small amounts of material from cowpox sores produced more likely immunity with less risk. Vaccination using the Jenner method, and improvements on it, became widespread in the nineteenth century. Smallpox epidemics declined.[1]

Smallpox continued as a serious health threat, though, killing on average 25–30 percent of the people it infected. New York State's Board of Health (elevated to the Department of Health in 1901) encouraged but did not require smallpox vaccinations, except in schools, as noted below. The department had a modest budget and limited staff, and most of the state's public health work was done through city and county health commissioners. These local health officials had the authority to quarantine afflicted people to prevent the disease from spreading during outbreaks. But there was widespread public indifference, opposition, and even resistance. Some people felt the vaccine was ineffective or actually led to diseases. Others resented being pressured by health officials to get vaccinated. Some people became concerned during epidemics and regional outbreaks but relaxed after the threat receded. In 1879, the Anti-Vaccination Society of America was founded in New York City to discredit vaccination and urge people to avoid or resist it. Other anti-vaccination organizations sprang up in New York City and elsewhere in the state. The champions of anti-vaccination set out to challenge public health officials.

The issue headed to court when a smallpox epidemic began to sweep through Brooklyn in 1894. Brooklyn was still a city in those days, and its aggressive health commissioner, Z. Taylor Emery, dispatched teams from his office to vaccinate people. Sometimes, Emery's employees asked politely; other times, they badgered and coerced; in still other cases, they were accompanied by police officers whose presence gave the vaccinators menacing backup. Resistance to coerced vaccination built, particularly in areas where German and Italian immigrants predominated; many had left Europe to avoid this sort of government coercion. Opponents organized the Brooklyn Anti-Vaccination League. In early May of 1894, Emery's staff forcefully detained a blacksmith, William Smith, and his employees in their shop in an area of the city where there was an outbreak after they refused to be vaccinated. Police stood guard outside his shop. Smith appealed to the state supreme court, asserting that Emery's act amounted to unlawful imprisonment. Justice William Gaynor, a brusque and irascible champion of the rights of the common citizen and opponent of government overreach (and future New York City mayor), ordered the quarantine on Smith be lifted on May 8, 1894. He ruled that the quarantine amounted to coerced vaccination. If the legislature had intended to make vaccination compulsory, it would have said so in statute, he argued. "Arbitrary power is abhorrent to our system of government," the judge declared. "[The law] does not confer on the Commissioner [Emery] the right to imprison any more than to take life."[2]

Commissioner Emery appealed, and the supreme court appellate division overruled Gaynor in February 1895. Three months later, in May, the court of appeals reversed the appellate division, holding that Gaynor had been right. Smith sued the city health department for damages due to his inability to operate his business. In December 1895, the Brooklyn circuit court awarded him $641 in damages. A year later, after a protracted legal battle, the appellate division overruled the circuit court and confirmed the validity of Emery's quarantine order. Showing striking deference to medical opinion, the court declared that these issues "present medical questions" and are properly "the subject of professional opinion."[3] By then, the epidemic had passed. But the judicial record on how far public authorities could go in combating smallpox was one of disarray.

Smallpox was always unpredictable, sometimes seeming to lie dormant and other times raging through the population. It continued in the late 1890s but in a milder form before reemerging as a more lethal strain in New York City in 1900 and reaching epidemic proportions the next year. The New York City Health Department, exercising its strong statutory powers to protect public health and combat infectious diseases, sent health officers backed by police into infected areas. Police banged on doors and health officials stormed in. They checked for vaccination scars on the arms of adults—evidence that they had been vaccinated—and where the scars were missing, they urged, coerced, and, in some cases with police assistance, forcefully vaccinated adults. When they found already infected adults, they removed and isolated them in "pesthouses" to let the disease run its course, stripped and removed bedding and infected clothes, and disinfected rooms. They transferred infected children to hospitals. There was resentment and some resistance, including people fleeing and hiding, but the health department teams continued their work. The city health officers' policy was harsh, but the results were dramatic. About one million New York City adults were vaccinated in 1902–4, around one-third of the city's population. Smallpox went into remission again.[4]

In these opening years of the twentieth century, as the epidemic surged and then subsided, debate over public health policy for smallpox intensified. These were the years of the emerging Progressive movement, whose proponents advocated government regulation and intervention in people's lives and the commercial affairs of the state for the common good. The state's "police power," explicit or implicit in the state constitution, was sufficiently strong to support such policy. Sometimes, the good of the people of the state as a whole would need to trump individual liberty; individuals would need to get vaccinated in order to keep smallpox from infecting others. The more people who were vaccinated, the fewer who would be stricken, and eventually the disease would wither and fade away. People who refused to be vaccinated created a susceptible group for the continual viability and spread of the disease. But "the vaccination question revealed a sharp uneasiness toward the authority of medicine and the power of the state . . . [at a] time when both institutions were reaching more ambitiously than ever before into American life."[5]

Anti-vaccinationists' organizations grew in number and influence. Their arguments had a libertarian flavor, and they cast the issue as one of personal liberty and rights against the overweening power of the state and the professional medical community. In the case of mandatory vaccination of schoolchildren, it was a question of parental rights versus state authority. The opponents of vaccinations began enlisting endorsements from within the medical community.

In New York City, Montague Leverson, who was both a lawyer and a doctor, became secretary of the Anti-Vaccination Society of America and president of the Brooklyn anti-vaccination organization. He lectured and wrote widely on the risks of compulsory smallpox vaccination. He had formerly been an advocate, he liked to tell his audiences, but, once he really investigated, had realized that vaccination was "a shameful superstition and a fraud." Edward Jenner had never really proven the effectiveness of his vaccine, data about its impact had been manipulated to exaggerate its effectiveness, and information about the numbers of people who died from inoculation had been suppressed. The medical community had gone along with it all in "a state of sleepy acquiescence." Leverson produced data from Britain that he said demonstrated that inoculation does not protect or mitigate. Most cases were of a "light character" anyway, and people recovered well.[6] The trend toward giving public health officials more power to coerce inoculation was leading to tyranny. Children should be subjected to vaccination only if their parents approved.

The argument that smallpox vaccine was sometimes contaminated or defective diminished when Congress passed the Biologics Control Act in 1902 imposing federal standards and regulation on manufacture of smallpox and other vaccines. Quality of and public confidence in the vaccine's reliability slowly rose. But New Yorkers were not willing to give their public health officials more power to compel vaccination or take other coercive steps. That same year, 1902, a bill introduced in the state legislature that would have given local health departments the power to require vaccinations of adults in times of epidemics found little support. Even Dr. Ernst Lederele, the New York City health commissioner, would not back it, warning it would just embolden the anti-vaccinationists and engender more public opposition. The bill died quietly in the legislature.[7]

An uneasy impasse set in. Public health officials had considerable powers of persuasion and even coercion during epidemics, but press exposure of strong-arm methods led to public skepticism or opposition. Vaccination's critics and skeptics kept criticism of vaccination going. On the other hand, the state's medical community kept insisting on the need for more statutory authority. The state's political establishment, viewing the strong diversity of opinion, was inclined to just stay with the status quo. "Measures directly affecting the person in his bodily liberty or integrity, represent the most incisive exercise of the police power," wrote law professor Ernst Freund in his authoritative 1904 book *The Police Power: Public Policy and Constitutional Rights.* "Only the emergency of present danger therefore can justify quarantine, isolation or removal to hospital and compulsory treatment, and it is at least doubtful whether vaccination can be made compulsory apart from such necessity." Mere "delegation of authority to administrative bodies" would not be sufficient.[8]

The status quo took root. Legislative attention and court activity over smallpox prevention measures in the general population diminished. Judicial attention shifted to vaccination of schoolchildren, where discussions had been ranging for a decade.

TAKING THE SCHOOL TO COURT

Smallpox was a particular menace to young people in school classrooms because of the necessity for close proximity, which fosters its spread. Vaccination was the only medically endorsed way to prevent kids from getting the disease. New York did not have a law directly requiring parents to vaccinate their children, but two sets of laws—compulsory school attendance and vaccination requirements—added up to the same thing.

Compulsory school-attendance laws, first enacted in 1874, were at first loosely enforced but were gradually tightened at the urging of educators and child labor reformers. Compulsory attendance requirements meant keeping young people in school, where they would learn. It also meant keeping them off department store and factory floors where they could be overworked and exploited and, because they were paid less than adults, their presence could contribute to low wages for adult workers. A 1903 statute banned child labor in factories and other venues and required attendance in school up to age fourteen. The courts sustained the law. Attendance enforcement was tightened after the creation of the New York State Education Department in 1904.[9]

School vaccination requirements were first enacted in New York in 1860 and updated and strengthened over the years. The version in effect at the turn of the century, adopted in 1893, declared that "no child or person not vaccinated shall be admitted or received into any of the public schools of the state."[10] Local school officials were charged to enforce the law including, if they wished, passing resolutions formally excluding unvaccinated children. Many local school boards did just that, citing the state law. The only legal way to avoid vaccination was to send your child to a nonpublic school, an option available only to parents with financial means.

Enforcement in the schools, though, was uneven. Some schools were strict, consistently requiring presentation of vaccination certificates and sending kids without them home. Others were more lax, accepting excuses in lieu of certificates—parents could not afford the vaccination (although the law provided that the schools could pay in cases where the parents could not pay), had religious or conscientious objections, or had not gotten around to it but would soon, they promised. In still other cases, it was a dead letter, with school boards, superintendents, and principals dismissing it as a meddlesome burden or something the state or local health officials, not the schools, should enforce.

Some parents went further, appealing to the courts to overturn the vaccination requirement as an unconstitutional infringement of personal liberty. In 1894, Charles Walters filed for a writ of mandamus to compel officials in Brooklyn's Public School no. 22 to admit his unvaccinated kids, Chester and Ada. The legal requirement amounted to an order to vaccinate the children against their and their parents' wills. Walters contended it was an unwarranted assault, similar to the coercive behavior that Justice William Gaynor had just nullified in the highly publicized case involving quarantined blacksmith William Smith.

Justice Willard Bartlett, writing for the supreme court in Kings County in 1895, turned down Walters's mandamus request. "The state can certainly exercise this discretion by debarring from attendance at the public schools such persons as are unwilling to adopt a precaution which, in the judgment of the legislature, is essential to the preservation of the health of the large body of scholars," he wrote. The judge dismissed the assault comparison. This was also different from what Gaynor had ruled, Bartlett explained. There, the borough health commissioner "restrained the petitioners from their liberty until they consented to be vaccinated, although the legislature had conferred no such power upon him." But "no such question as this, however, arises in the present case" because school officials had the compulsory attendance law on their side.[11] The only issue here was whether the legislature had acted constitutionally, and it certainly had in this case. The requirement was well within the state's "police power," said the judge. Walters appealed. The appellate division backed Bartlett. Walters gave up and did not appeal to the court of appeals.[12]

The school vaccination issue mostly went dormant in the courts for several years.

AFTER A DECADE, A MAJOR COURT CHALLENGE TO STATE LAW

Attorney Edmund C. Viemeister thought he knew the source of smallpox in his Queens neighborhood in the 1890s. He testified at a State Board of Health hearing in 1894 that it was "the stenches coming from the places along Newtown Creek," a three-mile-long waterway that formed part of the border between Brooklyn and Queens.[13] Fertilizer, chemical, oil, and copper smelting plants regularly discharged toxic wastes from their manufacturing into the creek. Brooklyn was still a separate city, and its health authorities could not agree with their counterparts in Queens, part of New York City, across the creek, on what should be done. Viemeister and his neighbors asked that the State order a mandatory cleanup. No action was taken, and the pollution intensified. Viemeister's experience convinced him that public health officials were not really interested in the causes of smallpox. He became skeptical about their claims that school vaccinations were essential to prevent its spread.

Viemeister's son William entered Public School no. 12 in Queens in 1898. His father refused to have him vaccinated for smallpox. Apparently, school officials looked the other way for a few years but in June 1902 denied William admission in the fall unless he could produce a vaccination certificate. Edmund Viemeister went to court, contending school officials' actions, and the laws behind them, deprived his son of a constitutionally guaranteed right to a public education.

Viemeister cited Article IX of the state constitution, adopted and approved by the voters in 1894, which said that "the Legislature shall provide for the maintenance and support of a system of free common schools, wherein all children of this State may be educated." That was a guarantee regardless of whether the child was vaccinated or not, Viemeister asserted. If the constitutional convention had intended vaccination as a condition for attending school, they would have put it in the document. It was a novel, clever argument. In addition, he added, smallpox vaccination was intrusive, ineffective, and even dangerous. He asked the Kings County Supreme Court to issue a writ of mandamus ordering school officials to admit his son. That court was presided over by Judge William Gaynor, the same judge who had challenged local health authorities' power in

Brooklyn a decade earlier. Viemeister hoped Justice Gaynor would use that precedent to rein in school officials and state law.

Viemeister produced four medical experts who condemned smallpox vaccination.

New York City physician Robert Gunn claimed to have made an extensive study of the Jenner vaccine and the more recent updates to the vaccine. Vaccination actually often led to people getting the disease or "general breaking down of the health." It often caused diseases, including tetanus, and in fact resulted in more deaths than it saved. Jenner and his followers invented excuses and adjusted evidence to cover their failures. "Men prominent in the [medical] profession" supported his views, Gunn insisted.[14]

Dr. Montague Leverson, the vocal anti-vaccine advocate referenced above, testified that he had been vaccinated himself to test the vaccination and had developed abscesses, boils, and rheumatoid pain and nearly died. He had since then made a years-long study and concluded that vaccination was "unscientific and barbarous . . . a curse to humanity and a superstition as baneful as was witchcraft." Vaccination was leading to "a degeneration of the race."[15]

Dr. Edward B. Foote told the judges he had made an investigation of the "forced vaccination" in Brooklyn in 1894 and found that healthy people who were vaccinated came down with the disease. He produced a sworn statement by Arthur Newman, whom he identified as an investigator but whose credentials were unstated. Newman claimed he had interviewed many Brooklyn residents after the smallpox epidemic. Some people said they simply could not afford vaccination. Others claimed the police came to their homes and they were handcuffed and forced to be vaccinated. One woman insisted she had been forcefully vaccinated just before giving birth to a child.[16]

Dr. F. H. Lutze testified he had seen healthy children sickened by the shots. Vaccination was a travesty, "a silly and ridiculous humbug." At the very least it should be a parent's choice, he argued.[17]

To counter all that alarming medical testimony, the city school district was represented by Samuel Hendrickson, a health officer with the Borough of Queens Department of Health. He was not a high-level official; the city did not see the need for one. City officials were confident of victory. Hendrickson reviewed the law and said there had been smallpox cases in Queens schools earlier in 1902, adding to the urgency of excluding unvaccinated pupils. Smallpox is highly contagious, and health authorities in New York City and the medical profession generally agreed that vaccination would act as a protection against it. That was all the argument that was needed.[18]

Viemeister's case was light on constitutional law and heavy on medical alarm. Justice Gaynor was not impressed. This case was different from the one involving forceful detention and vaccination that he had decided back in 1894. There, the health officials' statutory justification was lacking; here, the education authorities had the law behind them. On July 7, 1902, in a single-sentence opinion, he ruled that William Viemeister's expulsion was valid because the school vaccination law was within the legislature's constitutional power to pass.

Viemeister appealed to the Appellate Division of the New York Supreme Court.

Associate Justice John M. Woodward, writing the decision for a unanimous court in the Appellate Division, Second Department, on November 1, 1903, affirmed Gaynor's opinion and the law. The 1894 constitution did not make education an unconditional right but instead was intended "merely to insure a continuance and an extension of the privileges of citizens of this State." The legislature can impose "reasonable regulations upon this privilege" provided they apply across the state. "When the law operates equally upon all" and is "binding upon every person within the jurisdiction," the courts are bound to support it. Presiding justice Michael Hirschberg, who had been a delegate to the 1894 convention, in a helpful concurring opinion, affirmed Woodward's view: Viemeister's constitutional claim would not hold up. "No court in this State, so far as I have been able to learn, has ever declared an act unconstitutional which was simply designed to protect the public health."[19]

Undaunted, Edmund Viemeister appealed to the court of appeals. By that point, his cause had attracted widespread public attention and was regarded by both pro- and anti-vaccination communities as a test case.

The briefs he had submitted to the supreme court and the appellate division were included in his appeal. Viemeister engaged another attorney, John Leary, as co-counsel for the court proceeding. They prepared a new brief that went over by-now-familiar arguments and added some new ones. Forcible vaccination of a child—in this case, the power to "cut into his body and inject cow-pox, into the incision"—is an assault, they argued. The 1894 constitution guaranteed every child a constitutional right to an education; that right cannot be conditioned on being vaccinated. "Vaccination is not a new thing!" the brief reminded the court.[20] The 1894 constitutional convention delegates were clearly aware of it. If they had intended to require that schoolchildren must be vaccinated, they would have put that requirement in the document.

Could the legislature require it anyway, under its broad police power? "You are asked to *drive* this word 'vaccinated' into the Constitution by a vigorous swing of the judicial sledge hammer, 'police power,'" the brief admonished the judges. It continued: The appellate division was wrong in assuming that the legislature had a sufficient basis for action. In fact, the legislature really had no understanding of what it was requiring. It was just following "common knowledge," which is not sufficient. In fact, "vaccination is dangerous." The medical establishment was not to be trusted here. Doctors had cried in unison, "of course, try it!" when they discovered Jenner's invention but without insisting on scientific evidence to buttress their support. Since then, medical experts had padded statistics to document vaccination's efficacy. Moreover, lots of things had changed since Jenner's time, including hygiene, to decrease communicable diseases. (For one thing, there are more bathtubs in New York City now than in all the world in Jenner's time, the court was informed.) It really is not a matter of public safety. It amounts to "duress, to compel us to submit to a trespass upon our person in order that we might enjoy the right of instruction."[21]

New York City Corporation Counsel John Delaney submitted a short (seven-page) brief for the school board. Its brevity was evidence of the board's confidence. The brief advanced some technical legal arguments that the case was not appealable and Viemeister had no legal right to a writ of mandamus. But that was beside the point. The 1894 constitution did not nullify the 1893 vaccination law. By that reasoning, school authorities would not be able to send children with whooping cough, smallpox, scarlet fever, or other contagious diseases home to protect other students. Courts in Pennsylvania and California had recently affirmed similar laws there. This was a health-protection regulation, "pure and simple," within the legislature's authority and consistent with its obligation to protect public health.[22]

THE COURT'S DECISION: VACCINATION REQUIREMENT IS VALID

Judge Irving Vann wrote the unanimous decision for the court of appeals, sustaining the vaccination requirement, on October 18, 1904.[23] Vann emphasized three points:

THE REQUIREMENTS ARE CLEARLY WITHIN THE STATE'S POLICE POWER

"When the sole object and general tendency of legislation is to promote the public health, there is no invasion of the Constitution, even if the enforcement of the law interferes to some extent with liberty or property." Vann cited *Health Department of N.Y. v. Rector* (1895), which sustained a state law requiring clean water in tenement buildings. This principle is so well established "as to require no discussion," said the judge, but, apparently just to be on the safe side, he cited nine other court of appeals decisions, including some he had authored.[24]

Actually, Judge Vann's list of opinions did not fully sustain his contention. There was wording in each case asserting the state's authority but also counter-wording about limitations. Some related to health, but most were tangential at best. Vann's examples showed a mixed judicial record, typical of the court in this era:

> *Matter of Jacobs* (1885) invalidated a state law banning manufacturing of tobacco products in tenements.

> *People v. Marx* (1885) struck down a state law banning manufacture of oleomargarine.

> In *People v. Gillson* (1888), a statute making it a misdemeanor for people selling food to give gifts, prizes, or other rewards to the purchaser was called unconstitutional.

> *People ex rel. Nechamcus v. Warden* (1895) sustained a state law authorizing cities to license plumbers.

> *People v. Havnor* (1896) upheld a law banning barbers from working on Sundays.

> *People v. Arensberg* (1887) sustained a law proscribing "the manufacture out of any animal fat, or animal or vegetable oils, not produced from unadulterated milk or cream from the same, of any product *in imitation or semblance* or designed to take the place of natural butter produced from milk."[25]

> *People v. Adirondack Railway Co.* (1899) affirmed the state's power to restrict or prohibit railroad construction on state

land in the Adirondack forest preserve. That was far from a public health issue, but the opinion included a broad statement that "the power of taxation, the police power and the power of eminent domain, underlie the Constitution and rest upon necessity, because there can be no effective government without them. They are not conferred by the Constitution, but exist because the state exists, and they are essential to its existence."[26]

People v. Lochner, decided by the court the previous February, sustained a law regulating bakers' hours and working conditions. But it would be reversed by the US Supreme Court the next year.

THE REQUIREMENTS ARE REASONABLE FOR SCHOOLS

The right to attend public schools "is necessarily subject to some restrictions and limitations in the interest of the public health." Children with "dangerous and contagious" diseases can be banned from schools; otherwise, "a school might be broken up and a pestilence spread abroad in the community." Smallpox is dangerous and contagious, so "if vaccination strongly tends to prevent the transmission or spread of this disease, it logically follows that children may be refused admission to the public schools until they have been vaccinated."[27]

THERE IS A "COMMON BELIEF" IN THE VACCINE'S EFFECTIVENESS

Viemeister, as well as some laymen and "some physicians of great skill and repute," deny the vaccine's effectiveness. The judge asserted, however, that "we take judicial notice" of the prevailing opinion in the state about the vaccine's effectiveness. The term *judicial notice* is a concept in the legal tradition that allows a fact to be introduced into evidence if the truth of that fact is so well known, or so authoritatively endorsed, that it cannot be reasonably doubted. "The common belief . . . is that it has a decided tendency to prevent the spread of this fearful disease and to render it less dangerous to those who contract it. . . . it is accepted by the mass of the people as well as by most members of the medical profession." Nearly every state encourages vaccination, and some "directly or indirectly" require it. It is compulsory in several European nations. "A common belief, like common knowledge, does not require evidence to establish its existence, but may be acted upon without proof by the legislature and the courts. . . . The fact that the belief is not universal is not controlling, for there is scarcely any belief that is accepted by everyone."[28]

THE LIMITS OF A "COMMON BELIEF"

The *Viemeister* decision was unusual because it posited the "common belief" of the state's citizens without citing solid evidence of that consensus. But Edmund Viemeister apparently did not appeal to the US Supreme Court. The *Viemeister* opinion was widely cited as settling the issue once and for all.

Medical professionals regarded it as a ratification of their science, said an editorial in the *New York State Journal of Medicine*, the journal of the Medical Society of the State of New York. Moreover, it verified that the people of the state believed in the effectiveness of vaccination, and "what the people believe is for the common welfare must be accepted as for the common welfare." That seemed to raise the prospect that in other situations medical science might not prevail until most people understood and supported it. Not a problem to be concerned with now, said the doctors—the decision gave vaccination in schools "constitutional standing" and "the full force of the law."[29] Deputy Attorney General Sanford T. Church, addressing a state medical conference in the fall, assured his audience, with an almost audible sigh of relief, that the *Viemeister* opinion meant that now "we may . . . unqualifiedly assert" that vaccination is "valid and constitutional, and a valid exercise of the police power."[30]

By the end of 1904, the legislature, governor, attorney general, courts, educational and medical establishments, and, according to Judge Vann, the "common belief" of the citizenry, had all endorsed the smallpox vaccine requirement. The issue seemed at last definitively settled. By fortuitous coincidence, the frequency of smallpox declined. The strains that did appear were milder and less toxic than previous ones.

A 1905 US Supreme Court decision, *Jacobson v. Massachusetts*, sustained a Massachusetts law that authorized city and county public health officials to require smallpox vaccination for adults. That law was well within the state's "police power" to protect public health and safety, the court held. Justice John Harlan, writing for the majority, cited and quoted at length from the New York Court of Appeals' 1904 *Viemeister* decision and its references to "common belief" in support of his decision.[31] Of course, the Massachusetts law went well beyond school vaccinations, to the population as a whole. But having the highest court in the land cite *Viemeister* with approval confirmed and magnified its authority.

Jacobson and *Viemeister* were strong affirmations of state authority. The school vaccination issue seemed to have gone into eclipse. But soon there were cracks in Judge Vann's placid pattern of "common belief."

Over the next few years, parents sometimes neglected to get their children vaccinated or simply refused on the belief that it was not the state's business or could harm children. Press reports noted that some principals looked the other way and admitted kids whose parents did not submit vaccination certificates. In 1908, the New York State Education Department reported that there was "much hostile feeling in many sections of the State" over compulsory vaccination. Critics were saying that doctors pushed compulsory vaccination out of a "mercenary motive" (parents paid in most cases, but if they could not afford the shots, the law provided that the costs of vaccination should be borne by the school district).[32]

In 1911, the department surveyed city school superintendents about vaccination. Forty-one responded; only twenty-seven were enforcing the law. Some accepted physicians' certificates for children deemed "not in physical condition to be vaccinated." Others said they enforced it only in times of epidemics. The Olean school board reported that attempts to enforce the law were "strenuously resisted by a large number of citizens." Over half of the city's students dropped out of the public school and transferred to two parochial schools and a private school to avoid vaccination. A Staten Island father threatened to shoot anyone who tried to vaccinate his children. Vaccination did no good, he insisted. When the school refused to back down, the irate father withdrew them from school. "The children are now being instructed as best their parents can teach them in elementary subjects," his lawyer told reporters, "with a sprinkling of nature study in the fields and woods near their home."[33] Speakers at a Brooklyn rally denounced vaccination as a medical sham, unjustified by any reliable evidence.[34] Bills began to surface in the legislature to repeal the school vaccination requirement.

Faced with such adamant and growing opposition, and despite strong court support for vaccinations, the state education department, in concert with the state health department, developed legislation to eliminate the blanket statewide legal vaccination provision. Instead, school authorities would be required to exclude unvaccinated children from the schools whenever the local board of health certified that "an epidemic of smallpox exists or is threatened in the vicinity of such schools . . . or is threatened and that the public health of the community is menaced by the presence of such unvaccinated children in the schools."[35] That essentially would have left vaccination up to local school boards and health commissions. The medical community opposed the bill as an imprudent, reckless retreat from the state's responsibility. The bill passed the senate in 1912 but failed in the assembly.

Parents resumed testing the constitutionality of the law in the courts. In a 1914 decision, the court of appeals backed the requirement in another case where a father refused to get his son vaccinated as a condition of attending school. The issue had been settled in the *Viemeister* decision a decade earlier, wrote Judge Frank H. Hiscock for a unanimous court. In fact, he noted, states' rights to require smallpox vaccinations in the general population had been upheld by the US Supreme Court a year later, in the *Jacobson v. Massachusetts* decision. If parents could keep children home because they disagreed with the vaccination requirement, they could equally logically do so for other unlawful reasons, including putting them to work. That would make the requirement for public education "more or less of a farce." The father's real motive was to defy the State. He was "more interested in asserting his right to refuse to comply with the law than he was actuated by the purpose of protecting his child from some possible or supposed injury," the judge asserted. The vaccination requirement was sustained. Judge Hiscock's petulant tone made it clear that New York courts were not going to revisit this issue.[36]

BACK TO THE LEGISLATURE

Blocked in the courts, anti-vaccination advocates trudged back to the legislature. Politics had shifted. Democratic in-fighting and the impeachment and removal of Democratic governor William Sulzer in 1913 had led to voters electing Republicans for the majority of the legislature and a Republican governor in 1914. The 1915 legislature, considerably more conservative than the one before it, where Democrats had been the majority, set about rolling back some of its predecessor's labor-reform laws. Republican governor Charles Whitman, who was more liberal than his fellow Republicans in the legislature, vetoed most of these repeal bills. But a feeling against government regulation was in the air.

New York City–based anti-vaccination groups kept up their attack on the school vaccination requirement. But action this time came from an unexpected source, James A. Loyster of Cazenovia, an upstate town. Loyster was supervisor of the town and had ties to the state Republican Party. He was a political colleague of the powerful state party chair, William Barnes of Albany. Loyster was not part of any anti-vaccination group or even interested in the vaccination controversy until 1914. His son Lewis was vaccinated against smallpox on August 29 of that year, developed a fever, and died on September 21. The doctors diagnosed the cause as infantile paralysis—polio. Loyster concluded the smallpox vaccination had caused it. On his own initiative, he placed ads in upstate newspapers seeking to contact parents who had had similar tragic experiences. He contacted fifty-one of the people who responded, got them to summarize their stories and send him photos of their children, and assembled the results as a self-published book in January 1915.[37]

The book was a modest publication, but it turned out to be a brilliant polemic; Loyster sent it to newspapers, legislators, and other influential people. Lewis Loyster's tragic story was included along with a photo: a ten-year-old boy from Dunkirk, in "splendid health" when he was vaccinated on September 22, died October 13 of "lockjaw," a sign of a tetanus infection. A seven-year-old girl was in "perfect health" until vaccinated on July 25, then contracted meningitis, and died on August 10.[38] The book was full of heartrending stories and photos of beautiful, smiling children before vaccination. There was no information about the thousands who were vaccinated with no ill effects or about the general effectiveness of vaccination. Loyster blamed contaminated vaccine and the "germ-infested abrasion" that vaccination left, which allowed other diseases to enter and cause the tragedies he documented. "The cost in illness and destruction of child life is entirely out of proportion to the amount of protection against small-pox that is attained or needed," he concluded. "Vaccination of children is wrong in principle . . . and should be abandoned."[39]

Loyster persuaded two Madison County Republicans in the legislature, Senator Samuel A. Jones and Assemblyman Morrell E. Tallett, to introduce a bill to repeal the compulsory vaccination law. Loyster's book dramatized the issue and supplemented long-standing vaccine opposition. Anti-vaxxers rallied. The bill gathered lots of support in the legislature even as medical experts condemned it and presented evidence about vaccination's effectiveness. Benefits clearly outweighed risks. An editorial in the state medical journal admitted that contaminated vaccine occasionally turned up in the past—"a lamentable occurrence in its preparation" unlikely to recur now that vaccine was produced under federal guidelines. The real problem was "lack of antiseptic precautions subsequent to the vaccination," for which "stupid parents and thoughtless children" were to blame.[40] That patronizing tone did not mollify critics or win allies.

State Health Commissioner Hermann Biggs stepped in to work out a compromise. Biggs was New York's first prominent public health statesman. He served as New York City's chief medical officer for twenty-six years before being appointed to the state post in 1913. In New York City, he was responsible for the first use of diphtheria antitoxin in the US as well as developing a model program for treating tuberculosis and was an advocate for the science of bacteriology in the prevention of infectious disease. Before becoming state commissioner, he chaired a study commission that recommended modernization of the state Public Health Law and reorganization of the health department. During his tenure as state health commissioner, 1913–24, he increased the number of public health nurses, created local public health laboratories, and carried out public health education on an unprecedented scale. One of his mottos was "public health is purchasable. Within natural limitations a community can determine its own death-rate."[41] Another motto was that disease is an evil that is largely removable. Public education—making people aware of how diseases spread, the need for sanitation, and the efficacy of modern medicine—would be the key.[42]

Biggs proposed leaving the legal school vaccination requirement intact in large, crowded cities but exempting the rest of the state except in localities when the commissioner of health found the disease was spreading. The compulsory vaccination had never really been enforced in villages and rural areas anyway, due to local opposition, Biggs testified at a joint meeting of the senate and assembly health committees in February 1915. "The key-note of modern public health work is public health education—not compulsion," he argued.[43]

Biggs's testimony opened the door for the proposal to advance. In March 1915, the legislature passed a compromise bill leaving the smallpox vaccination requirement intact for cities of the first and second class— cities with 50,000 or more people, of which there were nine in the state according to the 1910 census. These nine cities had about 65 percent of New York's population.[44] In other areas, approximately 35 percent of the population, school authorities would have to require vaccination only when the state commissioner of health certified that smallpox existed in the school district "or in the vicinity thereof."[45]

Medical experts decried an abdication of state responsibility outside the big cities. The Anti-Vaccination League, by contrast, called it a surrender to the advocates of medical compulsion. Critics predicted it would be unworkable—by the time the state health commissioner had enough evidence to confirm smallpox in a community, it would probably already be too late to counter it by vaccination of schoolchildren. The law accomplished the main goal of Loyster and his upstate allies by removing the burden of compulsion from the state's upstate areas, where it had been most resisted.

STATE'S RESPONSIBILITY EVOLVES

The new law was a challenge to implement. Biggs and his successors were not always certain about when to certify outbreaks. But Biggs's larger point, that education rather than coercion should be the key strategy, was the crucial insight. Public education efforts converted skeptics and won support for compliance and voluntary vaccination of children. The health department reported in 1921 that in the cities where school smallpox vaccination was required under the law there were no outbreaks in schools (other than New York City), whereas there were outbreaks in smaller communities exempt from the law's requirements. The clear implication was that school vaccination mandates protected not only students but the community as a whole.[46]

That evidence led to more parents getting their kids vaccinated voluntarily. The disease began to subside among the population as a whole, and reported cases were less severe than in the past. Confidence in public health officials, particularly the state health department and city and county commissioners, continually increased. When smallpox was reported in a community, health officials strongly urged (but did not require) vaccinations, and people heeded their warnings, which helped contain the outbreaks. In turn, news of the vaccine's effectiveness encouraged more people to seek it out voluntarily and get vaccinated. By the end of the 1920s, smallpox had ceased to be a major menace. "Not a single case of smallpox was reported in New York State during 1934," said the state health department's annual report.[47] The last significant outbreak, in New York City in 1947, was contained by public health officials through a mass vaccination effort.

Thanks to vaccination, smallpox declined. Routine vaccinations for smallpox were ended in the United States in 1972, and the disease was eradicated by 1977. Other vaccine-preventable diseases such as diphtheria, measles, mumps, and polio were also eradicated or dramatically reduced through gradually increased mandatory vaccination of children.[48] New York was a leader. School-age children in the state are required to be immunized against all of these diseases.[49] Over the years, the other public health initiatives launched by Commissioner Biggs expanded. Schools hired school nurses. Health education entered the curriculum. Physicians gave free medical and dental examinations in New York schools.

Vaccination opponents continued their resistance campaigns, using some of the same arguments as their predecessors in New York's Progressive Era about individual rights and reliability of vaccines and incorporating new ones, such as religious objections.[50] The courts were consistently supportive of public health officials in expanding mandatory vaccinations. A 1922 US Supreme Court decision, *Zucht v. King*, upheld the right of states to give municipalities the authority to exclude unvaccinated students from school. Over the years, state courts and the US Supreme Court consistently upheld states' authority to require vaccinations for schoolchildren.[51]

New York allowed a religious exemption for some years but, after an outbreak of measles, repealed it in 2019. A number of parents sued. The state supreme court upheld the validity of the statute, citing federal and state court decisions including *Matter of Viemeister*. In that case, the state supreme court noted, the court of appeals had "upheld compulsory vaccination of school children. It upheld the mandate notwithstanding New York's constitutional duty to provide a system of free public schools, and notwithstanding the absence of a recent outbreak, based on historical and international experience."[52] The appellate division also upheld the decision.

The history of state smallpox vaccination policies in the Progressive Era illustrates the evolution of medical science, the role of public health officials, the evolution of legislation, and the role of the courts. The issues and tensions that surfaced during that era would play out again and again with other health issues in the rest of the twentieth century and the beginning of the twenty-first. The courts would continue to play a role akin to a rudder, supporting responsible public policy but also protecting individual rights.

Chapter 6

THE INSANITY DEFENSE ON TRIAL

Figure 6.1 and 6.2. Harry K. Thaw, at left, was tried in 1907 and 1908 for murdering Stanford White in retribution for a sexual assault years earlier on Thaw's wife, Evelyn, pictured at right. The Thaw case showed the challenges of determining the legal sanity of people who committed crimes of passion. *Source:* Bain News Service. Library of Congress Prints & Photographs Collection.

Can a man shoot another man to death but avoid capital punishment by claiming he was compelled to the act to avenge a sexual assault on his wife before he married her? New York's legal community, its medical jurisprudence community, and its court system wrestled with the issue in the case of Harry K. Thaw for nine years, 1906–15. The answer turned out to be yes. The Thaw case was in effect a trial of the insanity defense itself.

On June 25, 1906, Harry K. Thaw shot and killed Stanford White during a musical play at a rooftop theater at Madison Square Garden in New York City. "I did it because he ruined my wife," Thaw shouted as he calmly handed his pistol to a member of the audience. "He had it coming to him. He took advantage of the girl and then deserted her!"[1] Thaw, a wealthy, eccentric, and mentally unstable New Yorker originally from Pittsburgh, had married Evelyn Nesbit, a glamorous photographers' and artists' model, chorus girl, and actress, in 1905. Before their marriage, she told Thaw that White, a married man and famous architect (he had in fact designed the building where he was shot), had laced champagne with a drug during one of her visits to his apartment and, while she was passed out, had sexually assaulted her. She could not recall the exact date—sometime in 1901—and in fact her own birth date was uncertain because the records had been lost and sometimes her mother added to her age to get her modeling jobs. She would have been only sixteen or seventeen at the time.

It was an act of rape, but Evelyn introduced some uncertainty by changing her story over time. Evelyn's father had died years before, but her mother and guardian, instead of calling the police and having White arrested, allowed and encouraged her daughter to keep seeing him. White, in turn, showered both mother and daughter with gifts and money. Evelyn told Thaw the story of White's assault in 1903, when he was courting her, and he became enraged. Three years later, he killed White.

The Thaws had come to see the play, which White and his wife also happened to attend. Dozens of audience members and people in the musical saw the shooting. It seemed like a clear-cut case of murder. Thaw was quickly arrested, arraigned, and indicted for the crime. His fate thereafter would rest exclusively with men—the legislators who had made the laws, the New York County district attorney, his own attorneys, judges, and jurors were all men in those days. Thaw claimed the shooting was justified and that he had not planned it but that it was a spur-of-the-moment act when he unexpectedly saw White at the musical. He had been carrying the gun for his own defense, he said; that was legal in New York before the state passed a law banning concealed weapons without a permit in 1911. Could Thaw avoid being convicted of murder? A provision in New York law gave Thaw the prospect of getting away with the killing. It had been there since the beginning of the state. It resembled laws in England (an important source of legal authority in some areas in those days) and several other states and was based on the principle that defendants who committed murder and other heinous acts needed to know what they were doing and also that it was wrong.[2]

New York's version, most recently revised in 1882, provided the following:

> An act done by a person who is an idiot, imbecile, lunatic, or insane, is not a crime. A person cannot be tried, sentenced to any punishment, or punished for a crime, while he is in a state of idiocy, imbecility, lunacy or insanity, so as to be incapable of understanding the proceeding or making his defense. (§20)
>
> A person is not excused from criminal liability as an idiot, imbecile, lunatic, or insane person, except upon proof that, at the time of committing the alleged criminal act, he was laboring under such a defect of reason, as either (1) Not to know the nature and quality of the act he was doing; or (2) Not to know that the act was wrong. (§21)
>
> A morbid propensity to commit prohibited acts, existing in the mind of a person who is not shown to have been capable of knowing the wrongfulness of such acts, forms no defense to a prosecution therefor. (§23)[3]

Lawyers, judges, and juries wrestled with the meaning and implications of those ambiguous words. District attorneys and defense counsel sometimes engaged alienists (as doctors in the emerging field of medical jurisprudence were called) to testify for or against defendants' sanity. But the doctors were operating in "an inchoate medical environment absent of consensual agreement on classification and nomenclature."[4] They disputed with each other and tossed out terms like *moral insanity, dementia praecox, paranoia, mania, logorrhea,* and *unsound mind* that baffled judges and jurors. The "insanity defense" was used so often that it was derided as a fraud. Writer and humorist Mark Twain had declared:

Is not this insanity plea becoming rather common? Is it not so common that the reader confidently expects to see it offered in every criminal case that comes before the courts? And is it not so cheap, and so common, that the reader smiles in derision when the newspaper mentions it? Of late years, it does not seem possible for a man to conduct himself, before killing another man, as not to be manifestly insane. If he talks about the stars, he is insane. If he appears nervous and messy an hour before the killing, he is insane. . . . If, an hour after the murder, he seems ill at ease, preoccupied and excited, he is unquestionably insane.[5]

Several New York court decisions on capital cases tried to stem the tide of overuse of the insanity defense. They affirmed that "defect of reason" was meant to mean a serious mental disease. A spur-of-the-moment "irresistible impulse," a sudden welling up of passion, delusional feelings, or a desire for revenge would not excuse murder.[6] An 1893 court of appeals decision had explained that

partial insanity, or incipient insanity, is not sufficient, if there is still an ability to form a correct perception of the legal quality of the act and to know that it is wrong. If, when a specific act is contemplated, [the accused] has the power to know whether it is wrong to do it and the right to refrain from doing it, the law assumes he has also the power to choose between the right and wrong course of action, and will not permit either courts or juries to speculate as to its possible non-existence.[7]

The law permitted (but did not require) trial judges to appoint a "Commission in Lunacy" of medical or legal experts to determine a prisoner's sanity when the judge felt it warranted. Judges occasionally did this, but the commissions' impact was limited because often the experts themselves could not reach a definite consensus. Juries occasionally accepted defense counsels' claims of "temporary insanity" even if that stretched the law. One legal expert had scoffed at the plea of "lightning bug insanity, the kind that covers the time of the shooting and then goes out" wherein the accused killer, recovered from their insane episode, goes free.[8] Juries also sometimes acquitted on the basis of more durable insanity, existing at the time of the crime and continuing through the time of the trial, even when the evidence was thin. That verdict meant confinement in a state mental hospital until the prisoner was declared sane and released by the hospital director or a judge. That was a grim fate but better than the alternative: a guilty verdict for capital offenses meant death by electrocution.

Juries could be independent, even fickle. They sometimes acquitted men on what was called "the unwritten law": a man has the right to kill another man who had seduced or violated his wife.[9] In a famous case, in 1859, New York congressman Daniel Sickles had shot and killed Philip Barton Key II, the district attorney of the District of Columbia and the son of "Star-Spangled Banner" composer Francis Scott Key, in Washington, DC. Sickles had discovered that Philip Key was having an affair with his wife. Sickles's lawyers asserted that knowledge of the affair had driven their client temporarily insane. The jury acquitted him. (He later became a Union general in the Civil War and lost a leg in the Battle of Gettysburg.) In 1868, Civil War veteran George W. Cole from Syracuse shot L. Harris Hiscock, a leading Syracuse attorney, to death. "He violated my wife while I was at war; the evidence is clear," Cole declared. "I have the proof."[10] The jury found him not guilty. That case was well known in New York's legal community in part because Hiscock's son, Frank Hiscock, was a judge on the court of appeals at the time of the Thaw trials.

There were many other examples of juries substituting their own judgment for the letter of the law in cases where witnesses were inconclusive, prosecutors' and defense attorneys' arguments about insanity drowned each other out, medical experts undercut each other, or judges' directions left leeway for the juries. One legal expert, writing in 1906, decried the pattern of "juries' imprudence which recognizes rights that are forbidden by law and denies rights that are granted by law."[11] Over the coming years, Thaw's well-paid lawyers would exploit the inconsistencies in the law and court decisions, arguing that Thaw's killing of White was justified under the circumstances, that he was insane at the moment of the crime but sane before and after, and that he had been plagued by insanity for years but was now recovered.

SHOW TRIAL AND PUBLIC SPECTACLE

Thaw was tried for murder in a New York City courtroom January 23–April 12, 1907. His wealthy mother hired a prominent (and expensive) California defense attorney, Delphin Delmas, whose strategy was to pair the insanity defense with the "unwritten law" to portray the shooting as a single uncontrollable, aberrant but justifiable act. The prosecutor, the highly capable Democratic New York County district attorney William T. Jerome, was determined to prove Thaw a murderer. He and the judge, Justice James Fitzgerald, were Democratic Party insiders, as was Delmas, who had nominated New York Democratic congressman William R. Hearst for president at the 1904 party convention.

The trial proved to be an unprecedented, sensational public spectacle. Witnesses recounted the shooting in graphic detail. Reporters covered the trial every day, and many newspapers printed excerpts from lurid, sensational testimony. Evelyn Thaw was prominent for widely circulated photographs and ads with her posing as a model. She had been a dancer in the racy (by the standards of the day) *Florodora* musical ensemble on Broadway. The newspapers shamelessly exploited and victimized her to increase circulation and readership.

Delmas asked her to recount in detail what she had told Thaw about White's sexual assault in order, he said, to vividly document for the jury why Thaw was so enraged. Newspapers printed much of her testimony verbatim, titillating or outraging their readership but surely selling newspapers. Cameras were not allowed in the courtroom, but sketch artists were often in attendance to draw images of Evelyn, Harry, her mother, his mother, and other Thaw family members. Hints of hereditary insanity in the Thaw family came out in the trial. Thaw had hired detectives to shadow White, complained to New York's anti-vice crusader Anthony Comstock, and even wrote the district attorney's office about White's alleged assaults on other young women. Jerome produced a lawyer who testified that Evelyn had come to him for help after Thaw assaulted her with a whip. She denied it and sidestepped Jerome's attempts to shake her story. The Thaw family hired a writer to produce a short book on the shooting and commissioned a film, *The Unwritten Law*, documenting White's drugging and assault of Evelyn and defending Thaw's manly action to avenge her honor.[12]

ROUND 1: HUNG JURY

Delphin Delmas called a number of prominent mental health experts (well paid by the Thaw family) starting with Dr. Britton D. Evans, superintendent of the New Jersey State Hospital for the Insane (that state's equivalent of

Matteawan State Hospital in New York). Evans had examined Thaw shortly after he was jailed and recalled that he was in a nervous, agitated state and suffered from a "brain storm or a fulminating condition of mental unsoundness."[13] Evans used the same term, *brain storm*, in later testimony describing Thaw's mental state. *Brain storm* was a striking, graphic term, unknown to the law, that grabbed press and public attention. Evans had met with Thaw a number of times since then and attended the court proceedings most days. He was adamant that Thaw was deranged.

District Attorney Jerome tried to shake Evans's testimony by referring to other experts who argued that insanity might be misdiagnosed or feigned. Evans dodged by saying he could not say whether they were authoritative sources or not. Jerome tried to pin Evans down. Was Thaw insane? "He is not now and never was an idiot," Evans responded evasively. An imbecile, asked Jerome? "I believe not." How about his present state of mind? "It would be a matter of conjecture," the doctor replied. Asked the same question again, his response was "I have no intelligent opinion."[14]

In later cross-examination, Evans explained that Thaw was in "a state of mental instability" and exhibited "mental unsteadiness" and traits of "an unsound mind." Why had Thaw shot White, Jerome asked? Evans responded, "I believe it was a temporary attack owing to much strain and stress and anxiety and it was the insanity of adolescence." How was Evans sure it was a "brain storm?" Evans: "The agitation must have been there for the man to have done what he did in the manner that he did." How could Thaw have appeared so composed before and after the shooting? Evans: "The simple fact of outward agitation does not picture what is going on in the operation of the brain. A raging storm may be going on within. A lack of appreciation of what is being done sometimes causes a coolness in the manner."[15] Did Thaw know he was shooting White? Evans: "He may have had an insane knowledge that he was doing so."[16] Thaw's other medical experts all confirmed in their testimony, each using his own terms and explanations, that Thaw did not have a rational understanding of what he was doing when he killed White.

District Attorney (DA) Jerome had his own battery of medical experts, paid modestly by the DA's office for their time and expertise. Jerome's lead witness, Dr. Austin Flint, had a particularly weighty résumé: professor of physiology at Cornell University Medical Center, former surgeon general of New York, and former president of the state medical association. Flint was blunt and direct: Thaw "knew the nature and quality of his act and knew that the act was wrong." Six other authoritative prosecution alienists endorsed Flint's diagnosis. One of them, Dr. Carlos MacDonald, former professor of mental diseases at Bellevue Hospital Medical College and former chair of the State Commission in Lunacy, which supervised the state's mental hospitals, got more specific. Thaw was suffering from "a form of mental disease commonly known among men skilled in mental diseases as paranoia." But he insisted that Thaw "knew the nature and quality of the act that he was doing and that it was wrong." It was "reasonably certain that he would not recover"; releasing him "would be dangerous to public peace and safety," and therefore he should be committed to an institution for the insane.[17]

Justice Fitzgerald, as perplexed as the jury over the dueling expert testimony, appointed a Lunacy Commission on March 22 to advise on whether Thaw was sane enough to be tried. That would have made sense at the beginning of the trial, not two months into it, but the judge insisted he and the jury needed enlightenment. Fitzgerald appointed former appellate division justice Morgan J. O'Brien, former New York County DA Peter Olney, and Dr. Leopold Putzel, an expert in lunacy. Olney dropped off claiming lack of time and was replaced by David McClure, a prominent city attorney. The board called some of the same experts who had already testified and heard mostly the same contradictory themes. But two witnesses stood out.

One was Dr. Allan McLane Hamilton, grandson (and biographer) of Alexander Hamilton, professor of psychiatry at Cornell University Medical College with a specialty in nervous diseases and recognized as an expert on criminal insanity. Hamilton had been a consultant called in by the government to test the sanity of Charles Guiteau, President James A. Garfield's assassin, in 1881, and Leon Czolgosz, President William McKinley's assassin, in 1901. He had testified as an expert in several other capital cases. The Thaw family had asked him to visit Harry in prison shortly after the shooting. Hamilton talked with Thaw and decided not to sign on as a witness for him but also declined to testify in the trial on the grounds that his conversation had been privileged. But he attended court as an observer for most of the trial and decided it would be ethical to testify before the lunacy commission. Both sides expected he would be objective. In fact, he had criticized courts for putting too much emphasis on medical expert testimony, claimed that doctors often misdiagnosed insanity in their patients, and insisted that doctors sometimes failed to distinguish between harmless fantasies and genuine insane delusions. He had advocated replacing the current system with one where the court would name a neutral board of experts.[18]

Hamilton told the commission that during his visit to Thaw the previous June, Thaw "showed no remorse and did not seem to know his position." He imagined a conspiracy to convict him and had looked for intruders under the desk in his cell. Thaw had called White's killing "an act of providence" that had prevented him from ruining other young women. Now, during his trial, Hamilton continued, "he has no rational conception of the proceedings." As evidence, Hamilton said he noted that when District Attorney Jerome had reenacted the shooting during the trial, "Thaw turned to one of his attorneys and joked and laughed unconcernedly." Thaw was being poorly served by his counsel, Hamilton asserted. They should be arguing their client was insane.[19]

The other star witness before the lunacy commission was Harry Thaw himself. The commission decided to examine him directly as a way of cutting through the fog of expert testimony. Thaw was carefully prepared for his testimony by counsel Delmas and Dr. Evans. He answered every question clearly. He demonstrated he was following the court proceedings in detail, understood rulings made by the judge, and explained directions he had given to Delmas. Thaw was poised, calm, and even bantered with the commissioners. The commission reported on April 4 that "Harry K. Thaw was and is sane and was not and is not in a state of idiocy, imbecility, lunacy, or insanity"; fully understood the charges against him; and was capable of conducting his own defense.[20]

The commission attested to Thaw's mental state at the present time but had not said definitively whether he was insane at the time he shot White. That question fell back to his counsel and the DA when the trial concluded a few days later.

Delmas's summary reiterated the scoundrel White's assault and Evelyn Thaw's innocent victimhood. Harry and Evelyn were "two young persons whom fate, by inscrutable decree, had destined to link together, that they could walk through life together. It is a story—the saddest, most mournful and tragic which the tongue of man has ever uttered." He assured the jury that "I shall rely on no such unstable thing as the supposed unwritten law" but then set forth a variation of that very "law":

> Let me call the "insanity" of Thaw "Dementia Americana." It is the species of insanity that makes every American man believe his home to be sacred; that is the species of insanity which makes him believe the honor of his daughter is sacred; that is the species of insanity which makes him believe the honor of his wife is sacred; that is the species of insanity which makes

him believe that whosoever invades his home, that whosoever stains the virtue or his threshold, has violated the highest of human laws and must appeal to the mercy or God, if mercy there be for him anywhere in the universe.

When Thaw saw White that fateful night, Evelyn's story of being debased played out again in his mind. He was "goaded into frenzy" by the tortured memory and impelled to act.[21]

District Attorney Jerome's closing statement was forceful and persuasive. This was nothing more than "a vulgar, ordinary, low, sordid murder" by a violent, jealous man who feared White might try to win Evelyn back. Thaw's killing of White was "an act of sanity" when he "brutally and cowardly shot down his enemy." White, now dead, unable to defend his reputation, was being unfairly maligned. Evelyn Thaw was misleading and lying. She was not "the angel child that Mr. Delmas would paint her [Evelyn] to be, reared chastely and purely, as she herself tells you, drugged and despoiled! Why, what nonsense to come here and tell twelve men! She of the Florodora chorus!" If White assaulted her as she claimed, why did she "[meet] him again and again and again—this human ogre that had drugged her"? Evans's "brain storm" defense was phony: "if the only thing that lies between a citizen and his enemy is a brain storm, then . . . every man had better pack a gun and have the first brain storm!"[22]

Delmas's "Dementia Americana" defense was imaginative "legal meaning-making," basically a hoax designed to excuse murder.[23] Jerome, however, had not convinced the jury that the shooting fit the legal definition of murder. The jury deadlocked: seven for first-degree murder, five for not guilty by reason of insanity. That meant a hung jury. One juror, interviewed later, explained that the long, monotonous testimony of the alienists had confused and tired the jury and the opposing legal teams had in effect canceled each other out.[24] Some jurors insisted it was clearly murder, but others concluded from their own observations of Thaw's behavior in the courtroom that "this man is not right in his head," as one later told news reporters.[25]

ROUND 2: TEMPORARY(?) INSANITY

Thaw was tried a second time, in a much shorter, less dramatic trial that lasted from January 6 through February 1, 1908. Jerome dutifully led off with the reassertion that this was a case of premeditated murder. Witnesses described the shooting again, and Evelyn told her lurid story a second time. Jerome tried to rattle her on cross-examination, with no more success than the first time. He surprised the court by not calling any expert mental health witnesses this time, giving rise to speculation that he had despaired of convicting Thaw of murder and would be content to see him declared insane and committed to Matteawan State Hospital, the state's facility for the criminally insane.

The Thaw family dismissed Delmas and instead hired a Democratic Party political insider, Martin W. Littleton. He was a former Brooklyn borough president and protégé of David B. Hill, New York governor, senator, and power broker at the end of the nineteenth century. Through that connection, Littleton had been selected to nominate New York chief judge Alton B. Parker for the presidency at the 1904 party convention, burnishing his image as an orator. Littleton was known for his careful preparation and presentation. He had another advantage: he knew the judge, fellow Democrat Victor J. Dowling. Littleton took charge of the Thaw defense, promising his client and his family that the best way to avoid the electric chair was a conviction for insanity, commitment to Matteawan State Hospital for the Criminally Insane, and then an appeal that the insanity had abated and he should be released. It was a somewhat cynical strategy, designed to take advantage of the law's ambiguities.[26]

Littleton called Thaw's mother as a witness, and she testified to insanity in the family and to Harry's odd, rebellious behavior as a child. Littleton was able to bring in medical experts from Europe (at the Thaw family's expense) who insisted Thaw had exhibited insane behavior during vacation trips to Rome and Paris in the early years of the century. He called Dr. Britton Evans and two other doctors from the first trial, all of whom now insisted that Thaw suffered from "manic depressive" insanity, an affliction characterized by both "mania" and "melancholy."[27]

Jerome's closing statement was tame compared to the first time. Evelyn had not been truthful. She really had not been drugged by White but submitted voluntarily and after the alleged assault continued to visit his apartment and accept his favors. Thaw had lived a life of indulgence and dissipation. He had made Evelyn his mistress when she refused his first marriage proposal and beat her when he lost his temper. He was a sane coward with "no shame . . . no sense of honor or decency" who waited three years to kill White after first hearing Evelyn's story. He then went about "shielding himself in his wife's skirts" by directing her to commit perjury. But Jerome seemed dispirited, worn out by the two trials. He implied a conviction for manslaughter rather than murder would be satisfactory. Indirectly buttressing Littleton's case, the DA told the jury they should acquit Thaw if they believed he was a madman.[28]

Martin W. Littleton was a master of closing statements. He followed a formula: address the jury directly, make eye contact with jurors, present your facts succinctly, and use language they can understand. It does not really matter if your client is actually guilty or not. You are not passing on his guilt or innocence but rather defending "the ideal of justice for the guilty man as well as for the innocent."[29] Littleton's summary was the most persuasive of any in Thaw's several legal proceedings:[30]

- *There is a well-founded suspicion of the insanity defense, but Thaw really is insane.* Juries often felt the insanity defense was "invented for the occasion," Littleton admitted. But he portrayed his client as a shambling man with dull eyes and a distorted mouth. He mimicked the wild animal-like cries that Thaw's mother had testified he made as a child. Thaw had inherited insanity and was not to blame for what he did. It "derived its strength from heredity—grounded into the very history of the man." The killing was "a maniacal outbreak" rather than planned or premeditated.

- *The experts support the insanity defense.* Littleton summarized key points from Thaw's "alienists" in both trials. Jerome had offered only flimsy evidence, "innuendo, sneers, and insinuations."

- *Evelyn Thaw is a credible witness who was badgered by the district attorney.* Littleton made Evelyn a victim of both White and Jerome. Evelyn had been raised in poverty and exploited by White. "Thaw came into her life and loved her. He proved his love in the greatest way any man can." But Jerome was more intent on humiliating and destroying her than in proving Thaw sane. Evelyn had complained to the press about Jerome's harsh questioning, telling reporters that "all that is left for Jerome to do is to tear my little Buster Brown collar to pieces!" Littleton denounced Jerome's "antipathy . . . notes of savagery and bitterness."

The jury agreed and found Thaw not guilty by reason of insanity. He was remanded to Matteawan State Hospital to remain until discharged by due course of law.

ROUND 3: CONFINEMENT, APPEALS, ESCAPE

Leaving the courtroom, Harry Thaw expressed surprise that he was actually going to be confined at Matteawan, even though that was what his lawyers had been aiming for. Matteawan State Hospital had been established in Dutchess County in 1892 for the confinement and treatment of individuals found to be insane and committed to it by the criminal courts. Thaw was placed among the "mild" homicidal patients but given no special privileges and ate with and slept in the same room as other patients. There was no systematic counseling in those days, and antipsychotic drugs were several years in the future. Instead, doctors prescribed a benign program of "moral treatment"—a gentle, stress-free, highly routine environment. Patients who were capable were assigned to a work program, sometimes called "occupational therapy," that included cooking, maintenance, farming, and making baskets, rugs, and clothing. Patients had outdoor exercise twice a day. They could also play chess, checkers, softball, tennis, golf, and other games.[31] Thaw did not seem to mind at first. A few days after arriving, he told reporters he was perfectly sane and that his lawyers would have him out within a week.[32] His lawyers, Dr. Evans and other doctors who had testified at his trial, his wife, and friends who visited him were confident his stay would be brief.

There were only three ways a patient could get out of Matteawan alive—release by the hospital's director after he declared a patient sane, escape, or release by a judge issuing a writ of habeas corpus declaring the patient sane and authorizing their release. Harry Thaw, with the support of his wealthy family, well-paid attorneys, and medical experts, tried all three.

Thaw's mother filed multiple lawsuits against the prison's superintendent, starting almost as soon as Thaw reported for confinement. In 1908, his lawyers attempted to have him released from Matteawan on a writ of habeas corpus, claiming he was now sane. Jerome and the state attorney general appeared in court in opposition. Jerome produced a witness who had rented rooms to Thaw during 1902–5. She testified that he had used a false name, purported to be a theatrical agent, and whipped and terrorized young women he brought there. Thaw claimed he was interviewing them to get evidence against White, but that was not credible. Another witness testified that Thaw had given him money to pay the women to keep silent. That testimony, which had not come out at either trial, tipped the scales toward continuing confinement. The judge ruled that Thaw had been legally found to have "manic-depressive insanity" and that Matteawan authorities had not cleared him for release. The new testimony added to the evidence that "the petitioner would be dangerous to public safety and was afflicted with chronic delusion insanity."[33]

Thaw's mother petitioned to have her son moved to a private asylum; the courts refused. She alleged that legal costs were threatening the family with bankruptcy and sued in federal courts to have her son released to testify in a case involving the family's finances in Pittsburgh. She even hired former Pennsylvania governor William A. Stone to plead the case, all to no avail.[34]

Thaw appealed, arguing that the law under which he had been committed to Matteawan was unconstitutional. It amounted to an indefinite sentence. Thaw deserved a jury trial to determine his mental condition. The Thaw family tried a prominent Republican lawyer this time. They hired former New York governor Frank S. Black to argue the case in an appeal to the court of appeals. That court confirmed the lower court's ruling and dismissed the appeal. Thaw stayed confined.[35]

Thaw's attorneys mounted demands for a jury trial for their client to determine whether he should be set free. There was no provision in the law for that, but his lawyers argued it was justified anyway. Thaw had been sent to Matteawan as a patient, not a prisoner, they claimed, and he was now sane and should be released. William T. Jerome retired in 1909, but his successor joined the New York State attorney general in opposition each time an appeal was made. Matteawan officials and state alienists attested to Thaw's continued insanity. If a judge granted Thaw a trial, they feared, others confined at Matteawan might try to follow the precedent.[36] But even the legal community began to question New York's policies. Confining a sane man in a madhouse was "an outrage, heinous in effect, and a plain violation of all fundamental constitutional principles," said a law journal editorial. Harry Thaw deserved a trial by jury to determine if he was sane and therefore could leave Matteawan a free man.[37]

Thaw's mother in press interviews called Jerome and state authorities vindictive for keeping her son in the madhouse. She even hired a publicist to discredit Matteawan authorities for holding onto sane patients.

After years of appeals, determined to escape confinement, in August 1913 Thaw walked out of the asylum's front gate and was driven north to New Hampshire and then over the Canadian border to Sherbrooke, Quebec. His escape had been planned by his family, and the automobile and driver financed by his mother. Once in Canada, he fought extradition, claiming he had been confined without a trial to determine his sanity. The Canadians handed him over to New Hampshire authorities near where he had crossed their border. He fought extradition from New Hampshire to New York in federal court, resulting, among other things, in a federal commission on lunacy, which found him sane. In December 1914, at the order of the US Supreme Court, Thaw was extradited to New York. He was not tried for his escape—he had just walked out the gate, had not bribed anyone, and had not assaulted any guards. State authorities charged him with conspiracy and remanded him to prison in New York City rather than return him to Matteawan, unsure of what to do next.[38]

ROUND 4: FREEDOM

After Thaw was extradited to New York, the Thaw family engaged a capable new counsel, John B. Stanchfield, like Littleton, an accomplished Democratic Party insider. He had been a law partner of Democratic Party leader, governor, and senator David B. Hill and had been the party's candidate for governor in 1900. The judge for the next appeal was someone he knew well, Justice Peter A. Hendrick, who was a leader in Tammany Hall and had served as counsel to its leader Charles F. Murphy. Justice Hendrick was unwilling to issue a writ releasing Thaw and would not grant him the jury trial that he demanded.

Stanchfield had been a pitcher for the Amherst College baseball team when he was an undergraduate. One day, reportedly, he had pitched the first recorded curveball. That was a pitch that was notoriously hard to hit, but the term became a metaphor for something totally unexpected. Stanchfield now proposed something of a judicial curveball: a jury should hear Thaw's plea but only to advise the judge on the defendant's state of mind. Based on that, the judge would then make the final determination, as the law provided. Hendrick liked the idea. Thaw had not been convicted of a crime, the judge reminded everyone. He was confined at Matteawan "as a precaution to the public. . . . In view of the different conclusions reached in the various judicial proceedings heretofore . . . the question of Thaw's insanity should be determined by the court with the aid of a jury of twelve men who are not lawyers or doctors." Hendrick insisted this would not set a precedent.[39]

The State attorney general, Republican Egburt Woodbury, disagreed. If Thaw got a jury trial to determine his sanity, then presumably anyone confined at Matteawan could do the same, despite Hendrick's reassurance. In another twist in this long legal saga, the State's attorney general appealed State Justice Hendrick's decision to the Appellate Division of the New York State Supreme Court. That court sustained the judge. The attorney general then appealed to the court of appeals, which rendered its verdict on June 28, 1915. In a unanimous decision (one judge took no part), the court ruled Hendrick could have his jury proceeding. The appeal, the court noted dryly, represented "another chapter in the long history of the attempts of the defendant Thaw to regain [his] freedom." Hendrick was not evading his responsibility to make a decision but "simply intends to take the verdict of such jury by way of advice." Nothing in the law, "expressly or by fair implication, prohibits . . . the advisory employment of a jury as is now proposed." In fact, the courts have broad leeway to call juries into existence when they feel they are warranted. "Justice Hendrick had the discretionary right to call to his aid a jury."[40]

The judge quickly assembled a jury. Eleven out of the twelve jurors were married men, the press noted, presumably giving Thaw, a married man who had avenged his wife's debasement, an advantage. Stanchfield was better organized, articulate, and more forceful than his opponent, Attorney General Woodbury, and his courtroom manner was superior to that of Deputy Attorney General Frank Cook, who handled most of the trial. Evelyn Thaw declined to testify this time, claiming illness but privately admitting she was through defending Harry's violent act as being justified to avenge her loss of virtue. Stanchfield had the reports of the 1907 state lunacy commission and the 1913 federal commission, both of which pronounced Thaw sane, read into the record. A member of the federal commission testified that Thaw was rational and admitted that he knew killing White was wrong and he regretted it. Canadian authorities testified that Thaw was sane and quiet in their country until he was told that he would be extradited, which naturally upset him. Eleven men and three women from New Hampshire testified he was a model citizen during his stay in their state. A Concord policeman who was assigned to monitor Thaw got to know him well, went fishing with him, and said he never seemed irrational. A retired US marshal played friendly card games with him. The proprietor of the hotel where he lodged said he was a model guest. Mrs. Eugene W. Sargent told the court that the finest families in Concord had welcomed Harry Thaw into their homes.[41]

Stanchfield produced alienists who told the jury that Thaw was sane. Dr. Charles F. Bancroft, superintendent of the New Hampshire state hospital for the insane, testified for Thaw. He was absolutely rational, though he might have a "constitutional inferiority." Asked by Cook if that meant he was insane, Bancroft said not necessarily, but that he might be right on the line. "The act itself seems to have been a passionate, compulsive act growing out of anger and jealousy and a final combination of influences that disturbed Thaw." He had nursed his "anger and jealousy," and, "after an extended period of dissipation, he lost control of himself." Pressed to be more definite, the doctor said Thaw had never been insane. Dr. Charles F. Mills insisted that "Harry K. Thaw is a sane man."[42] Dr. Austin T. Flint, whose testimony had helped send Thaw to Matteawan in 1908 and keep him there through his previous appeals, admitted, under Stanchfield's withering cross-examination, that Thaw suffered from "constitutional inferiority with paranoiac trend" but was now acting sanely.[43] That undermined the state's case for returning him to Matteawan. The woman who had testified at the second trial about Thaw's luring young women to the room she rented to him was called and testified again, but Thaw again denied the accusation.

Stanchfield's star witness was Harry K. Thaw himself, reprising his role in the 1907 state and 1913 federal lunacy commission hearings. By that point, the trial had taken on an air of frivolity. Thaw spoke and shook hands with well-wishers in the courtroom audience. He laughed and told newsmen he expected to go free in a few days. Justice Hendrick allowed Thaw to dine with New York County sheriff Max Grifenhagen in the evenings at the swank Hotel Biltmore, where he also listened to music. The sheriff and Thaw also strolled on Fifth Avenue when the court was in recess. In introducing his client, Stanchfield noted sarcastically that the state's alienist experts in the courtroom had been determined to keep Thaw confined. He asserted—and they denied—that they had hired a lip reader to sit in the courtroom and tell them what Thaw was saying to his counsel. They had watched Thaw closely in court in the hope of catching him doing something odd. "If he laughs on the stand, they will say he is insane; if he cries, he is insane."[44]

On the stand for five hours, Thaw did neither. His testimony was calm and credible.

Stanchfield took his client through carefully rehearsed questions and answers. Justice Hendrick jumped in with requests for clarification or follow-up questions that indirectly helped Stanchfield make his case. Thaw said the state was keeping him locked up because they said he was a "paranoic" who had "delusions founded on nothing." But Thaw said his mind was clear and he had information to back up his beliefs. The state's "bug doctors" were determined to keep him confined even if that meant they had to testify untruthfully about his condition. Deputy Attorney General Cook asked, Was he insane when he shot White? Thaw: "At the trial, the jury, on the basis of a reasonable doubt, agreed that I might have been insane when I shot Mr. White. No one believed I was insane at the time of my acquittal." Asked to elaborate, Thaw said he had not planned to kill White but did so on impulse, then handed the pistol to "a sensible looking man" and did what he could to prevent panic in the theater. Why had he waited three years after Evelyn told him of her affair with White to deliver retribution? Thaw: "There is no answer to that question. I cannot give you one."

What about reports from one of his alleged women victims that he had treated her roughly? "Well, I was not a Sir Galahad," Thaw responded, referring to a legendary medieval knight known for his gallantry and purity. What about other alleged degenerate acts? "It is pure nonsense." White was the real evil culprit. He had lured Evelyn to his apartment, given her champagne, and "the next she knew it was all over. She was ruined." He told of his courtship of Evelyn, his deep love for her, and his motivation to avenge her debasement.[45]

Over two thousand people showed up on the final day of the trial on July 14 to cheer Thaw. Cook in his summary speech reminded the jury that insanity ran in both sides of Thaw's family, that Thaw had lived a worthless, aimless life, and that he exaggerated his love for Evelyn as a justification for killing. "This man never completed anything in his life except the killing of Stanford White." He should be returned to Matteawan.

But it was John Stanchfield's summing up that carried the day. Harry loved Evelyn, and her tragic story had touched his heart and impelled him to action. He harbored fears that White might use his wiles to try to steal her away. Thaw was not perfect—he had traveled in Europe with Evelyn before marrying her—but "this case is the story of a married libertine on the one hand and of a man who loved her well enough to give her his name." The public authorities were vindictive. Dr. Flint was the best example—he admitted Thaw was rational now but still tried to sow doubts by alleging continuing afflictions using baffling medical terms. But it was Thaw's own testimony that was most persuasive: "on his appearance and manner I am going to take the result of this trial." Thaw had fended off attacks on his character and veracity, explained his motives and actions clearly, and shown the world that he was a sane man. He had earned the right to go free.[46]

Justice Hendrick narrowed the jury's responsibility in his charge to them: they were only to state whether in their opinion Harry Thaw was now sane. They were not trying to pass judgment on his state of mind on June 25, 1906, or retrying him for shooting White. The jury unanimously found Thaw sane. The next day, Hendrick, citing their finding, ordered him freed.

Harry Thaw walked out to a cheering crowd. He took a train to his home in Pittsburgh, stopping in Atlantic City, where another crowd cheered him. A crowd of eight hundred people met him in Pittsburgh and surrounded his car as he went home. "Harry, the world is with you!" one well-wisher shouted. His trials had cost him a fortune in legal fees, cost New York State even more, and robbed him of nine years of freedom, he told the crowd. The next day, from his home, he issued what he called his "Final Statement." His 1908 acquittal had been "a swindle" because it was supposed to result only in his confinement for a few weeks. New York law was anachronistic. "It sent a citizen to the madhouse with no hearing whatever as to his sanity, which violates the fundamental principles of the New York State Constitution." The appeals judges before Hendrick had been duped by the government's "bug doctors" into keeping him locked up for years. Now, exonerated, he just wished to live quietly as a citizen in his beloved native city.[47]

In a bizarre final note to the trial, jury foreman David Robinson followed Thaw to Atlantic City. There, he held his own mini–press conference. The jury had ignored Justice Hendrick's charge, he told reporters. They always believed Thaw sane. They based their decision on the "unwritten law," which Robinson called the "natural law." Thaw was justified in killing White. Robinson had come to Atlantic City in the hope of meeting Thaw to urge him to commence a libel proceeding against the newspapers who had defamed him by their reporting during the trial. Dramatically, Robinson reached into his pocket and pulled out a pen, which he said the jurors had used to sign their decision document. He seemed to be offering it for sale. Thaw ducked Robinson, refusing to meet, but endorsed his statement, adding that the state's case against him had been built on "hot air." The next day, several other jurors told newsmen that Robinson was not being truthful. The unwritten law played no part in their deliberations. They had followed the judge's charge. Robinson, challenged, claimed he had been misquoted and that they did not ignore the judge. The bizarre Thaw case finally settled into the history books.[48]

Harry Thaw and his wife divorced soon after his release. He lived quietly for awhile but was arrested again in 1917, this time for kidnapping and whipping a young man. He was found to be insane and sent to a Philadelphia asylum, where he remained until gaining his freedom in 1924. In 1926 he published a memoir entitled *The Traitor*. There, he claimed that on the night of the shooting in 1906 he had seen White approaching young women in the cast before the play began with an evident intention of seducing and ruining them, as he had Evelyn. He never publicly expressed regret for what he had done. Thaw died of natural causes in 1947.[49]

Evelyn Nesbit Thaw had a child in 1910. She claimed Harry was the father; he denied it. Harry and Evelyn divorced in 1915. Evelyn took up a dancing career, then married her dance partner, but divorced him a few years later. She ran a tearoom for a while and tried painting, sculpting, and acting in nightclubs and movies, without much success. Evelyn Thaw published her own memoir, *Prodigal Days*, in 1934. She served as a consultant on a 1955 movie, *The Girl in the Red Velvet Swing*, based on her life, in 1955. She died in 1967.[50]

THE INSANITY DEFENSE ON TRIAL

Two years before Harry Thaw's release, in July 1913, on the fiftieth anniversary of the Battle of Gettysburg, Thaw had sent Daniel Sickles an envelope containing ten $100 bills and a note thanking him for his service as a "gallant Union officer." Thaw's sympathy was heightened by the fact that he had two uncles in the Union army, he added. Thaw made sure reporters learned of his generosity. But, as usual with Harry Thaw, you never knew his real motives. Thaw had often said his shooting White was like Sickles killing Philip Key back in 1859, justified to avenge ruining his wife. Sickles was aged, ill, and needed money. But he had grown weary of Thaw's citing him as a model. He sent Thaw's money back.[51]

By the time Harry Thaw went free two years later, many people in New York and elsewhere in the nation would have agreed with Sickles—they were tired of hearing from and about Harry K. Thaw. The Thaw affair had become a wearisome, multiyear spectacle. The turmoil relating to the insanity defense that his case raised had agitated New York's legal and medical communities. Thaw and his lawyers had demonstrated that the system was broken. Dr. Allan McLane Hamilton, the highly respected insanity expert who had testified at Thaw's 1907 lunacy commission hearing, called the trials "farcical," marked by "prostitution of scientific testimony" by "so-called experts . . . chosen because of their pliability, self-importance and preparedness to make a case out of the rottenest of elements, and to obstinately swear it through."[52] A New York City attorney noted in 1910 that the case had "abused the public ear, outraged the public decency and cost thousands upon thousands out of the public funds," and showed the insanity defense to be at best in "a confused condition" and easily manipulated to killer's advantage.[53]

The Thaw case had demonstrated the flaws of the insanity defense, but fixing it proved to be difficult. In 1910, at the urging of the New York State Bar Association and the State Commission in Lunacy, the legislature passed a law enabling trial judges to appoint three disinterested physicians to examine a defendant who pleaded insanity but still allowing either side to call their own experts during the trial.[54] That was not much of an improvement over the authority for judges to appoint "commissions in lunacy," which had been on the statute books for a generation. Over the years, it came in for criticism because judges overused it, often appointing less-than-qualified (and sometimes politically connected) "experts." One proposed remedy was a change in statute to provide for compulsory examination of defendants claiming insanity by a permanent group of state-employed specialists, an approach taken by Massachusetts and some other states, but it found little support in New York until years later.[55]

A New York State Bar Association committee recommended in 1911 restricting applications for habeas corpus writs for discharge from state mental hospitals to patients who could get two "qualified medical examiners" to attest to their sanity. But the proposal found little support. The committee floated a proposal for a new "guilty but insane" verdict. A person so convicted would be confined in an insane asylum as long as they would have served in prison if not insane and convicted of the same crime. If the penalty would have been execution, the "guilty but insane" person would be confined for life unless pardoned by the governor. Not surprisingly, that proposal met with a good deal of skepticism and opposition. If defendants are insane, then they cannot be guilty of a crime, some lawyers argued. If they regain their sanity, then they should automatically go free. The committee floated the idea of abolishing the insanity defense altogether. The "guilty but insane" proposal and the proposal to abolish the insanity plea went nowhere. The committee reported in frustration that cause and effect seemed impossible for the legal community to disentangle: "A man is insane because he does certain acts, and he does the acts because he is insane."[56]

Taking another tack in the hope of building a consensus, in 1914 the bar association sent a questionnaire to the leading alienists in the state asking for their advice on twenty-four questions, starting with "What is the medical definition of insanity?" and concluding with an inquiry as to their reaction to the "guilty but insane" proposal. Perhaps not surprisingly, there was no consensus on the definition or any of the proposed reforms.[57]

Over the following years, the intersection of mental health and the justice system continued to be the scene of continued debate. The legal and medical communities continued to dispute the insanity defense and often went their separate ways.[58] Lawyers want things clear-cut; mental health professionals advocate analyzing the brain's complexities and assert that *knowing* the difference between right and wrong is not really the same as *understanding* the reality and consequences of a violent act. The "unwritten law" gradually withered away with changes in mores that no longer viewed sex outside of marriage as scandalous or excused killings motivated by jealous rage.[59] In 1939, New York set aside the provision for judges to select their expert medical witnesses to testify in insanity trials and replaced it with a law enabling courts to appoint qualified psychiatrists from city or state hospitals to examine defendants who claimed insanity.[60] A 1965 law changed the definition of criminal insanity: "A person is not criminally responsible for conduct if, at the time of such conduct as a result of mental disease or defect, he lacks substantial capacity to know or appreciate either (a) the nature and consequence of such conduct; or (b) that such conduct was wrong."[61] That definition, with some minor word changes, is still in effect.[62] Advances in psychiatry and technological advances such as MRIs, which enable detection of physical brain defects, have added to the assembling of scientific evidence in court cases.[63]

Despite these advances, the issues raised in the Harry Thaw trials still reverberate. Just what is insanity? What impels people to kill? Do wealthy people who can hire stellar lawyers have an advantage over others? What are the courts' obligations to assemble and consider the evidence and reach verdicts that are fair to the accused but also punish wrongdoing and protect society? How should the state take care of people with mental problems who are found guilty of committing crimes?

Chapter 7
THE DEBUT OF THE ADMINISTRATIVE STATE

Figure 7.1. Saratoga Springs required a robust supply of electricity and gas to power its homes, industries, a thoroughbred racetrack, and tourist facilities, including the Grand Union Hotel, pictured here. The village's appeal to the New York State Commission of Gas and Electricity to order lower utility rates led to a precedent-setting court decision sustaining the commission's authority. *Source:* Library of Congress Prints & Photograph Collection.

Can the legislature deal with complex utility oversight and regulatory issues through creation of a commission that promulgates rules with the force and effect of law and makes binding decisions on service and rates? New York State tried that with a pioneering example of what would be later called the administrative state, the Commission of Gas and Electricity, in 1905, and the courts supported it.

The Commission of Gas and Electricity of the State of New York, created by the legislature in 1905, was arguably the first example in New York of the emerging concept of what would sometimes later be called the administrative state—powerful administrative agencies with the authority to promulgate rules with the force and effect of law, enforce regulatory compliance, and make binding decisions about public rights and services. The commission was active for only two years before being superseded by the Public Service Commission in 1907, an even more robust administrative agency with more extensive delegated powers, discussed in chapter 8.

In its brief tenure, the Gas and Electricity Commission was a model of judicious, objective regulation. Its constitutionality was challenged and tested in court, however. A Saratoga company, whose gas and electricity rates the commission ordered reduced, challenged the law as an unconstitutional delegation of legislative powers to an executive branch commission. A key court of appeals decision in 1908 affirmed the commission's validity and helped open the way to a growing list of administrative oversight agencies in the twentieth century.

THE NEED FOR A NEW APPROACH TO REGULATION

By the early years of the twentieth century, New York's population growth, urbanization, and industrialization had outdistanced state government's capacity to regulate economic affairs in the public interest. State government was a loose-fitting structure. The governor was nominally head of the executive branch, but his appointment of department heads needed senate confirmation, and departments secured their budgets by lobbying the legislature (there was no unified executive budget until the 1920s). Agencies issued annual reports to the legislature rather than the governor. The state health, banking, and insurance departments all had sparse regulatory laws to enforce. The Department of Labor was responsible for enforcement of state regulations about labor and working conditions in factories enacted in 1886 and revised later. The regulations were loose, though; the number of inspectors limited; enforcement spotty; and fines for violation rare.

There were a few commissions, including a state Board of Railroad Commissioners created in 1881. Its decisions, though, were not much more than recommendations since enforcement depended on seeking action by the attorney general, which the board rarely did.

New York State's regulation of its companies was mostly light, non-intrusive, and unobjectionable from a corporate viewpoint. That changed with the upsurge of the Progressive movement beginning in the late 1890s, which emphasized activist government to rein in irresponsible corporate practices and protect the public.[1] One of the Progressives' tools was what came to be called the administrative state. That term was not used until later, but the concept, still inchoate, was beginning to crystallize by the early twentieth century. The model is one of concentration of three governmental functions in powerful agencies: legislative (the power to make binding rules), executive (the power to carry out and enforce those rules), and judicial (the power to evaluate and issue orders in disputes between companies and citizens). The administrative agencies represented extensive delegation of authority and power by Congress or state legislatures. They were, legal historian Lawrence Friedman has observed, "the child of necessity" because of "a need for specialists and specialized bodies" to deal with complicated economic issues and exert control in the public interest.[2]

The emerging concept was a particularly good regulatory fit for "public utilities" such as gas and electricity companies and railroads. Competition was not an effective mode of keeping rates down and service quality up. It was not feasible, for instance, to run multiple competing gas pipes under city streets or competing electric lines on poles along sidewalks. Public utilities' municipal franchises usually gave them a monopoly. The legislature and courts lacked time and expertise to tend to complicated issues of utility rates and service in communities throughout the state. Progressives contended that something new, a specialized commission, was needed to do that work.[3]

But blending powers that the state (and federal) constitution segregated from each other caused concern and resistance. In the debate over the constitutionality of New York's gas and electricity commission law, critics often cited Thomas M. Cooley, an influential legal scholar of the era, who maintained that legislatures could not delegate their regulatory powers to executive agencies or commissions: "One of the settled maxims in constitutional law is that the power conferred upon the legislature to make laws cannot be delegated by that department to any other body or authority. Where the sovereign power of the State has located the authority, there it must remain."[4]

Judicial guidance was mixed. The federal government and some states—for example, Wisconsin—had delegated authority to commissions to deal with complex issues, and the courts mostly approved. Courts had validated the Interstate Commerce Commission (ICC) law, passed in 1887, which required that railroad rates be "reasonable and just" but did not actually empower the commission to set rates (that would come in 1906). But court decisions had circumscribed the commission's powers, often siding with railroads when they protested commission decisions.

In 1892, in a decision that proponents of the New York gas and electricity commission statute would cite, the Supreme Court sustained Congress's delegation of power to the president to impose a retaliatory tariff whenever the president determined that American exports were subject to "unequal and unreasonable" duties in a foreign nation. The US Constitution reserved legislative authority to Congress. But, the court reasoned, Congress had defined the goal, and the president was just carrying out what Congress intended—in this case, identifying inequitable duties and imposing appropriate retaliations.[5] Proponents of state administrative agencies asserted that similar judicial reasoning should apply at the state level: the legislature defines what needs to be done; agencies fill in the blanks and apply legislative intent on a case-by-case basis.

Change was precipitated, as it often was in New York, by public exposure of malfeasance and corruption. The Consolidated Gas Company, which controlled most of the gas market and a good deal of the electricity market in New York City, was exposed in the press in 1905 for gouging the city on gas prices. The Republican-controlled state senate established a committee to investigate. The committee hired an industrious, capable Republican attorney and former law school professor, Charles Evans Hughes, as its counsel. Hughes proved to be a brilliant investigator and examiner of Consolidated officials under oath. His investigation exposed a pattern of overcapitalization, bloated profits, fraudulent bookkeeping, and tax evasion.

The public demanded action. A bill was introduced to set the gas rate in New York City at eighty cents per cubic foot by law. Maverick New York City publisher and congressman William R. Hearst, an independent candidate for mayor in 1905, spearheaded a campaign for more drastic action: the City taking ownership of Consolidated.

Counsel Hughes advanced a better idea, which he convinced the committee to endorse and send to the legislature: a powerful new commission with unprecedented, broad powers to investigate and establish standards for services and maximum rates for gas and electricity. This was a historic new model for New York. Utility companies lobbied against it, complaining it would meddle and interfere in their business. Under media scrutiny and public pressure to act, however, the legislature passed and in June 1905 Republican governor Frank Higgins signed the bill drafted by Hughes to set up a Commission of Gas and Electricity. Most Republican legislators reluctantly voted for it; a few opposed or abstained. All the Democrats, the minority party in both houses, voted no. Assembly minority leader George M. Palmer told reporters it was "another grand move toward centralization of power and toward paternalism in our state government."[6]

THE POWERFUL NEW COMMISSION CHARTS A CAUTIOUS PATH

The law gave the Gas and Electricity Commission unprecedented authority. Three commissioners, appointed by the governor but requiring senate approval, headed the agency. The law gave the commission "general supervision" of gas and electric utilities and power to regulate the price of gas and electricity and related operations and services. Commissioners or staff members could "examine all persons, corporations and municipalities under its supervision," "keep informed as to the methods employed by them," and "enter in or upon the property" of the companies at any time to inspect their facilities. The commission could "prescribe methods of keeping accounts and books," "examine the books and affairs" of the companies, and require submission of annual reports. Commission approval would be required prior to the issuance of company stocks or bonds.[7]

New companies needed commission approval before going into business. That authority would enable the commission to either minimize or foster new competition, which dovetailed well with its regulatory power.

Local governments or groups of one hundred customers or more could bring complaints about the price or quality of gas or electricity or the adequacy of service. The commission would then hold a hearing where complainants and the company's representative would be heard, investigate with its own staff, and then fix a maximum price "within the limits prescribed by law."[8] (That phrase became a point of contention because the law did not actually prescribe any limits.) Commission orders went into effect right away or by a close deadline established by the commission.

The price would be in effect for three years and after that could be changed only through a complaint by a local government or a hundred-person customer group. The law made no provision for *companies* to appeal or ask the commission for a change during the three years. But companies, local governments, or aggrieved groups of customers could appeal commission decisions to the Appellate Division of the State Supreme Court.

The commission got to work, including handing down a series of decisions on rates for gas and electricity. Many of its decisions were compromises between what customers insisted on and what the companies demanded. The commission dithered with the politically charged New York City gas issue, so frustrating Senator Frederick Stevens, who had sponsored the commission legislation, that he introduced a bill in February 1906 to abolish the commission.

By then, though, most utilities had decided they really did not want that. Commission oversight seemed preferable to unpredictable rate setting by the legislature and agitation by Hearst and others for municipal ownership. At a hearing on Stevens's bill, a representative of Consolidated Gas endorsed continuing the commission, insisting that "rate fixing," so long as it did not involve excessive "governmental interference" with operations, was far preferable to municipal ownership. The commission, motivated by Stevens's abolition bill, ordered the gas rate in Manhattan cut to eighty cents per cubic foot later that month. Consolidated Gas complained, but not too much, because by early 1906 its critics were demanding something even more drastic: seventy-five-cent gas. Companies might grumble to the press when the commission cut their rates, but, overall, they conceded the commission was fair and evenhanded.[9]

Eventually, though, a constitutional test case emerged, not from the huge New York City utility but from a company in Saratoga Springs. Trustees of that village (it was not yet a city) complained to the commission that the rates set by its public utility, Saratoga Gas, Electric Light, Heat and Power Company, were too high. The commission investigated and agreed, ordering a reduction in the price of gas and electricity on June 29, 1907.

The company appealed the commission's decision to the New York State Supreme Court Appellate Division, Third Department, in Albany in July, asserting that the rates set by the commission were too low and, more important, that the commission's authority was invalid because the law was unconstitutional.

Ironically, the Gas and Electricity Commission's Saratoga decision turned out to be one of its last acts. Charles Evans Hughes had gone on to even greater achievement as counsel for a legislative investigation of insurance companies later in 1905. His skill in the investigations and fashioning reform legislation led to his being nominated by the Republicans for governor in 1906. His successful campaign stressed the need for knowledgeable experts to regulate companies in the public interest. Hughes's most important initiative when he took office in 1907 was to propose a Public Service Commission (henceforth PSC), which would supersede the Gas and Electricity Commission and also supervise railroads and rapid transit lines. The PSC law passed in May, and the new commission began work on July 1, 1907, superseding the Gas and Electricity Commission three days after its Saratoga order.

Administrative regulation seemed to have acquired momentum. But was such unprecedented regulation constitutional? The *Saratoga* case quickly acquired an outsized significance. If the Gas and Electricity Commission's authority was constitutional, then the new PSC would presumably enjoy the same legitimacy, and other administrative commissions might follow later. The first test of the constitutional viability of the administrative state in New York started its journey through the court system.

THE SUPREME COURT APPELLATE DIVISION ENDORSES THE LAW

The case was argued in the fall of 1907. Counsel for the state contended that the law was an appropriate delegation of power by the legislature. The commission had acted pursuant to law, so the rate it established was valid. Attorneys for the Saratoga company acknowledged that the legislature had the power to establish rates but insisted it could not delegate them to a regulatory commission. They also argued that the rate set by the commission was too low.[10]

Presiding justice Walter E. Smith wrote the majority opinion for the appellate division court on November 20.[11] The company had submitted a brief with detailed information on production and operating costs, stock prices, and shareholder profits—mostly the same data it had submitted to the Commission of Gas and Electricity. Smith judiciously declined to delve into that thicket of data or to rule on whether the rates set by the commission were appropriate. That was not the court's business, he explained. The commission had acted according to the law, and if the law was constitutional, then the commission's decision was presumed to be valid.

The only question for the court, according to Smith, was the constitutional one: "whether this [rate-setting] function is so purely legislative that it cannot in any degree be delegated to an administrative body as a commission named, as provided in this statute." Smith found plenty of judicial precedents to support his contention that it could be delegated. The US Supreme Court had upheld a Mississippi law authorizing a railroad commission there to set rates and had confirmed "the necessity of leaving the application of such a law to some administrative body."[12] The court approved a similar law in Minnesota, with the caveat that rate-setting decisions must be open to judicial review, as they were under New York's gas and electricity law. Smith cited other Supreme Court decisions approving similar rate-making authorities in other states.

The issue was new to New York's courts, the justice conceded, but the principle that rate-making authority could be delegated was "established in analogous cases." Smith cited four decisions in support of that view but did not discuss them. There were no federal or state court decisions forbidding such delegation, he said, "provided the determination of the Commissioners is directed by some standard which is presented in the statute."[13]

The legislature could not practically set a limit on what could be charged for gas and electricity by every company in every community in the state. That wasn't needed anyway, said the judge. The phrase in the law "within the limits prescribed by law" was sufficient guidance. "The standard which is to guide this Commission in the exercise of its administrative duties in fixing rates is a reasonable charge for the product of the public service corporation, one reasonable to the public and reasonable to the corporation. Such a standard is sufficiently defined within the authorities which have been referred to."[14] It was up to the commission to determine what was "reasonable." That dovetailed well with the administrative-state rationale: expert agencies would determine what was fair and in the public interest in particular circumstances.

The three-year duration for a commission decision was a shortcoming, Justice Smith noted, but not a substantial burden—a company could appeal to the courts or to the legislature in the interim.

The company had asserted but had not proven that the rates set by the commission would deprive it of a reasonable profit or deprive its stockholders of a reasonable return on their investment. Smith concluded with a broad principle: courts should begin with a presumption in favor of a governmental order and should not interfere unless there was a clear violation of constitutional safeguards or law. There were none here. The commission's decision should stand, and the law that gave it authority was constitutional.[15]

Justice John M. Kellogg wrote a long dissent endorsed by one other judge making the argument that the regulatory law was unconstitutional. The state can require that "the price [of gas] must be reasonable—that is, the common-law price." That was up to the legislature, though, not an appointed commission. "It is difficult to understand how the Legislature may delegate its functions and allow some other body to impose a new duty upon persons and property" in this state. A business owner's submission to the will of the legislature "does not allow the Legislature to impose upon him the judgment and discretion of an unknown commission."[16]

The appellate court had explored the constitutional issues thoroughly, but its 3–2 decision left room for reservation and appeal. Saratoga Gas and Electric appealed the decision to the court of appeals. The appellate division endorsed the appeal, recognizing the importance of the case. The court of appeals agreed to hear the case. The briefs submitted by the village and state supporting the commission and by the company opposing it illuminated the constitutional issues that came to define the debate over the administrative state. The case was about the Gas and Electricity Commission, but by the time the court considered the case that commission was defunct. It was apparent that something larger was at stake: the constitutionality of that commission's successor, the Public Service Commission, and potentially other administrative agencies that might be created in the future.

THE COMPANY'S APPEAL: DELEGATION OF RATE SETTING TO A COMMISSION IS UNCONSTITUTIONAL AND DANGEROUS

The company had hired a prominent Saratoga attorney, Edgar T. Brackett, to represent it before the commission, the appellate division, and now before the court of appeals. Brackett, a Republican, had served in the state senate from 1896 to 1906. He had abstained on the vote to authorize the Gas and Electricity Commission in 1905 out of concern that it gave the governor too much power by authorizing him to appoint the commissioners. Once the bill passed, Governor Frank Higgins had spurned Brackett's request to appoint a friend to the new commission. Brackett launched his own unsuccessful campaign for the 1906 Republican gubernatorial nomination. Regarding Brackett as something of a maverick, the Republican Party's leaders redrew the lines of his senate district that year and nominated a Schenectady politician in his place. Brackett, capable and widely respected as an attorney but disaffected from both his party and the novel regulatory commission concept, was a strong choice for a counsel to oppose the law.[17]

Brackett attacked from several angles:

The rate set by the commission was too low to allow a fair profit. But that was almost beside the point; the law itself was invalid. He cited court decisions that had struck down state regulatory statutes and argued that Justice Smith had underestimated or misinterpreted other decisions that supported such laws. There were really no decisions that authorized a legislature to give an administrative body power to fix rates in the absence of a specific provision in the state's constitution authorizing it to do so. The company could not appeal for a change for three years, an outrageous burden. The company could appeal to the courts, as Saratoga Gas and Electric was doing now, but that was burdensome, time-consuming, and expensive.[18]

Brackett dramatized the menace of the law. The people responsible for it were "iconoclasts, not constructionists." The law was intended to provide a means for "political control" of companies and to create jobs with high salaries for the governor to fill. The law gave the commission "the right to absolutely control the details of the business of a corporation." It was part of a pattern, "the passing craze of the hour," where politicians insisted that modern conditions demanded bold action and the right approach—amending the constitution—was ignored. It could open the door to worse abuses, even "an act saying that the Governor may issue such edicts as he sees fit (of course in constitutional phrase) and let it go at that." It was all part of "the mad race of the present toward centralization, the grasping after power, unspeakable silly things."[19]

The Saratoga Gas and Electric company also hired two other attorneys to prepare a separate brief on the law. John B. Stanchfield, a prominent Democratic leader and the party's candidate for governor in 1900, had debated Governor Hughes on the pending Public Service Commission law at a public meeting in Elmira earlier in 1907, arguing forcefully that commission regulation was unconstitutional. Attorney Charles B. Tuttle was in the early stages of a political career that would include US attorney and the Republican nomination for governor in 1930.

The Stanchfield/Tuttle brief cited and discussed dozens of court decisions to the effect that the legislature's power to delegate its authority was limited. It argued that Justice Smith had misinterpreted a number of the decisions he cited in favor of the commission. But the brief took up where Brackett left off and went much further, with larger arguments about the menace of government by commission. It was a manifesto aimed more at the new Public Service Commission, and at the emerging administrative-state notion generally, than at the now-defunct Gas and Electricity Commission:

- *The legislature can handle this work directly.* Despite the number of companies and the complexity of the issues, "the Legislature itself has ample power and ability" to carry out, through committees, all the work the commission is doing.[20]

- *The gas and electricity commission law transfers legislative authority to a nonelective body and to the court.* The brief argued that the law ceded power to the commission, which would act as a "vice legislature" with a power of "general supervision" over public service companies. The power of the appellate division to review makes it "a sort of higher or supervisory Commission. . . . The effect is to throw non-judicial duties on that Court," which is already burdened with genuine judicial responsibilities.[21]

- *The law gives the commission too much power.* The real object of the law is "to effect the control, management and restriction of the gas and electric business by a Commission wielding practically all the police powers of the State." The commission "carries the power of correction, suggestion and compulsion." It is "autocratic" with "full paternal power" constrained only by its own "policies, rules or standards."[22]

- *It does not establish any standards or limits on the rates the commission may impose.* The words "within the limits prescribed by law" do not provide concrete guidance. The common law is not much help; it does not limit the power bestowed on the commission in the law. Catch-all terms such as "just and reasonable" and "reasonable to the public and reasonable to the corporation," cited as standards by the law's proponents, are vague. "The so-called standard is really no standard at all." In reality, the law "left the whole matter of price up to the Commission."[23]

- *The gas and electricity law is a forerunner of worse things to come.* The theory of "Government by Commission" is being hailed "all over the land as the newly discovered panacea for all evils, real or imaginary" in any industry "affected with a public use." It is "an unprecedented experimentation in State socialism," taking property without compensation. If this law stands, the legislature "can create as many Commissions as there are industries to be affected," making "infinite mischief in the future."[24]

VILLAGE, ATTORNEY GENERAL, AND PUBLIC SERVICE COMMISSION: THIS LAW IS CONSTITUTIONAL

The Village of Saratoga Springs teamed up with the state attorney general and the new Public Service Commission to defend the constitutionality of the Gas and Electricity Commission.

Saratoga Village attorney Frank Gick's brief was mostly a reprise of the evidence the village had submitted to the commission documenting that the company's rates were too high. It cited a range of court precedents endorsing strong regulation power. Its most notable feature was a short statement of easily understood "Principles of Law," which sought to reduce his case to its essentials. The principles included were as follows:

- The presumption is that the commission's order is valid. The burden is on the company to prove it is not.

- Each case must be decided on its own merit. That is the commission's purpose and just what it has done very well here.

- The court should not interfere except in "a flagrant case of unreasonableness."

- Whether the prescribed rate will yield a profit to the company is "not conclusive" from the evidence the company submitted. Lots of factors go into the issue of profit, including the ability of management.[25]

State attorney general William S. Jackson, a Democrat elected in 1906, was not a fan of regulatory commissions. Earlier in 1907 he had floated his own proposal for an elected rather than an appointed Public Service Commission. His office's brief was a strong one, though, in part because he realized that winning in this high-visibility case would probably mean he wouldn't need to defend the constitutionality of the new PSC. As he noted in the document, "the special attention of this court is invited to the importance of this case as the precursor of attacks upon the validity of the Public Service Commission Law."[26]

The first question was whether the commission had proceeded according to the law; Jackson summarized its Saratoga investigation to show that it did. The appellate division's opinion was so persuasive that it was "almost unnecessary" to delve into the constitutional issues. The legislature created the commission because it could not decide the prices of gas and electricity in every locality in the state. The legislature passed laws enabling the creation of companies and could, therefore, regulate them. State courts had approved the concept. Jackson quoted the court of appeals decision *People v. Budd* (1899), which validated a state law regulating grain-elevator charges. Chief Judge Charles Andrews had written there that "constitutional legislation permits impositions and restrictions upon the use and enjoyment of property which may seriously impair the value of property and abridge freedom of action." The US Supreme Court had approved. Since then, the courts had approved other state regulatory laws such as a franchise tax on corporations passed in 1899. Courts had approved the concept of "action to be taken by public officials possessing no power to legislate."[27] The courts had approved the decisions of the Rapid Transit Commission and the State Board of Railroad Commissioners.

As a practical matter, utility rates need to be determined on a case-by-case basis. Neither the legislature nor the courts have set concrete standards for "the reasonableness of a rate." The rate had to be "just from the standpoint of the interests of the company and the consumer, and of their mutual rights and obligations." Jackson ventured a working definition of what constituted a "confiscatory" rate—one that would yield a return that is "clearly and palpably lower than the rate of return which invested capital ordinary earns from an investment of the same or a similar degree of security." The commission had worked diligently to avoid that, made no legal errors, and exercised its "sound judgment." The burden was on the company to prove that the rates the commission had set were unreasonable or confiscatory, and it had not done that.[28]

The new Public Service Commission Second District, which covered areas of the state except New York, Kings, Queens, and Richmond counties, submitted a brief from its counsel, William A. Sutherland. The PSC, as successor to the Gas and Electricity Commission, had an obligation to defend its actions in courts. But, more importantly, the PSC realized that the constitutionality of its own statute would be confirmed or undermined by the decision in the *Saratoga* case.

Commission regulation was a necessity of modern economic life, the PSC's counsel insisted. The appellate division's reasoning was unassailable. "The vast and constantly increasing business of the country renders rate making more and more complex," necessitating expert commissions. Twenty-four states had some form of public service commissions, and Congress had recently (1906) given rate-making authority to the Interstate Commerce Commission. Courts had held that rate making is an administrative act. Sutherland cited an array of court decisions from several states including California, Illinois, Florida, and Minnesota as well as the US Supreme Court. Chief among them was *Reagan v. Farmers' Loan and Trust Co.*, an 1894 Supreme Court decision that "affirmed the constitutionality of the statute creating the [Texas Railroad] commission and deputing to it the administrative office of ascertaining and declaring reasonable rates."[29]

Though Saratoga Gas and Electric's attorneys had also invoked judicial precedents, Sutherland's document pointed out that in some places their briefs were mistaken. In others, they cited court decisions limiting commission authority that were later superseded by decisions endorsing that authority.

Sutherland also refuted appellate justice Kellogg's dissent. "The absurdity of limiting the Legislature to sitting as a committee of the whole in constant review of the changing conditions which may give rise to needed changes in the rates" proved the need for a commission. Kellogg's only substantive objection was that the commission had the final word. Actually, as this very case proves, the courts can step in if the commission rules unfairly or if the constitutionality of the law is attacked.[30]

Rates set by the commission must be "fair and just and in conformity to the common law, whether ascertained and declared by a commission or by the legislature" or by the new PSC. If the rate fixed is "an invasion of the rights, either of the stockholders of the Public Service Corporation, or else of the general public, and constitutes a wrong upon one party or the other," the courts are open to redress that wrong.[31]

Two supplemental briefs prepared and submitted in response to the ones discussed above rounded out the judicial record. The Village of Saratoga Springs' brief reiterated that setting gas and electricity rates is a judgment matter for the skilled commission created by the legislature specifically for that purpose.[32]

The final document, angry and alarmist in tone, came from the company's counsel Edgar Brackett, now assisted by three new attorneys, including a former assistant US attorney general and a counsel for Consolidated Gas in New York City. Its secondary target was undoubtedly the new Public Service Commission rather than the Commission of Gas and Electricity, but it went after that defunct commission as if it were still in existence. The Gas and Electricity Commission law makes the commission "a kind of third House" of the legislature because "to make a rate is to make a law" rather than carrying one out. The caveat that the rate has to be "within the limits prescribed by law" was too vague to act as a constraint. No court had ever ruled that such a delegation was constitutional. The brief again attacked Appellate Division Presiding Justice Smith, arguing that he had misinterpreted the decisions he cited or that they were not germane to the case at hand.[33]

The brief practically boiled over with dire warnings. "There is a growing tendency on the part of Legislatures in this country to meddle with business matters." Legislatures are constantly shifting power to "irresponsible commissions." It is part of a pattern to bow to "the popular caprice of the moment" and "convert representative government into a socialistic bureaucratic government." Other states were watching to see if New York would stand as a bulwark against this "tidal wave of socialism."[34]

COURT OF APPEALS:
THE LEGISLATURE'S DELEGATION OF AUTHORITY IS CONSTITUTIONAL

Chief Judge Edgar M. Cullen wrote the opinion for a unanimous court of appeals on February 18, 1908. The court had a mixed record regarding regulatory statutes, approving some and striking down others. Cullen, a Democrat, had served as an associate judge on the court and had been appointed chief judge by Governor Benjamin Odell after the incumbent,

Alton B. Parker, resigned to run for president of the United States in 1904. Highly respected, he was nominated by both parties to run for the chief judge's position that year. Cullen was a judicial moderate. He emphasized judicial precedent. He was fond of exhorting his colleagues on the court to go "back to the books!" to seek guidance from previous court decisions. Cullen was wary of government programs that infringed on personal liberty. But he was also supportive of reasonable regulatory legislation. In 1905, he issued a dissent in the case of *Wright v. Hart*, where a majority of the court had struck down a law regulating the bulk sale of goods.[35]

Cullen's opinion verified the constitutionality of the gas and electricity commission law, but, in a twist at the end, it declared the law invalid because of one relatively minor feature.

The central question, Cullen began, was, Can the power to fix rates charged by a public utility be delegated by the legislature to a commission it creates? Cullen argued that it certainly could. The US Constitution was quite explicit in reserving legislative authority to Congress, but it did not explicitly forbid delegation. The state constitution was even more flexible. It did not actually mandate that the legislative branch and the executive branch had to be strictly separate in all matters. In fact, "there never has been in this state that sharp line of demarcation between the functions of the three branches of government which obtains in some other jurisdictions." For instance, the legislature has delegated the power to grant divorces to the courts. It authorized the courts to require construction of public highways that connected two or more jurisdictions. An early statute gave the New York Court of Common Pleas the power to grant licenses for ferries. It authorized the Board of Regents to incorporate colleges and academies. It granted the Board of Railroad Commissioners the power to determine whether new rail lines should be constructed. All of these powers had been confirmed by court opinions.[36]

Legislative bodies in towns, villages, and cities often granted their administrative officers the power to carry out laws—for instance, licensing plumbers and boards of health. The power to do so has been upheld in the courts. Cullen stated, "I cannot see why, on principle, powers that can be delegated to the administrative officers of a municipality for exercise within the municipality are not equally subject of delegation to state administrative officers throughout the state."[37]

Cullen then cited federal precedents. Congress gave the secretary of war the power to approve construction of bridges across major rivers. The secretary of the treasury was given power to prohibit the importation of low-quality tea. Congress had recently (1906) given the ICC power to set railroad rates. The courts went along with each delegation of power except the ICC's new authority, still to be tested in court but likely to be approved.[38]

Having made the general case for delegation, the judge turned to the practical issue at hand. "It is plain that no uniform rate of charges could be established that would be just and reasonable" for all situations. That meant the need for "an investigation into the particular facts in each case" by experts, work beyond the capacity of the legislature. The legislature has decreed that there shall be maximum rates for gas and electricity but delegated responsibility for determining them to the commission. "What is entrusted to the commission is the duty of investigating the facts, and, after a public hearing, ascertaining and determining what is a reasonable maximum rate." The common-law prescription that the rate must be "reasonable" was more than sufficient. Indeed, "a lawmaker might exhaust reflection and ingenuity in the attempt to state all the elements which affect the reasonableness of a rate" only to find that he had overlooked or ignored something. An objective administrative commission would determine what was fair and reasonable in each case.[39]

Cullen devoted less than a page to decisions by courts in other states cited by Brackett and his colleagues. Those decisions were not in accord with New York law or court decisions in our state, he said dismissively. No state court had stated definitely that the power to fix rates could not be conferred on a commission. The chief judge had built a strong case for the constitutional validity of commission regulation.

But the opinion ended with a surprising conclusion. There was a provision that "necessarily renders it invalid": the requirement that the rate fixed by the commission would continue for three years, and even longer unless a new complaint was filed by the municipality or one hundred or more customers. Of course, the company could appeal to the legislature or the courts in the meantime, but that would burden the company. It would also shift the burden of rate determination from where it belonged, with the commission, to the legislature or the courts, neither of which had the expertise to deal with it. Companies should have equal rights with consumers to appeal for a revision of the rates. This presumed "inadvertence" in the law caused the court of appeals to reverse the appellate division's decision and vacate the order of the commission it had endorsed.[40]

That flaw could easily be corrected by the legislature, Cullen added. The chief judge must have known that was a moot point. The PSC law, passed in 1907, which authorized the Public Service Commission to supersede the Gas and Electricity Commission, included just the sort of provision the judge wanted, an ability for companies to ask for the commission to revisit and review the decisions it had made.

A FOOTHOLD FOR THE ADMINISTRATIVE STATE

Cullen's opinion had emphatically endorsed the legislature's power under the Constitution to delegate rate-setting authority to a commission. A unanimous vote of the court of appeals and an opinion written by its chief judge gave the decision visibility and weight. As Attorney General William Jackson noted, "the decision in this case will undoubtedly constitute a settlement of the law on this point."[41] That prediction was accurate. The administrative state had debuted in New York and survived its first court challenge. Other decisions aligned with it. The constitutionality of the Public Service Commission law would not be seriously challenged.

Cullen's decision offered judicial sanction for Governor Hughes's new Public Service Commission, discussed in chapter 8. Hughes had in fact foreseen the continuing role that the courts could play in erecting judicial guardrails to keep the regulators on track. But the original PSC legislation had not included any provision for judicial review. In a speech in Elmira on May 3, 1907, defending his Public Service Commission legislative proposal against critic John Stanchfield, the governor had remarked that "we are under a Constitution, but the Constitution is what the judges say it is, and the judiciary is the safeguard of our liberty and of our property under the Constitution." Critics of judicial activism then and later cited the phrase "the Constitution is what the judges say it is" as evidence that judicial review could be erratic and arbitrary. Hughes later tried to walk back the statement. He was not condoning "judicial caprice." He meant to emphasize "the essential function of the courts under our system in interpreting and applying judicial safeguards" and, therefore, not throwing on them "the burden of dealing with purely administrative questions" by giving them responsibility to analyze and judge the soundness of complicated commission decisions.[42] Hughes compromised, and the final version of the PSC bill had a provision that the commission could suspend its orders while they were under appeal to the courts.

Cullen's broad justification for delegation of legislative power to regulatory commissions was echoed in New York and other state courts and at the federal level in the following years.[43] Since that time, courts have mostly confirmed and justified the power of Congress and legislatures to delegate broad responsibilities to administrative agencies, provided there are "intelligible principles" for them to follow, in the words of a 1928 Supreme Court decision.[44] Occasionally, the courts stepped in, asserting that the delegation had been too open-ended. Hughes himself, when he was chief justice of the Supreme Court in 1935, wrote an opinion striking down a New Deal law giving the president authority to promulgate "codes of fair competition" in the poultry industry under the National Industrial Recovery Act. That involves "the coercive exercise of lawmaking power," said Hughes. "The Congress is not permitted to abdicate or to transfer to others the essential legislative functions with which it is . . . vested." Courts must enforce "the limitations of the authority to delegate." Hughes later relented, and his views on regulatory authority became more liberal, closer to what he had advocated as governor of New York.[45]

The debate continued. As legal scholar Roscoe Pound noted in 1944, "what such agencies do is law because they do it." There may be "a tendency of administrative agencies to act on policies of their own devising rather than on those prescribed in the statutes" and to issue binding rules and regulations without adequate investigation or assessment of impact. There was bound to be "a certain friction with the courts," which were obligated to push back in cases of "administrative absolutism" by agencies that lacked "an ethos as to their quasi-judicial function."[46] Recent US Supreme Court decisions indicate a renewed interest in the issue of delegation.[47]

Advocates continue to support the concept of broad legislative delegation of regulatory authority to executive agencies, boards, and commissions. Critics of government regulation may criticize it as legislative abdication of oversight responsibilities, executive overreach, and unwarranted meddling in social and commercial affairs. The US Supreme Court has again explored the issue in recent cases.

The major issues—how far legislatures should go in authorizing administrative boards to regulate and make binding rules, how extensive and binding those regulations should be, and when the courts should step in and overrule those agencies—have been debated for more than a century. They all have roots in New York's 1905 gas and electricity commission law and the 1908 court of appeals decision in the *Saratoga* case.

Chapter 8

THE ADMINISTRATIVE STATE IN ACTION

Figure 8.1. Charles Evans Hughes, New York governor from 1907 to 1910, was the architect of the State Commission of Gas and Electricity and the Public Service Commissions, forerunners of the administrative state. *Source:* Oscar Marshall/ Moffett Studios, 1908. Library of Congress Prints & Photographs Collection.

The Public Service Commissions, created in 1907, constituted a robust example of the administrative state, pioneered by the New York State Commission of Gas and Electricity, covered in chapter 7. There were two public service commissions until 1921—the First District, covering New York, Kings, Queens, and Richmond Counties, and the Second District, covering the rest of the state. The commissions had broad powers that included regulation of railroads, the state's most important industry. That was the priority work of the Second District commission and the main topic of this chapter.

TAKING STATE REGULATION TO A HIGHER LEVEL

The state Commission of Gas and Electricity, established in 1905, discussed in chapter 7, was the pioneering example of what would sometimes be called the administrative state later in the twentieth century. Its successor, the Public Service Commissions, established in 1907, had an even more powerful blend of legislative, administrative, and judicial authority and a much broader sweep, including railroads and rapid transit lines. The PSC First District covered New York, Kings, Queens, and Richmond Counties; its main focus in the early years would be New York City rapid transit issues. The PSC Second District covered the rest of the state. Its major focus in its first decade or so would be railroad regulation. This chapter concentrates on the Second District commission and its work vis-à-vis railroads, the state's largest industrial entities. That commission succeeded in building public support, strengthening responsive railroad management, improving service to the public, sidestepping political opposition, and for the most part prevailing in the courts.

Charles Evans Hughes was the masterful architect of the administrative state in New York's Progressive Era. Hughes served as counsel to a legislative committee that recommended the Commission of Gas and Electricity, enacted by the legislature in 1905. He was counsel to another committee that crafted legislation to strengthen state insurance regulation the same year. Those stellar achievements garnered him the Republican nomination for governor in 1906. His campaign stressed the need for executive administration by knowledgeable experts to deal with the complexities of modern government. He promised new public service commissions with responsibility to regulate gas and electric companies but also the state's railroads and rapid transit in New York City. Hughes's moderate, progressive appeal contrasted with the strident campaign of his Democratic opponent, congressman and publisher William Randolph Hearst, who attacked railroads and other businesses and called for municipal ownership of public utilities. Hughes won handily, and the Republicans also kept their majority in the legislature.[1]

Hughes introduced his proposal for a public service commissions' law in his first address to the legislature in January 1907.[2] Hughes recalled in his autobiography that the sweeping proposal was "a distinct shock to the corporate interests concerned." He summarized the commissions' powers:

> To act upon its own initiative as well as upon complaint; to pass upon the issue of stocks and bonds; to examine property, books, and accounts; to require detailed support in prescribed forms; to prescribe reasonable rates; to require adequate and impartial service; to provide for the safety of employees and for the protection of the public; and generally to direct whatever may be necessary or proper to safeguard the public interests and to secure the fulfillment of the public obligations of the corporations under its supervision.[3]

The unprecedented proposal quite predictably engendered opposition. Democrats expressed alarm that "government by commission" would interfere with business management. The railroads lobbied against the bill, though with an intent of diluting its powers rather than defeating it entirely, which they realized would be impossible. Railroad leaders had mixed feelings. They dreaded a hostile and powerful state commission that might second-guess management. On the other hand, they were critical of the regulatory confusion that prevailed in New York in the opening years of the twentieth century.[4]

The railroads were tired of having to lobby in the legislature. Every year, bills were introduced to require an increase of train-crew size ("full crew" legislation); fine the railroads when they failed to provide freight cars requested in advance by shippers in a timely fashion (called "reciprocal demurrage" by shippers who claimed it was the reciprocal of the fines the railroads charged for excessive delays in loading and unloading cars), fine the roads for each day that they failed to move loaded cars at least fifty miles (a way of forcing the roads to curtail delays in moving freight, sponsors claimed), and address passenger rate inequities. Rail lobbyists killed the bills, but public sentiment for more legislative action seemed to be growing. Perhaps a new public service commission could deal equitably with these issues.

The State Board of Railroad Commissioners, established in 1882 after years of shipper agitation over unfair rates, had limited power and could enforce rulings only by resorting to the attorney general, which it rarely did. The railroads were required to pay its expenses. They regarded it mostly as a nuisance. But it had authority to approve or deny applications for new railroads. In the early years of the century, it approved several new interurban electric railroads, the product of new electricity technology. Early in 1907, a new company, the Buffalo, Rochester, and Eastern, announced plans to build a major new cross-state railroad from Troy to Buffalo to compete with the overloaded New York Central for freight shipments. The state railroad commission seemed likely to approve; a new public service commission might not.

Shippers often brought lawsuits to force improved railroad service and rate reductions. Courts' views were unpredictable. It wasn't clear from a legal standpoint just what constituted adequate service and fair, equitable rates. Courts lacked investigatory staff and were often uncomfortable having to make decisions based on contradictory evidence presented by the roads and users. Decisions in favor of shippers angered the railroads, and those in favor of railroads alienated shippers. A new commission could take these contentious issues into a new venue.

Hughes worked with progressive Republicans in the legislature to build support and hold the line on his proposal, refusing to compromise or weaken the bill. Shippers and travelers, angry over railroad rate inequities and inadequate service, concluded that a new commission would force improvement. An evenhanded administrative commission would be fairer and more predictable than the current system, the railroads hoped, a view the governor himself promoted. Hughes gave about forty public speeches for the bill in the spring of 1907. Republican president Theodore Roosevelt, himself a former New York governor, lobbied legislators from his party to support it, asserting it would be good for their party. Support overbalanced criticism.

Critics demanded a provision for judicial review to protect companies from arbitrary commission rulings. Hughes was reluctant. Decisions of the gas and electricity commission were being challenged in court. The *Saratoga* court case, discussed in chapter 7, was still making its way through the court system, its outcome uncertain. The courts lacked expertise to decide on complicated matters of service and rates, said the governor. He did not want "to convert the court into an administrative board" or "cast upon them such burdens of administration" as would be required if they had to review commission decisions. He countered that the commissions would regulate, not dictate to, the companies. "You must have administration by administrative officers," he told one group. If the commissions were to exercise "arbitrary power" or deprive companies or individuals of property without "due process of law," the courts could intervene.[5]

The governor did not explain just how that would work. He refused to include a specific provision for judicial review in the bill. But, in the end, he allowed a placeholder of sorts—a provision that the commission could suspend fines for violation of its orders when litigation to challenge those orders was pending. That seemed to presuppose that litigation would be permitted. Governor Hughes, progressive Republicans, and reform-minded newspapers had done a remarkable job of selling the bold commission proposal. It passed the assembly unanimously in May, with even some Democrats reluctantly supporting it, and overwhelmingly in the senate, with only six Democrats voting no. The new law filled forty-nine closely printed pages, spelling out the PSC's sweeping authority.[6]

It was the most powerful regulatory board in the nation, surpassing New York's past entities (including Hughes's 1905 handiwork, the Commission of Gas and Electricity), other states (Wisconsin had a powerful commission, but it regulated railroads only), and the federal government (the PSC in some ways had more extensive powers than the Interstate Commerce Commission). Implementation was almost immediate—the new law took effect July 1, 1907.[7]

BENIGN REGULATORS

The new commissions got down to work right away. The Second District commission's work regarding railroads was its main focus. Railroad regulation and the courts' review of it are the most revealing about the commission's work and the courts' perspectives on administrative regulation. In the rest of this chapter, *PSC* or *the commission* refers to the Second District commission unless otherwise indicated.

The law gave the governor authority to make appointments to the commission (with senate approval, which would turn out to be pro forma in most cases). Hughes appointed as chairman Frank W. Stevens,

Jamestown counsel for the New York Central Railroad's Lake Shore and Michigan Southern line. Stevens was a highly regarded attorney. But the appointment of a lawyer who was employed by the state's most powerful railroad to head the state's railroad regulatory agency signaled the governor's expectation that the commission would not be hostile or coercive toward public utilities. In a speech soon after the commission began its work, Stevens acknowledged that railroad service fell short of public expectations but said that was the result of business exceeding the roads' capacity. The PSC would "assist the railroads . . . in making things better" and would do nothing to "coerce" or "cripple or to harm" them since they were "absolutely indispensable to the welfare of the public." "Corporations have their legal rights," and the commission would respect them.[8]

Hughes appointed wealthy Auburn industrialist Thomas M. Osborne, who had led a Democrats-for-Hughes initiative in the 1906 election, to the commission. Osborne insisted the PSC would actually help the railroads and other utilities address their critics by putting the companies and the public on "an open and honest footing" where differences could be resolved.[9] A third gubernatorial appointee, Martin S. Decker of New Paltz, had served as deputy commissioner on the ICC. Decker wrote an article for a railroad journal soon after his appointment predicting that the PSC would be a "fair play" commission that would pursue "practical regulation," shy away from "disturbance of railway values," and in fact ensure "the conservation of railway revenues."[10]

The other two original commissioners appointed by Hughes had little influence over policy. Stevens, Osborne, and Decker shaped the new administrative state agency to assert and protect the public interest, but in a manner that usually benefited the railroads and other utilities being regulated. Stevens wrote reassuringly in the commission's first report, at the end of 1907, that the commission would exercise "judgment and discretion." Its decisions would "be determined by consideration of facts and figures and not by fancy or sentiment." It would "enhance the value of the services of the railroads to the public" and also aid "the railroads themselves in rendering them business investments capable of affording fair and satisfactory returns" to their stockholders.[11]

Railroad companies were relieved and reassured by Stevens's judicious, evenhanded approach. They gradually, sometimes grudgingly, adopted a stance of cooperation with the commission in improving service to the public and ironing out rate inequities.[12] If the railroads were content, so also were the Progressive reformers. They began pointing to the PSC as an excellent model for government regulation in the public interest. Progressives asserted that utilities had changed their attitudes, improved their services, and adjusted their passenger and freight rates just because the commission was overseeing them and urging, nudging, and occasionally ordering better service.[13]

The PSC developed mostly lenient policies toward railroads. The railroads gradually improved services at the commission's urging and sometimes under its orders. Freight moved faster and rate inequities diminished. Commuters and long-distance rail travelers noted that railroads' on-schedule operations increased. The PSC used several strategies:

- It carried out lengthy investigations and held public hearings on complaints to allow tempers to cool, reveal previously unrecognized misunderstandings, and bring out bases for compromise solutions.

- It settled disputes informally, amicably, and on a compromise basis whenever possible to avoid having to issue formal orders.

- It issued extensive reports on railroad finances, new equipment, passenger train delays, rate of movement of loaded freight cars, and so on, emphasizing improvement over time. The commission intervened in isolated instances of freight car shortages and sluggish freight movement with helpful suggestions and, occasionally, orders for improvement. Problems melted away as the railroads increased their equipment and freight-handling facilities and built parallel trackage.

- The commission pushed, and sometimes ordered, railroads to adjust the most glaring passenger rate inequities. In some cases, it persuaded the roads to increase on-time operations by simply changing their published schedules to coincide with the realities of their operations.

- It exercised its authority to approve all railroad stock and bond issues by requiring documentation and justification but then approving in almost all cases. The railroads welcomed the PSC's stamp of approval as evidence against potential charges of "stock watering." Financial journals claimed that the commission's approval actually made the securities more attractive to investors.

- The law included a provision requiring PSC approval for construction and operation of new utilities. The commission used its veto to block new companies that would have competed with existing lines. For instance, it twice (1908 and 1909) rejected an application from a new company, the Buffalo, Rochester, and Eastern Railroad, to build a new line parallel to and competing with the New York Central's main line from Troy to Buffalo. Chairman Stevens wrote that the Central was improving its freight-handling capacity at Buffalo (long a bottleneck), adding more trackage, and moving freight faster. Rather than a new line, Stevens explained, New York's policy was to have the PSC keep effecting better service.[14]

A SMOOTH PATH IN COURT

Given the reciprocal relationship between the PSC and the railroads, the commission had a relatively easy time in court.[15]

The court of appeals' 1908 decision discussed in chapter 7, *Village of Saratoga Springs v. Saratoga Gas, etc., Co.*, validating legislative delegation of regulatory power to the Gas and Electricity Commission, discouraged substantial constitutional challenge to the PSC.

The PSC law had been meticulously drafted by Governor Hughes, himself a constitutional expert (he would join the US Supreme Court three years later, in 1910), and his colleagues to fend off constitutional challenges. One of those behind-the-scenes architects, William M. Ivins, New York City attorney and the Republican party's 1905 candidate for mayor of New York City, joined a colleague in publishing a book in 1908 that laid out the constitutional basis for each provision of the law. The section on "scope of regulatory power" cited multiple court decisions from New York, other states, and the US Supreme Court that buttressed state police power.[16] That book gave the commission another shield against constitutional assault in courts. Ivins became something of a champion for the law, filing an amicus brief that led to the state supreme court's dismissal of one complaint and occasionally serving as special counsel to the PSC, First District.

Frank Stevens and his colleagues carefully wrote orders to avoid making them vulnerable on constitutional grounds. Railroads and other companies, finding the commission's oversight mostly salutary, did not seriously challenge its constitutional right to exist.

When the courts intervened, they generally supported and justified PSC decisions.

COURTS HAVE POWER TO REVIEW COMMISSION ORDERS

Public utilities may have accommodated themselves to commission regulation, but they also asserted the right to challenge it in court. The PSC law did not specifically authorize judicial review of commission decisions, but, as noted above, it provided a placeholder of sorts by declaring that fines for violation of PSC orders could be suspended where decisions were appealed to the courts. The courts dealt themselves into regulatory policy in 1908 by asserting a right to review PSC decisions where appropriate.

In that case, the PSC First District had ordered two adjoining New York City street railroads, Metropolitan Street Railway and North and East Railroad Company, to establish a through route and joint fare for passengers. The order provided criteria for how the joint fare should be apportioned between the two lines. The rail lines objected—this was just the sort of meddling that critics of the administrative state had feared. The companies convinced the state supreme court to issue a writ of certiorari—a technical legal order directing a court to deliver a ruling to a higher court for review. The commission demurred, arguing that it was not a court and its orders were not subject to certiorari review. It asked the First Department of the New York Supreme Court Appellate Division to vacate the order.

The appellate court sided with the lower court. Presiding justice Edward Patterson acknowledged that "there is no specific method . . . by which the action of that Commission can be brought within the judicial cognizance of the courts of the State." Patterson also conceded that the commission's authority was legislative in character and it was "in a sense acting legislatively." But here it was "substantially acting as a court" because "its inquiry and action in the premises was judicial in its nature," particularly in determining the "proportionate share of a joint rate to be allowed to each operating company." Moreover, judicial review apparently was "within the contemplation of the Legislature" when it inserted the provision for suspending fines during court review.[17] The certiorari order would stand.

The unhappy PSC appealed to the court of appeals, citing a US Supreme Court decision handed down a month after the appellate division's ruling. The Supreme Court had ruled that a Virginia commission's role in fixing railroad rates was legislative rather than judicial in nature.

Chief Judge Edgar M. Cullen, writing for a unanimous court of appeals, affirmed the appellate court's decision. The US Supreme Court's decision was for Virginia's situation only, he said: "It is not controlling upon us," and in fact "it is opposed to the uniform current of judicial authority in this state." Cullen conveniently cited his own opinion in the *Saratoga Gas* case a year earlier. That confirmed that the legislature could bestow rate-making authority on a commission but that "the very question of what rates are reasonable could be given a judicial or *quasi* judicial aspect."[18] That seemed like a stretch for the *Saratoga* opinion, but Chief Judge Cullen had written it, so his interpretation went unchallenged.

The court of appeals decision secured a foothold for the courts in the administrative state's regulatory hierarchy. Public utilities would thereafter often ask the courts to review PSC decisions.

COURTS SHUNT DECISIONS TO THE COMMISSION

The courts might review some PSC decisions. But they used the PSC to avoid being drawn directly into complicated railroad-service and rate-regulatory issues. In a tangled 1909 lawsuit by competing companies wanting to build a switching railroad in Buffalo, the supreme court appellate division declined to enter the thicket of conflicting claims. Both sides should appeal to the PSC, "the body which is especially delegated with authority" to deal with railroad questions. "It has the opportunity of frequent inspection of conditions prevailing and is especially equipped for the solution" of such issues.[19]

When a Jamaica shipper sued the Long Island Railroad for removing a switch and siding that he had used to ship goods, the appellate division invalidated a lower-court injunction against the railroad and ordered a new trial. But the judge suggested there was a better way of settling the dispute—an appeal to the PSC. The commission "is enabled by its superior facilities to investigate and to determine whether the plaintiffs should have a siding."[20]

The courts showed reluctance in other decisions. A shipper sued the Lehigh Railroad to compel it to furnish bulkheads in its freight cars for the shipment of grain and other bulk products. The court of appeals sided with the shipper but noted that "the power of fixing rates and making regulations concerning intrastate traffic is clearly within the jurisdiction of our state public service commission." The courts could decide such issues but only "until the commission had exercised its power over the subject."[21]

COURTS DEFER TO THE COMMISSION

The courts usually proved reluctant to overrule commission decisions. Both of the commissions were well administered, their staffs professional, their investigations thorough, and their opinions well documented, courts said. "The public service commissions were created by the legislature to perform very important functions in the community, namely, to regulate the great public service corporations of the state in the conduct of their business and compel those corporations adequately to discharge their duties and not to exact therefor excessive charges," said a unanimous 1916 court of appeals decision. "The court has no power to substitute its own judgment of what is reasonable in place of the determination of the public service commission." The court's only responsibility is "to keep them within the law and protect the constitutional rights of the corporations over which they were given control."[22]

In one of the few major cases where it overruled the commission, the court of appeals came close to apologizing, noting that "the Public Service Commissions Law is an advanced step in legislation of great importance to the community."[23]

In another decision, affirming the commission's authority over issuance of stock, the court said that the PSC law "was enacted in response to a pronounced and insistent public opinion and was a radical and important modification of the relations and policy of the people toward the corporations which are its subjects. Its paramount purpose was to protect and enforce the rights of the public. . . . It provided for a regulation and control which were intended to prevent, on the one hand, the evils of the unrestricted right of competition and, on the other hand, the abuses of monopoly." Restricting the commission's power over stock issues would constitute "a bait and a trap for ensnaring the investing public."[24]

COURTS SUPPORT THE COMMISSION

Court decisions endorsing commission orders often included wording that highlighted the commissions' roles. Long Island commuters asked the Long Island Railroad to establish a new passenger station between its Cedar Mountain and Jamaica stations. It would be 0.8 miles from the first and 0.7 from the second. The railroad refused, saying the other two stations were sufficient and a new station stop would disrupt its express freight service. The PSC ordered the station built anyway. The company appealed and prevailed on the state supreme court to issue a certiorari writ. The court reviewed the decision but backed the commission. "The establishment of stations, requiring adequate facilities for the traveling public, is peculiarly within the power of the Public Service Commission," and there was no evidence that the order was "unreasonable or unjust." The harried Long Island commuters got their new station.[25]

The New York Central Railroad established an "equipment trust" to issue certificates to finance the purchase of equipment in 1909. It was a clever legal ruse—four of the Central's vice presidents were designated proprietors of the trust. The railroad asserted that the trust was separate from the company and the issuance of certificates therefore did not need PSC approval. The appellate division saw that as a sham. "To hold that by this device the railroad companies might escape the requirement of the approval of such securities by the Public Service Commissions would be to annul the force of the statute," declared the court. "The defendant cannot accomplish by indirection through a fiscal agent what it has been forbidden by statute to do directly."[26]

The courts were usually solidly behind the commission on the all-important issue of approving freight rates. In a significant test case, a New York Central freight agent had allowed a discount rate for a milk processor shipping milk from Carmel to Melrose Junction. The court held that was illegal. Special rates and discounts were not allowed. A railroad could transport goods only at the rates legally established and on file with the commission.[27]

The courts sometimes struck down PSC rulings that interfered with utilities' city charter requirements or ordinances passed *before* the law took effect. But they usually sided with the commission to prevail over ordinances passed *after* the law went into effect. In a Troy case, the commission ordered the United Traction Company to run its trolley cars on Oakwood Avenue on a twenty-minute schedule. The city council later passed a resolution requiring operation on a ten-minute schedule. Not so fast, said the company, appealing to the courts to enforce the PSC's slower schedule. The courts obliged. The PSC was established "for the purpose of promoting uniformity and consistency in authoritative directions to be given to public service corporations . . . and to direct and supervise their relations to and dealings with the public as their patrons." To permit this ordinance to stand "would permit any municipality to disregard and set at naught the orders of the public service commission" in cases like this and "would not only cause confusion of authority but would make of no effect some of the work of the commission."[28]

In another case, the PSC First District denied a bankrupt railroad permission to issue bonds to help it emerge from bankruptcy. The company appealed. The court cited "the spirit of the Public Service Commissions Law against the issue of 'watered' stock or bonds." The courts had affirmed the commissions' responsibility to protect the investing public. When stock was issued after PSC approval, the public could have confidence in the adequacy of the corporate assets and resources behind it. That meant that the commission had "a fuller and further duty" than just looking at the company's proposal. It had "the power or duty of inquiry" into the actual operational capacity and plans for the company.[29] If the commission concluded the proposed stock issue was not based on the company's value and its potential earning capacity, it had the right to disallow the proposal.

COURTS LIMIT THE COMMISSION

The courts sometimes drew the line and overturned commission decisions that intruded too much into company management.

In a 1909 decision, the PSC Second District turned down an application from the Delaware and Hudson Railroad to issue bonds to pay indebtedness on a small railroad and a coal mine it had purchased. The D&H appealed, saying that the decision intruded into managers' prerogatives. The appellate division sided with the railroad. The commission appealed and lost at the court of appeals. "We understand that the paramount purpose of the enactment of the Public Service Commissions Law was the protection and enforcement of the rights of the public," said the court, identifying the commissions as "the guardians of the public." But "we do not think the legislation alluded to was designed to make the commissions the financial managers of the corporation or that it empowered them to substitute their judgment for that of the board of directors or stockholders of the corporation as to the wisdom of a transaction." The commission could scrutinize whether the stocks were to be legally issued "for the discharge of the actual and not the fictitious debts of the company." But "beyond this it appears to us that the power of the commissioners does not extend."[30]

In another case involving the Delaware and Hudson, the commission approved a bond issue by the railroad to purchase an electric company.

But Chairman Stevens imposed a condition: the portion of the issue said to be in support of construction of a new plant should be switched to the railroad's regular budget since it was actually replacement of an old, obsolete plant and not really something new. The railroad appealed; how it interpreted the proposed construction was a matter for its own management, not the commission. The appellate division supported the commission, but there was a strong dissent from one judge to the effect that the commission had overstepped its authority. The court of appeals sided with the dissenter and the D&H, saying "the condition imposed by the commission . . . was wholly unauthorized."[31]

In 1919, the court of appeals disallowed the commission's informal "reparations" policy under which it had sometimes negotiated refunds from railroads to shippers for freight rates that the commission had ordered reduced. The New York Central had usually complied in the past. But in 1916 it dug in, refusing to pay a shipper for what the commission had determined to be an unfair fee it had been charging shippers for track space occupied by their freight cars beyond a certain fixed or "free" time. The case made it to the court of appeals late in 1918 and was decided in February of the next year. The court acknowledged that the refunds were usually voluntary but also noted that the commission sometimes directed them through a "binding adjudication." The policy had continued for years. But "there is not any language" in the law "which suggests, and much less justifies" this authority: "we cannot discern in the statute such legislative intent."[32] The practice was discontinued.

THE COMMISSION USES THE COURTS AS A BUFFER

Occasionally, the commission apparently made a decision against a company in the expectation—probably hope—that the court would reverse its order and thereby divert public criticism from the commission to the court.

Westchester County residents battled with the New York Central and the New York, New Haven and Hartford railroads over commuter rates for several years in the early twentieth century. The press took up the cause, fanning the flames of public anger with the railroads. The commission held hearings, urged dialogue and compromise, and generally delayed in the hope that the railroad and its riders would work things out and the controversy would abate. When that did not work, and the rail lines increased rates again, Chairman Stevens issued a decision in 1913 ordering the rates lowered. But it was not a typical airtight Stevens decision—only seven pages long and based on the assertion that the railroads had not proven the increases were justified. That ran counter to the commission's usual approach, where most of the burden was on the complainants rather than the utilities and the commission decided whether the rates were unreasonable or not.

The New York Central hurried to test the PSC's decision in court. The court of appeals invalidated the commission's order because "the public service commission was not justified by the facts in casting upon respondent [the railroads] the burden which it did." Judge Frank Hiscock, writing for the majority, added, "I do not attach any importance to the idea . . . that the burden should be cast upon the railroad of explaining and justifying its increase of rates."[33] Judge Benjamin Cardozo dissented, but without a written opinion. The court also invalidated the PSC's order reducing the New Haven's rates.

The commuters were disappointed and frustrated. They suspected that the shrewd Stevens might have written a deliberately weak opinion with the expectation the court would overturn it but the commission could maintain its reputation as champion of commuters. Apprehensive of their chances in the courts, they had prevailed on Westchester legislators to introduce a bill in the spring of 1915 to roll back the rate increases. The legislature passed it, but Governor Martin Glynn vetoed it because the issue was still in the courts. After the court had spoken, legislators declined to revisit the issue on the argument that the courts had settled it. The commuters had won before the commission but lost before the courts, and the governor and had been abandoned by the legislature. The commuter rates continued at the level the railroads had established.[34]

THE ADMINISTRATIVE STATE ENDURES

The PSC was mostly sustained by the courts. Beyond that, it garnered public interest and support as railroad passenger and freight service improved, electricity and gas companies were held to reasonable standards of rates and service, and, in New York City, the realm of the First District commission, surface transit improved and subway construction accelerated. Railroad regulatory proposals in the legislature diminished to a trickle. Railroad lobbyists bottled them up with the rationale that the PSC could handle the issues. Governor Hughes vetoed a "full crew" bill the legislature passed to mandate the number of engine crew members on the grounds that the PSC could address the issue.

In the 1908 gubernatorial contest, Hughes's Democratic opponent, Lewis Chanler, decried "government by commission" that violated "personal liberty." But Hughes defended the PSC's record and said repeal would be a victory for corrupt politicians and selfish utility companies. He challenged his opponent to propose something better; Chanler declined, and Hughes won reelection handily. That was another boost for regulation by commission.[35]

In 1909, the legislature extended the commissions' authority to cover telephone and telegraph companies. The next year, the legislature strengthened the commission's rate-setting power. Democrats regained control of the governor's office and the legislature in 1910 but left the commissions alone. Governor John A. Dix (1911–13) appointed a former business partner as a commissioner. Governor William Sulzer (1913) proposed two political cronies as commissioners; both were rejected by the senate. But when Frank Stevens retired as chairman in 1913, Sulzer relied on merit rather than politics and appointed the highly regarded PSC commissioner Martin S. Decker to succeed him. Stevens, who had set the tone of the commission as a firm but friendly regulator, went to work for the legal staff of the New York Central Railroad and later wrote a history of the early years of the road.[36]

The Republicans regained control of state government in 1915. A joint legislative committee investigated the operation of the commissions in 1915 and recommended their continuation. A constitutional convention that year made no recommendations for changes, in effect implying approval. The two commissions were consolidated in 1921. The leading-edge pioneering agency of the administrative state had become a permanent part of state government.

In January 1916, Charles Evans Hughes visited New York for something of a victory lap. His governorship (1907–10) had been a success, and he had been appointed to the US Supreme Court in 1910. He was being touted as a Republican presidential candidate, which he would in fact become later in the year, nearly winning the presidency. His ideas about administrative commissions were being written into statute books across the nation. The Public Service Commissions were cited as examples of responsible regulation in the public interest.

In a valedictory address to the New York State Bar Association, Hughes decried the "evil of needless multiplicity" of laws at the federal and state levels. Too much legislation was not the answer to regulating modern economic life. Administrative agencies with "both legislative and quasi-judicial powers" would address the need for agile government regulation. Legislatures could enact "appropriate standards" and authorize agencies to apply them. After all, "complaints must be heard, expert investigations conducted, complex situations deliberately and impartially analyzed, and legislative rules intelligently adapted" to varying circumstances. Administrative agencies with "special knowledge, flexibility, disinterestedness, and sound judgment" would carry legislative intent into practice. Commissions have the capacity for calm "deliberation and conference," in contrast to legislatures, where partisan concerns can interfere.[37]

The courts were standing like sentinels just offstage, Justice Hughes added reassuringly. Judges had the obligation to "construe legislation according to the intent of the Legislature" but also show flexibility as "the interpreter of legislation in the expanding life of democracy." Courts could be counted on to keep administrative commissions within their legally prescribed boundaries and constitutional limits, but it was up to administrative agencies to deal with "the complexity of the facts" in their areas of expertise. Don't expect the courts to interfere unless clear statutory violations or constitutional issues were presented, Hughes said: "to put upon the Courts the burden of considering the details of administrative problems would be to overwhelm them" with work.[38]

Hughes himself would express some reservations about legislative delegation of too much authority to executive agencies when he served as chief justice of the US Supreme Court in the 1930s. But the administrative state would become a hallmark of public policy and government in the twentieth century. It would also continue to be controversial, as critics continued to voice concerns that it sometimes put too much power, without accountability or responsibility, in the hands of unelected officials. It was a question of balance and judgment, as New York's first public service commissioners had demonstrated and as the courts had endorsed.

Chapter 9

STATE PROTECTION DENIED
FOR WOMEN WORKERS

Figure 9.1. Mary van Kleeck, pictured here, wrote *Women in the Bookbinding Trade* in 1913, documenting the work of women in factories that produced books and magazines. New York City publishing companies' court challenges to New York's ban on women's night work in factories resulted in the New York Court of Appeals invalidating a law in 1907, as described in this chapter, and validating a revised law in 1915, as related in chapter 10. *Source:* Harris & Ewing Collection, Library of Congress Prints & Photographs Division.

Can the state ban women from night work in factories in order to protect their health and welfare? The courts said no in 1907, declaring that women workers are not "wards of the state."

New York State Department of Labor factory inspector William W. Walling made a surprise inspection visit to Williams Printing Company on Eleventh Avenue in New York City on the night of January 31, 1906. He recorded seeing about forty women at work at 10:20 p.m. The work they were doing—folding and collating pages for assembly into periodicals and books—was easy and unremarkable. It was not physically demanding, and it appealed to many women. Some were unmarried, supporting themselves. Others were wives and mothers, supplementing their families' income. It was the sort of work done routinely at dozens of print shops around New York City, the center of newspaper and periodical publishing and printing in the nation. Factories like Williams Printing employed nearly 20 percent of all the workers in printing and publishing in the nation.[1] Women were employed in many other New York industries, too, most more physically demanding than publishing, including factories that made clothes, boots, shoes, cigars, and other products and canneries that processed and canned food. Women were usually hired at lower wages than men and were displacing them in some industries.[2]

But what Inspector Walling observed and reported that night was illegal. It was a violation of section 77 of the state labor law, enacted in 1899 and reenacted in 1903, which read, in part, "No minor under the age of eighteen years and no female shall be employed at labor in any factory in this state before six o'clock in the morning or after nine o'clock in the evening." Inspector Walling took down the names of several of the women workers. The law was worded to put the burden of compliance on factory owners, not women workers. Charging the company's owner, David Williams, with one specific violation would make prosecution in court easier than charging multiple violations. Walling's report therefore identified one woman worker, Katie Mead, who was engaged in "gathering"—"tacking pieces of printed paper together and putting them in the shape of a book, which was subsequently bound."[3] Williams was charged with violating state law for employing Mead that night.

It was only a misdemeanor offense, but it constituted the first step in a case that would make history.

BENEVOLENT PROTECTION OR INTRUSIVE PATERNALISM?

New York's "factory laws" dated to 1886. The first one prohibited the employment of women under twenty-one and men under eighteen for longer than sixty hours a week and excluded children under thirteen years of age from all factories. Subsequent legislation extended safeguards covering two protected classes, children and women. Child labor was largely prohibited by a series of laws enacted in 1903. Factory labor by women was restricted to no more than ten hours per day or sixty hours in a week, and "night work"—work after 9:00 p.m.—was forbidden.

Women could not vote in those days; that did not occur in New York until 1917. The legislature that enacted the night-work prohibition, the government attorneys who were about to defend it in court, the factory owner and his counsel who would assail it, and the courts that would decide it were all men. News reporters (all men) did not interview Katie Mead to see why she worked at nights. They did not stake out at the doors to the Williams factory to interview women who worked there. The voices and desires of working women were largely left out of the picture.

But other women, mostly middle class and well educated, had been a moving force behind the legislation restricting women's night employment. They were not factory workers themselves but believed night work was injurious and exploitative. They would be even more involved as advocates after the law prohibiting night work was struck down, as chapter 10 explains. Their advocacy for working women had mixed results:

> Protective legislation was clearly a mixed blessing for women and the working class. Maximum-hours laws could safeguard the health of wage-earning women, but at considerable cost. Women had to give up their freedom of contract. Worse, they were defined as weak and dependent, the inferiors of men. Special protective legislation also widened the sexual divide within the working class: male and female wage earners had still less reason to recognize their common plight; male unionists had still less incentive to organize laboring women.[4]

Employers complained that the laws disrupted hiring practices, increased labor expenses, and violated their right to employ women under contracts that both parties found satisfactory. Many provisions of the factory laws were routinely evaded or violated. Employers regarded them more like a nuisance than a strict legal requirement. The state had a small force of factory inspectors, and they concentrated on enforcing the restrictions on women and child labor. "We are not specially concerned about overtime or nightwork in factories where adult males only are employed," the commissioner of labor reported in 1903, "but, where women, minors and children are at work, special care is necessary to see that the statutes applicable to their labor are properly observed."[5]

Even there, though, the labor department frequently just issued warnings or citations to violators. They usually promised to comply with the law in the future, and the department admitted in its reports that it lacked staff for follow-up inspection visits to check. Its 1904 report complained that "the Bureau of Factory Inspection is struggling with the problem or enforcing a constantly growing set of regulations against a constantly increasing number of industrial enterprises."[6]

When scofflaws were hauled into court, county district attorneys often proved to be indifferent prosecutors. Many of them believed the laws were impractical and close to unenforceable—it was hard to prove whether someone had worked more than the permissible number hours, particularly when both employers and employees were often vague or evasive if questioned about how many hours they had worked. The proscription of work after 9:00 p.m. was easier to enforce because a violation would be clearly visible to an inspector. If women were observed working on a factory floor after that time, the owner was clearly in violation. The fine for violation of the law was $100, a relatively hefty sum in those days, but convictions were rare.

ENERGETIC ENFORCEMENT

By 1905, the factory inspection division of the labor department had acquired a reputation of laxity, compromise, and indifferent enforcement of the factory laws. That changed when Philemon Tecumseh Sherman became commissioner in May of that year. Sherman, who went by "P. Tecumseh," was appointed by Governor Frank Higgins on the recommendation of a coalition of social workers, philanthropists, and others who had lobbied for child labor legislation in 1903 and demanded that those new laws—and others on the books—be more vigorously enforced.

Sherman, an independent Republican, had gotten his political education through serving for several years on the New York City Board of Aldermen. He brought the same energy to enforcing the labor law that his father, William Tecumseh Sherman, had brought to leading Union troops in the Civil War.

Sherman secured legislative support to increase the inspection force. Inspectors began making more surprise follow-up visits to check on compliance. Sherman publicized violators. He pushed for convictions and fines. There were fewer friendly warnings, more orders summoning violators into court. Sherman left no doubt that the law would be enforced. Inspector Walling's visit to the Williams factory was part of that crackdown.[7]

Enacting and enforcing protective labor legislation for women was a priority of the emerging Progressive movement. Some advocates worried about women's health and the toll that long hours in factories would take. Others fretted that married women and mothers working outside the home subverted their natural roles as homemakers and caregivers for children. Moralists feared night work in the proximity of men would tempt women into moral lapses or prostitution. Walking home alone at night on deserted city streets after work could be dangerous for women. Catching up on sleep during the day was not the equivalent of resting at night, the natural time for recuperative sleep.

"Anemia, nervous exhaustion and general susceptibility to disease" as well as "lowered vitality or chronic ill-health" afflict women who work at night, wrote Josephine Goldmark, one of the leading advocates for banning night work by women, in 1906.[8] She was the legislative manager for the National Consumers' League, initiated in 1899 to lobby for better factory working conditions. Goldmark and other advocates admitted they lacked solid documentary evidence to prove their case. Their contentions were mostly based on observation and conjecture about the impact of night work rather than actual experience. Furthermore, the League had other priorities in New York state, including suppressing child labor, which was largely accomplished in a series of laws in 1903.

Moreover, the absence of documentary proof about the harmful effects of night work on women opened the prohibition of such work to criticism. Critics asserted that women should be able to work when they wished. They really did not need the hovering protection—or the intrusive interference—of the state; that was condescending and paternalistic. In fact, opponents of the law said, forbidding night work discriminated against women. It ran against the rising demands of the woman suffrage community for not only the vote but also equal rights. It also violated their right to contract for their own labor.[9]

Many women needed to work nights in factories to support themselves and their children, said the law's critics. Denying that right put them at a competitive disadvantage with men. Cynics went further, alleging that restrictions were really intended to squeeze women out of the workplace where they competed with men and were paid less, keeping men's wages low. Judges had tended to agree, often looking askance at state laws that restricted women's working hours. In an 1895 Illinois case, *Ritchie v. People*, the state's supreme court had invalidated a state law imposing maximum-hours limits on women's work week. The court cited women's liberty of contract, saying women "are entitled to the same rights under the Constitution to make contracts with reference to their labor as are secured thereby to men."[10]

By the time the *People v. Williams* case started its journey through New York's court system in 1906, courts had reached a workable if inexact method of determining which protective laws to uphold and which to strike down. To secure courts' approval, there had to be a convincing case for the purpose and the goals to be achieved by the law. There also had to be a clear connection between means and ends—the judges needed to be convinced that legislators had legitimate reason to act as they did. When laws failed to pass muster, by contrast, judges ruled that they were arbitrary, that they contravened constitutionally guaranteed rights such as liberty of contract, that they were out of line with previous relevant court of appeals or US Supreme Court decisions, or that their proponents had failed to present the court with convincing arguments about the reasonable nature of the statutes.[11]

Courts found it challenging to apply this formula in cases like *Williams*. "In cases involving women, the legal community began to consider the laborer in question more closely than the nature of the labor. Questions about police power quickly became questions about the state's capacity to regulate in favor of morality and in favor of women's reproductive health."[12] Gender differences might, under appropriate circumstances, provide justification for protective legislation for women. On the other hand, if the judges felt that women and men were, or should be, equal under the constitution and before the law, then discrimination in favor of restricting and protecting women was not justified.[13]

CONSTITUTIONAL CHALLENGE

Labor commissioner Sherman pushed inspection and enforcement. But he also harbored—and shared—second thoughts about the law's specific provision forbidding night work by women. In his 1905 annual report, he urged the legislature to make it more flexible—for instance, to allow for overtime in emergencies and at peak work times. In his 1906 report, he conceded that "a shadow of a doubt as to its constitutionality has always rested heavy upon the prohibition of night work" and that his department was "afraid to test the question" in court.[14] He conceded that the requirement made it easier for his inspectors to enforce the provision about maximum hours. But that was because in some cases where women were the majority of employees, prohibiting night work in effect meant the factory had to close at night.

If fully enforced, forbidding night work "would deprive some mature working women, employed by night only, at skilled trades, for short hours and for high wages, of all means of support."[15] It seemed discriminatory, too, said Sherman, applying only to women in factories and not in mercantile operations, laundries, or buildings where thousands of women toiled at night as cleaners. "This law has never been fully and strictly enforced," he admitted, because doing so would be too disruptive to some industries. It "has stood upon our statute books to a great extent as a mere expression of a moral aspiration."[16]

This time, the accused would resist on constitutional grounds, as Sherman had predicted would eventually happen. In fact, David Williams's counsel would use some of the same arguments that Sherman expressed in his reports. If the night-work law was really "a mere expression of a moral aspiration," it needed to fall. Commissioner Sherman's skepticism helped pave the way for the demise of that section of state law.

Williams's trial in the New York City Court of Special Sessions on March 30, 1906, lasted only a few minutes. New York County's highly capable, politically savvy district attorney, Williams T. Jerome, sent a deputy to prosecute. He asked Inspector Walling to relate what he had observed at Williams Printing on January 31 and to affirm it was a violation of the law. Under cross-examination by Williams's counsel, Frederick B. House, a partner in the prominent Manhattan law firm House, Grossman & Vorhaus, Walling admitted that "respecting the light, air and general sanitary conditions," Williams Printing was "the best factory of its kind in New York City."[17]

The people and the defense then both rested. Williams's counsel offered no defense against the charge against him. The court found Williams guilty. It was expected that the judges would levy a fine, as in past cases.

But counsel House surprised the judges. He immediately moved for an "arrest of judgment"—a legal term meaning postponement or stay of a court's decision where the defendant desires to mount a legal or constitutional challenge. Williams was going to fight the decision on the grounds that the law itself was unconstitutional.

House explained that the section of the law prohibiting night work constituted a violation of the Fourteenth Amendment to the US Constitution by denying women the equal protection of the laws. It contravened provisions in both the state and federal constitutions forbidding depriving a person of their liberty or property without due process of law. In short, the law was unconstitutional. House was borrowing and applying the reasoning that the US Supreme Court had used in its *Lochner v. New York* decision the year before, 1905, to strike down a New York law restricting the working hours of bakers. That gave House's petition more weight. The judges agreed to suspend decision on the *Williams* case and review the legal issues.

Everyone interested in laws surrounding women's working hours recognized the potential importance of the case. "The protection of children is pretty well conceded to be a proper exercise of police power," said a *New York Tribune* editorial. What was at stake here was the health of women who were mothers or potential mothers: "the protection of women is the protection of the children of the next generation." Young women in particular needed the state's protection from "the evils of night work and subsequent night exposure on the streets."[18] Opponents of the law, though, saw the *Williams* case as an opportunity to kill the oppressive night-work prohibition.

TRIAL COURT: THE NIGHT-WORK BAN IS UNCONSTITUTIONAL

Frederick House presented his argument that this provision of the law was an unconstitutional denial of a woman's right to enter into a contract for her labor and deprived her of liberty without due process of law. His contentions closely followed the Supreme Court's dicta in *Lochner v. New York*: the courts should invalidate laws that unduly restricted liberty of contract.

Because of the importance the *Williams* case had now taken on, state attorney general Julius Mayer stepped in for the New York County district attorney to present the people's case. The law was a valid exercise of the state's police power, he argued—the power to enact and enforce laws protecting the welfare, safety, and health of the public. It was essentially the same case that Mayer had made the previous year, unsuccessfully defending the state in the *Lochner* case.

Justice Willard H. Olmsted sided with House. He wrote the unanimous decision for the three-judge court on August 3, 1906. "The right to labor and to contract for that labor is both a liberty and a property right," the judge began. For the state to violate it, there must be evidence that the law was enacted "to protect the comfort, welfare and safety of the whole people, and the individual must suffer this curtailment of his granted rights in the interest of the common good."[19] Olmsted found legal guidance and precedent in US Supreme Court decisions, particularly *Lochner*. There, the court had decided that a New York law regulating bakers' working hours and conditions was "not within any fair meaning of the term, a health law, but is an illegal interference with the rights of individuals, both employers and employees, to make contracts regarding labor upon such terms as they may think best."[20] The Supreme Court's reasoning there, justice Olmsted made plain, was admirable, convincing, and directly applicable to the *Williams* case.

He found Attorney General Mayer's brief about the need for and intent of the law unconvincing: "the Attorney-General finds and urges no other reason than that the general welfare of the State demands that the progeny of women of the factories shall have mothers with healthy bodies to the end that the State may have sturdy citizens." On that reasoning, the state could regulate the work of "the housewife, the woman who toils at home" and even "the society woman," all of whom might become mothers.[21]

Besides, women were now equal to men before the law, the judge insisted. "Legislative emancipation" has given them the right to hold property, operate businesses, and sue in court. "Modern social development" has resulted in their employment in all sorts of callings. They competed with men, and indeed in some fields "to the extent of almost wholly supplanting men." The law in question grouped them with children as a class of citizens needing "paternal protection." It was really "an attempt to relegate women to their old position as dependent State wards."[22]

Mayer's state brief had also claimed that the law was really a "health regulation" to protect women in factories. Other legal requirements, such as requirements for fire escapes, cleanliness, and ventilation, might well do that, Olmsted observed. But forbidding night work could not pass muster as a health regulation. There was no real evidence that night work harmed women's health. The legislature had not imposed similar restrictions on women in nighttime mercantile work. It was inconsistent: a woman dressmaker who was proprietor of her own shop might work as long as she wished, but if she had a woman employee, the employee would have to stop work at 9:00 p.m. "Why this distinction between two possible mothers of future citizens if this be simply a health regulation?" the judge asked.[23]

This was no health regulation for the good of women or the general welfare of the people of the state. Instead, the justice wrote, it is "an unreasonable and unwarranted infringement of the constitutional right of the individual, and not only of her right but also of the right of him who would contract for her employment."[24] The court ruled the law's provision banning night work was unconstitutional. It dismissed the case against Williams. Katie Mead and others could legally work past 9:00 p.m.

The *New York Times* had supported the protection of women in factories, but its editors found Justice Olmsted's reasoning persuasive. The law was inequitable and discriminatory because it "creates classes and treats one of them differently from the way in which it treats the others."[25]

THE SUPREME COURT APPELLATE DIVISION: THE NIGHT-WORK BAN IS UNCONSTITUTIONAL

The state appealed the verdict. Attorney General Mayer, realizing now that the night-work law might be doomed, made a stronger case than before. But it still fell short. His brief did not explain the significance of the case or the injury to women working long hours at night. Florence Kelley, director of the National Consumers' League, called the attorney general's brief "a disgraceful exhibition of ignorance."[26] By contrast, House, again representing Williams Printing, strengthened the case that the law contravened the Fourteenth Amendment.

The appellate division of the state supreme court issued its decision on December 7, 1906. Three judges voted to confirm the Court of Special Sessions' decision; two dissented, supporting overturning it.

Justice Francis M. Scott wrote the majority opinion. It was only two pages long, mostly endorsing the lower court's decision. To overturn it, the court would need to find that "owing to some physical or nervous difference, it is more harmful for a woman to work at night than for a man to do so." But no such difference had been proven. The decision declaring the law invalid should stand.[27]

Justice James Houghton dissented. Not every statute that interferes with the right of individuals to contract for their labor is unconstitutional, he argued. The test is whether it is "reasonable and appropriate." Houghton cited decisions where the courts had validated such use of the police power. *Lochner* did not apply, Judge Houghton argued. That pertained to limiting the number of hours bakers—almost all men—could work. The *Williams* case was different, focusing on whether working at night was likely to induce "generative weakness" in women. The state had a legitimate interest in the health of its woman citizens and their children. Factory work was automated by machines and required constant exertion, which "tends to dull the mental and moral perceptions and leads to degrading recreations, especially when the work ceases at an unseemly hour of the night." The law should stand.[28]

Justice George Ingraham agreed with Houghton. *Lochner* was not a deterrent; it pertained only to hours of bakers. The legislature had "recognized difference in the strength and capacity for manual labor between men and women" in passing the section of the law under review. Employers "under modern industrial conditions" took advantage of women, working them hard to extract "the greatest amount of work possible." The legislature had every right to ban night work by women, which could "overtax their physical strength and break down [their] health."[29]

THE STATE'S CASE: THIS LAW APPROPRIATELY PROTECTS WOMEN

By the time of the appellate division's decision, Attorney General Mayer was a lame duck. In the November 1906 election, Democrat William S. Jackson defeated the lackadaisical Mayer with a pledge to be aggressive in pursuing labor law violators. Jackson believed the state had lost in the Court of Special Sessions and at the appellate division because its case was too weak. Mayer wrote the appeal to the court of appeals, which agreed to hear the case, but it was up to Jackson to prepare a new case for the state.[30]

Jackson's brief was powerful. Proscription of women's night work was part of a benevolent system of New York laws designed to protect workers' lives and ensure safe, sanitary working conditions, the brief noted. The law was intended to "protect the health of females" by limiting their workday to ten hours and "protect their health and guard their morals" by preventing night work. Several other states had some statutory protection for women in factories, Jackson noted. Night is "a natural time for rest," and rest during the day is inadequate, "broken and unsatisfactory." Of course, that applied to men, too, but "with much greater force . . . to women, who by nature are more weakly constituted, less able to endure hardship, and endowed with a highly sensitive organization." The law has always recognized "the physical limitations of women with reference to labor," the attorney general added.[31]

Night work is objectionable from a "moral standpoint," the brief insisted. "The married woman is compelled to assume a double burden. To the labor of night is added the cares of her household during the day. Her children are neglected at a time when her influences and training should supplement the day at school." Young women in particular are at risk of moral lapses when working with men late at night or walking home with them after work when "opportunities for evil are multiplied."[32]

New York was in good company in its legal protection of women, the brief argued. Forty-three states forbade Sunday labor. Six prohibited women from working in mines; eight banned it where "traffic in liquor is carried on." Fifteen states, including industrial ones similar to New York such as Massachusetts and Pennsylvania, restricted the number of hours women could work. Indiana, Massachusetts, Nebraska, and many foreign nations prohibited night work by women. Britain had done so for more than fifty years.[33]

The brief called the state's proscription of night work "a reasonable and good faith exercise of the power vested in it" to protect its citizens. It cited a dozen opinions by New York and other state courts and the US Supreme Court supporting state regulations.[34]

Of course, the law impinges on right to contract and personal liberty, but "all laws are more or less restrictive of the liberty of the citizens." The brief cited *People ex rel. Nechamcus v. Warden* (1895), where the court of appeals had held that "the natural right to life, liberty and the pursuit of happiness is not an absolute right. It must yield whenever the concession is demanded by the welfare, health or prosperity of the State." New York City alone had 39,000 factories employing 130,000 female workers, the brief stated. Those numbers showed the potential "injury to the State" from night work.[35]

Supporting this law really would not be inconsistent with the Supreme Court's *Lochner* decision. That pertained to men in bakeries; this law, to women in factories. The state's responsibility to protect women was comparable to its role in protecting children. The brief cited a few court decisions supporting the principle of the state protecting women. Its main references, though, were to two authoritative law textbooks of the era, *The General Principles of Constitutional Law in the United States of America* by Thomas Cooley (1880) and *The Police Power, Public Policy and Constitutional Rights* by Ernst Freund (1904). Both authorities, according to the attorney general, sanctioned regulations to protect women workers and restrict their hours.[36]

THE DEFENDANT'S CASE: THIS LAW VIOLATES WOMEN'S RIGHTS

The firm representing Williams—House, Grossman & Vorhaus—engaged Henry B. Corey, an independent attorney in the capacity of counsel to the firm, to handle the appeal to the court of appeals. House had been effective in the lower courts with his skillful appeals to law and judicial precedent. Corey, by contrast, had a knack for putting things in terms that everyone, not just lawyers and judges, could understand. He was the author of the popular book *Law without Lawyers: A Compendium of Business and Domestic Law, for Popular Use*. He called it a book for "people who have not enjoyed a legal education" written in terms "as simple as the nature of the subject would admit . . . clear, accurate and popular in the best sense of the word."[37]

His brief for the court of appeals had plenty of legal citations and liberal quotations from *Lochner* and other court decisions that had knocked out state regulatory laws. But he believed the legal issues had been thoroughly aired in the trial and appellate courts. His strategy would focus on the *human* implications of the law being challenged. He intended to give the court of appeals a convenient and convincing basis for invalidating the law that citizens could appreciate.[38]

The printing and bindery business was important to New York's economy and employed thousands of people, Corey began. It required night work to make sure that newspapers and periodicals, published under tight deadlines to ensure timeliness, were produced on schedule. Working conditions in the Williams plant were excellent, as state factory inspector Walling had testified in the Court of Special Sessions trial. Some female employees there were the sole supporters of parents or children. They worked only at night, not also during the day, so they were not fatigued. They needed the work. The women received "liberal wages, much in excess of wages paid to shop girls or for ordinary day work . . . they earn a good living." The work was light and easy. "These women have, by training, acquired great manual dexterity, undoubtedly assisted by natural feminine delicacy of touch."[39] Their work was a skill. They were proud and content with their jobs, with good reason.

The question boils down to whether these women, and thousands like them, were "to be deprived of their means of livelihood, their right to labor at the only skilled trade they know; to be supplanted by men workmen, and to be forced out to compete for a harder task, for longer hours and for a smaller wage in unskilled employments."[40]

Corey explained that the section of the law prohibiting night work in factories actually harmed women by denying them equal protection of the laws guaranteed by the US and state constitutions and the right to compete with men for night labor. "An equality of opportunity for work with men is denied to women by the statute. They are shut out from night employments. . . . Should [women] not have an equal right to seek and obtain that employment as men?" The law was an anachronism; women were now men's equal in the eyes of the law. "The old conception of woman as a weak, helpless, irresponsible, protected member of society, whose identity was merged with that of her husband before the law, has almost entirely disappeared," Corey argued. That meant that "society cannot hold woman to all the responsibilities of man under the present industrial system, without granting her an equality of rights."[41]

The state's argument that night work hurt women's health was baseless, Corey maintained. This was light employment, and in any case permissible under law during the day. "It would be absurd to think that it would be harmless to a woman's health to work eight or ten hours during the day, and seriously injure her to work eight or ten hours during the night." In a parting jab at the state's "police power," Corey added that "this legislation only illustrates a prevalent tendency toward vexations and unfair regulation of private rights and liberties."[42]

THE COURT OF APPEALS: WOMEN ARE NOT "WARDS OF THE STATE"

Judge John C. Gray wrote a unanimous opinion for the court, issued on June 14, 1907.[43] It confirmed the appellate court's decision. The night-work provision of the law was unconstitutional.

The legislature overstepped the limits set by both the state and federal constitutions for state interference with the rights of citizens. Both constitutions "protect every citizen in the right to pursue any lawful employment in a lawful manner. . . . Any arbitrary distinction against, or deprivation of, that freedom by the legislature is an invasion of the constitutional guaranty. Under our laws men and women now stand alike in their constitutional rights and there is no warrant for making any discrimination between them with respect to the liberty of person, or of contract."[44]

Limiting the total hours that could be worked during a day or week, as other provisions in the law do, might be construed as protecting and promoting women's health. This part of the law, though, simply barred work between certain hours "without any regard to the healthfulness of the employment." Paraphrasing a contention in Henry Corey's brief for Williams Printing, Gray said that the law "is, certainly, discriminative against female citizens, in denying them equal rights with men in the same pursuit."[45]

Judge Gray had favored the court supporting legislative regulations tied to the welfare of people in the past. He had written the majority opinion in *People ex rel. Nechamcus v. Warden* in 1895, which Attorney General Jackson cited in his brief. He had written a concurring opinion in the 1904 court of appeals decision in *People v. Lochner*, which validated the state's limitation on the working hours of bakers. There, he had said that "we must presume that the legislative body was animated by a reasonable intention to promote the public welfare and if the courts can give effect to it, because tending to guard the public health, they should, unhesitatingly, do so."[46]

But in this *Williams* opinion, Judge Gray went in the opposite direction. The main reason was the Supreme Court's decision in *Lochner v. New York* in 1905, which reversed *People v. Lochner* and dramatically circumscribed the state's police power. Gray felt his opinion had to follow that Supreme Court precedent.

Prohibiting women's night work was simply too intrusive, said the judge, and "it is time to call a halt." Referring to women generally, Judge Gray concluded that "she is entitled to enjoy, unmolested, her liberty of person, and her freedom to work for whom she pleases, where she pleases and as long as she pleases, within the general limits operative on all persons alike, and shall we say that this is valid legislation, which closes the doors of a factory to her before and after certain hours? I think not." He concluded that "an adult female is in no sense a ward of the state [and] she is not to be made the special object of the paternal power of the state." Instead, "she is entitled to be placed upon an equality of rights with the man."[47] Judge Gray sounded like a women's rights advocate asserting women's equality.

The appellate division's opinion was confirmed. David Williams had won. The court of appeals had repudiated the state's prohibition on women's night work in factories.

PONDERING THE DECISION

The *Williams* decision was limited in its scope; it struck down the night-work prohibition but left the rest of the law intact. But some factory owners believed, or said they believed, that it freed them to employ women as they pleased for longer hours than the law's limits. The Department of Labor explained repeatedly that the court's decision focused only on night work and that the other provisions, limiting the number of hours women could work per day and per week, remained in effect.[48]

But Commissioner Sherman, in his 1907 annual report, noted that "hours of labor of women. . . . is a most unsatisfactory subject. In general the hours of work in New York factories are moderate and the natural tendency of industry is to shorten them. But the letter of the law on the subject has been generally disregarded in certain classes of establishments and both its letter and spirit have been habitually violated in many factories during short rush seasons, without the factory inspectors being able to prevent [it]." He continued, "Very earnest efforts . . . were made to enforce the rest of the law" after the *Williams* decision, particularly the sixty-hours-per-week limitation, "and even that proved so heavy a task that prosecutions had to be limited to gross or long-continued violations." The 1907 legislature made some changes in the law, including defining adult women workers as age twenty-one and older and minors as younger than that. The New York State Department of Labor asserted that the *Williams* decision applied only to *adult* women and announced that it would enforce the night-work proscription for younger women. That proved challenging, though, due to the difficulty in verifying workers' ages. Sherman insisted he needed more factory inspectors to enforce the labor law and a legal staff to ease reliance on local district attorneys.[49]

Commissioner Sherman, tired after two years of intense leadership and service, resigned on October 3, 1907. His successor, John C. Williams, appointed by progressive Republican governor Charles Evans Hughes, who had been elected in 1906, had served as Sherman's deputy. Williams met with Florence Kelley of the National Consumers' League and the heads of other reform organizations. He pledged vigorous enforcement of the labor code. But he insisted that any new regulations, including reimposition of the ban on night work by women, would need to depend on documentation of the effects of long hours on women.[50]

The court of appeals' *Williams* decision got lots of attention, most of it positive, in the legal community. A commentator in the popular legal journal *Green Bag* cited with approval Judge Gray's view that "when it is sought, as here, to arbitrarily to prevent an adult female citizen from working any time of day or night that suits her, it is time to call a halt. Such a law arbitrarily deprives citizens of their right to contract with each other." The real motivation for the law was not women's health at all. It was actually "to save young women employed in the factories from the temptations, insults, and exposure" they were likely to endure walking home on city streets after leaving work. The court was right in striking down this example of "the growing tendency of the legislatures to interfere with the lawful pursuits of citizens."[51]

Soon, courts in other states were referring to the *Williams* decision in their own opinions on women's labor legislation.

The *Williams* decision also brought a good deal of criticism. To Progressives, it was another example of an insensitive conservative court favoring business interests by voiding an appropriate measure to protect women workers. Josephine Goldmark, reflecting the views of the National Consumers' League and other proponents of the night-work ban, criticized its narrowness. The court had concentrated on a "single narrow aspect of the matter"—whether working at 10:20 p.m. was injurious and illegal. It had ignored "all those intricate social aspects of night work, its effects upon health and the home and general welfare." The decision reflected the court's "inability to see the purpose of the law."[52]

A few commentators saw ironies and inconsistencies. Women workers had not asked for the law in 1903, but neither had they protested or challenged it in court. Since the time of its passage, they did not "clamor for the right to toil at night in factories." Most women seemed indifferent to or unconvinced by the state's claim that night work was an "unnatural and harmful . . . mode of life." When the *Williams* decision was rendered, however, judging by the criticism from women's advocates, "those whom the court professed to protect felt themselves most aggrieved."[53]

Apparently, no one in government or the media interviewed women factory workers for their reactions to the *Williams* decision.

The *Williams* decision seemed to leave everyone dissatisfied and feeling that the issue had not been finally resolved. P. Tecumseh Sherman agreed. In his last *Bulletin* just before leaving office, Sherman included a long, reflective essay on factory laws and the courts:

He disagreed with the sentiment of "antagonism towards the courts and some despair of protecting labor under our constitutions."[54] After all, New York courts had approved restrictions on maximum hours for women and laws requiring cleanliness in factories.

Previous court decisions criticized at the time they were rendered had turned out to be valid. For instance, the 1885 court of appeals decision *In re Jacobs*, overturning a law prohibiting tenement-house manufacture of tobacco products, was valid because the purported purpose, protecting public health, differed from the actual goal, banning manufacturing in tenement houses altogether. The point was soon moot in that case because tobacco work moved into factories for economic reasons.

The court of appeals was wrong, and the US Supreme Court right, in the *Lochner* case, said Sherman, because baking is not an unhealthy profession, and public health was not really a valid justification. The court of appeals was right in *Williams*, too, Sherman admitted. His inspectors had found no evidence that night work by women in factories was unhealthy.

On one hand, legislatures needed lots of leeway in enacting laws within the state's police power. On the other hand, constitutions are also meant to limit the powers of legislatures, and courts are not swayed by popular passions or "the changing opinions of temporary majorities" in legislatures. Laws needed to be "reasonable."[55]

In determining that, courts needed to ignore restrictions "supported only by individual opinions (although numerous and loudly voiced), or based upon scientific hypotheses or social or economic theories." European labor regulations, sometimes cited by proponents of restrictions, were limited guides, not necessarily compatible with our "free form of government" or "our constitutional guaranty of liberty." The *Williams* decision was a warning against "pushing statutory restrictions upon hours of labor beyond the requirements of necessity." Working hours are moderate in New York, said Sherman, and labor unions' work was leading to even shorter hours without the need for government interference. The legislature, in considering future legislation, and the courts, in reviewing it, should use as criteria that which is "generally admitted to be reasonably *necessary* for the public welfare. . . . There must be a public necessity."[56]

Commissioner Sherman, exiting state service, had provided guidance for the future. The debate over whether proscribing factory night work by women was "a public necessity" would continue. Proponents of the night-work ban redoubled their efforts. The night-work proscription would be reenacted in 1913. It would be challenged again in the courts, but this time, as discussed in the next chapter, it would be validated.

Chapter 10

STATE PROTECTION AFFIRMED FOR WOMEN WORKERS

Figure 10.1. Florence Kelly, a leader of the National Consumers' League, built a network of activists and advocates for labor and other reform legislation, including laws protecting women and children in New York State. *Source:* Underwood & Underwood, c. 1925, Library of Congress Prints & Photographs Division.

Can the state ban women from night work in factories in order to protect their health and welfare? The court of appeals said no in 1907. But, presented with new evidence about factory working conditions, much of it assembled by women labor-reform advocates, the court reversed itself and said yes in 1915.

The early years of the twentieth century were the time of the rising tide of Progressivism, a widespread social and reform movement designed to address the problems caused by urbanization, industrialization, and political corruption. Many states, including New York, passed protective labor legislation for women, including restricting the number of hours they could work. But it was not a priority for labor unions, which were mostly focused on men's work issues, or even rising women's unions such as the New York Women's Trade Union League and allied organizations. They were more interested in direct action, such as strikes to secure better hours and working conditions and higher wages. Unions in the opening years of the new century were at least mildly skeptical about state government labor regulations. Too often, the regulations were not well enforced. Labor laws could be repealed. Courts could void legal protections by ruling them unconstitutional, as happened in New York's 1907 *People v. Williams* decision, described in chapter 9.[1]

That attitude shifted after the *Williams* case. Reformers redoubled their efforts to assemble evidence on the evils of night work, secure legislation forbidding it, and defend the laws in the courts.

A strong push for a reenactment of the night-work ban after *Williams* came from the Consumers' League of New York City, founded in 1890, and the National Consumers' League, founded in 1899 and headquartered in the city. The national and city leagues worked in tandem for legislation to improve working conditions for women and the health of women and children as well as to eliminate child labor. The leagues' officers were mostly middle- and upper-class women rather than frontline women workers. The national league's highly effective and energetic general secretary, Florence Kelley, made child labor elimination a priority and led a campaign that largely eliminated it in New York in 1903.

Kelley and her colleagues lobbied for limitations on women's hours and defended them in the courts. Working long hours and, particularly, laboring at night was unfair to women, exploitative, and tiring. Kelley and the league's chief legal advocate, Josephine Goldmark, approached Goldmark's brother-in-law, prominent Massachusetts reform attorney Louis

Brandeis, to prepare a brief in the US Supreme Court case of *Muller v. Oregon* in 1908. The case was a test of the constitutionality of that state's law restricting women's factory hours to ten per day. Goldmark and her colleagues assembled reports and data showing the harmful effects of long hours, which Brandeis compiled into a masterful and convincing document. Impressed by the evidence in the document as well as the cases assembled by state attorney general about the states' "police power" to enact labor reforms, the Supreme Court upheld the law. The "Brandeis brief," with variations, was used by the league and other advocates to help secure judicial approval of similar laws in other states over the following years.[2]

Kelley lectured widely on the topic of protective labor laws for women, and her lectures were assembled and published as books. The league sent investigators into factories to document working conditions. Kelley built a network of advocates and lobbied legislators directly for labor reforms. Goldmark's 1912 book *Fatigue and Efficiency* connected long working hours with lowered productivity, particularly for women. A book by another activist, Mary van Kleeck's 1913 *Women in the Bookbinding Trade*, documented the exhausting conditions of thousands of women working in printing plants, many at night. Both studies were published by the Russell Sage Foundation, which supported research into social and working conditions. The Consumers' League and other proponents helped secure European commitments to ban night work at an international conference in 1906.[3]

Tragedy accelerated labor reform in New York. On March 25, 1911, a fire in the Triangle Shirtwaist Factory in New York City killed 146 workers, most of them young women. The tragedy led the state legislature to establish a Factory Investigating Commission (FIC), chaired by Democratic majority leader of the senate Robert Wagner, with Democratic majority leader of the assembly (and speaker of the assembly during 1913) Alfred E. Smith as vice chair. The commission assembled a stellar staff of investigators and cooperated with labor unions and organizations like the Consumers' League. The league worked out an arrangement for some of its investigators to work for the commission at the league's expense. Highly effective advisors to the commission, particularly Frances Perkins and Mary van Kleeck, brought women's labor issues to the forefront. The commission held hearings, visited factories, and commissioned studies by its staff. During the next few years, it formulated a battery of reform laws that easily passed the legislature, including fire safety and building codes and restrictions on maximum hours of work for women.[4]

The commission investigated the impact of night work by women. Its investigators visited a twine factory in Auburn, reporting that after a night's work, "the appearance of the women workers is very disheartening. They are stolid, worn looking, and pale. Their clothes, faces, and hands are covered with oil and . . . dust." That and other factory visits and evidence from studies affirmed that women who work at night suffer from "symptoms which mark lowered vitality, if not actual disease, such as loss of appetite, headache, [and] anemia." The factories were noisy, dirty, and often hot. Studies revealed a higher infant mortality rate among women who returned to work after childbirth. Women returning home alone late at night after work risked "unusual moral dangers and temptations" and "the possibility of insult or attack on the streets." Josephine Goldmark testified that night work undermined women's health. Banning night work would aid enforcement of a law recommended by the commission and passed by the legislature limiting the number of hours women could work in a factory to ten per day and fifty-four in a week.[5]

The commission's report brushed aside potential objections to banning night work. None of the women interviewed asked for a ban. The reason, the report explained, was that they didn't fully realize the harm night work was doing to them. Women told FIC investigators they needed the work to support themselves or their families. But the commission asserted that "such work is unnecessary from an economic point of view." The courts had struck down similar legislation in the past, notably the *Williams* decision in 1907. That should not be an obstacle, either, said the commission, because since *Muller v. Oregon* in 1908, "the current of judicial opinion has flowed in another channel." There was an additional benefit, the report added, reflecting Goldmark's influence: banning night work would help state labor officials enforce the statutory limits on women's work hours. "None of the investigations carried on by the Commission has shown conditions more disastrous to health and public welfare than the employment of women a night in the factories of the state." Considering all the evidence the FIC had turned up about safety and fire risks, injuries to workers, long hours, and harmful chemicals, that was a dramatic claim.[6]

The commission recommended a law banning women's night work in factories. Women laborers were not asked their opinions. Mary Dreier, president of the Women's Trade Union League, was a member of the commission. That league endorsed the FIC's proposals generally but did not identify this one in particular as a focus for advocacy. The city and national citizens' unions actively lobbied for it. Only representatives of the printing industry, which routinely employed thousands of women at night to meet production deadlines, opposed. The legislative proposal passed the legislature easily in 1913. The new law incorporated the exact wording the commission recommended: "In order to protect the health and morals of females employed in factories by providing an adequate period of rest at night, no woman shall be employed in any factory in this State before six o'clock in the morning or after ten o'clock in the evening of any day."[7]

LAUNCHING A TEST CASE

Getting the night-work prohibition law onto the statute books was relatively easy. Protecting it there from a hostile court ruling was the next piece of work at hand for its supporters. After all, as the chair of the New York City Consumers' League committee on legislation pointed out, "this law is practically a re-enactment of the provisions declared unconstitutional in the *Williams* decision" except that it was cast as a "health measure."[8] Representatives of industry, particularly the printing industry, also welcomed a court test. They were confident that the courts would invalidate the new law, just as they had the previous one in the *Williams* case back in 1907.

The league held informal discussions with the FIC about how to bring a successful test case. Republicans in the legislature had been lukewarm about the FIC's labor reform package. But the Republican New York district attorney, Charles Whitman, had been enthusiastic. He had prosecuted the owners of the Triangle factory for manslaughter after the tragic 1911 fire and lost. In the process, he had learned a great deal about women's working conditions in factories. He hoped to secure his party's nomination for governor in 1914 and wanted to run as a progressive. His office would gladly prosecute blatant offenders of the new night-work ban. He assigned assistant DA William DeFord to cooperate with the league. (Whitman's defense of labor laws and record as a crime fighter helped him garner the Republican gubernatorial nomination and win the 1914 election.)

Esther Packard, an investigator for the FIC whose salary was being paid by the New York City Consumers' League, identified a prospective test case. She made a surprise visit to Charles Schweinler Press, a company that occupied an entire block and was ten stories high, on Hudson Street in Manhattan, on the evening of February 8, 1914. Schweinler Press, one of the largest in the nation, printed several popular magazines, including

McClure's Magazine, The Ladies' World, and *Harper's Weekly.* More than six million magazines emerged from its presses each week. To meet production schedules, the machinery ran twenty-four hours a day. A reporter for *McClure's* visited and observed "row upon row of gigantic, roaring presses turning forth thousands of copies per hour; type-casting machines clicking out, at a furious rate, line upon line of type; great steaming foundries pouring forth page after page of plates."[9] Ironically, *McClure's* had advocated for state progressive reforms. But Charles Schweinler employed many women at night, in open defiance of the new state law. Packard targeted Schweinler in part because he had already been cited a number of times for violation of the night-work ban.[10]

At 10:24 p.m. that night, Packard observed a woman employee, May Cashel, who was employed as a "fly girl." She picked up loose printed sheets emerging from the presses and laid them on a cart that was taken away (by a man because the carts were heavy) to another part of the plant for binding. Inspector Packard observed Mary Cashel doing the work for only five minutes, but that was enough to document a violation of the law. Cashel was married, with three children, ages four, twelve, and fourteen. That would strengthen the prosecution of the employer and defense of the law, proponents felt. One of the rationales for passing it the year before had been that night work stressed and exhausted mothers and led to them neglect their families.[11]

Schweinler was cited for violating the law and tried in the City Court of Special Sessions. Esther Packard related the violation of the law she had observed.

May Cashel, however, appeared as a witness for the company. The work was light and easy, she explained, and she needed to work to supplement her husband's salary as a stevedore. Her husband had breakfast waiting for her when she returned home after work in the morning. He took care of the household work. The older children went to school, and she was able to sleep during the day. The four-year-old played around the house or snuggled beside her mother in bed in the daytime. The children were well cared for and "you see I look sturdy and well," she told the court. Schweinler's attorney, former city judge Alfred Ommen, who also represented several other printing companies on labor issues, insisted that the law itself, and this test case, were the handiwork of "some distinguished ladies [and] social workers." The court of appeals' decision in the *Williams* case was a binding precedent. The night-work ban was unconstitutional. Ommen said that employers throughout the state were anxious to have the constitutionality of the law resolved.[12]

The Court of Special Sessions found Schweinler guilty but issued a suspended sentence on the grounds that the night-work law was unconstitutional. That added up to a mixed, ambiguous verdict, not the sort of test-case result the law's proponents had wanted. The Consumers' League convinced DeFord and Whitman to push to reopen the case for more review of the constitutional issues. The court agreed. The New York league furnished more extensive information to DeFord from the Factory Investigating Commission and research for a brief that the National Consumers' League was developing for the case, discussed below. The court reviewed the evidence and reaffirmed that Schweinler was guilty. But this time the judges declared the law constitutional.[13]

Josephine Goldmark, who by this time had become the most prominent public defender of the law, celebrated it as a victory. Charles Schweinler appealed. Both sides understood this would be a high-profile test case that would make judicial history.

DOCUMENTING THE CASE AGAINST NIGHT WORK

As the Schweinler case advanced to the state supreme court's appellate division, Brandeis and Goldmark were finishing the latest, and longest, version of the briefs they had developed since *Muller v. Oregon* in 1908.[14] It would be submitted as an amicus curiae ("friend of the court") brief in support of the one DeFord was preparing and also later to the court of appeals. The Brandeis/Goldmark brief in the 1908 *Muller* case had been 112 pages long. The one they prepared for *Schweinler* was 529 pages. Much of it was devoted to the harmful effect of factory work on women, in line with the Brandeis/Goldmark briefs stretching back to *Muller*. But this new brief was different in two ways.

Over two hundred pages were devoted to the dangers of night work for women. It cited and quoted from dozens of studies and reports from the US, including Factory Investigating Commission information, and from European nations. There were "anatomical and physical differences" between men and women, but in addition women were weaker than men in "muscular strength and in nervous energy." Night work took a toll, and sleeping during the day was less refreshing and did not compensate. Night work, "involving loss of sleep and sunlight, has been found disastrous to the health of women. . . . All the dangers to health involved in industrial work—continuous standing or continuous sitting, speed, monotony, and the like—are intensified in night work." Night work in factories is "disastrous upon the female functions and childbirth," increasing infant mortality. Moreover, "night work inevitably destroys all family life. Women who work at night and try to make up sleep by day must inevitably neglect domestic duties and lose the benefits of family life."[15]

The second distinct feature, specifically included because the defendant was a printing company, was a section on the bookbinding trade. It consisted of long quotations from Mary van Kleeck's recent book, *Women in the Bookbinding Trade.* The work might look easy, but it was hard and demanding, consisting of standing, lifting, and operating heavy machinery. Many women were kept on the job from morning until after midnight during peak production periods, despite the statutory limit on working hours. Insufficient lighting, noise, and poor ventilation constituted additional threats. Women returning home after work faced threats on the streets.[16]

APPEALING FOR PUBLIC SUPPORT

Both sides in the *Schweinler* case appealed to public sentiment while the case was under consideration by the appellate division and the court of appeals. They hoped to sway the judges who would decide the case.

Josephine Goldmark wrote a long letter to the editor of the *New York Times.*[17] She cited the FIC's evidence and recommendation for the law. In some trades, including printing and laundries, it was common practice to require women to work all day and then in the evening as late as midnight to meet peak production timetables. "The commission recognized that the only way to control such excessive overtime is to set a definite closing hour after which all night work [by women] is prohibited."

Goldmark and her allies had deliberately selected a married woman as the object of their test case. She cited the FIC's assertion that married women who worked in factories at night were too exhausted to care for their children and carry out housekeeping. The commission had addressed the objection that women themselves did not want to be excluded from night factory work. She quoted from the FIC report: "Ignorant women can scarcely be expected to realize the dangers, not only to their own health, but to the next generation from such inhuman usage." This was not a "new or visionary proposal," she went on. New York was aligning with the laws of several other enlightened states and European nations.

Goldmark repeated a familiar theme about the drain of night work on women: "physicians and scientists who have studied the physiological effects of night work" show that "women who work at night have neither the privacy nor quiet to make up adequate sleep by day. For them, the loss of night sleep is uncompensated."

Alfred Ommen responded a couple of days later with a letter of his own.[18] He had interviewed scores of women who worked in factories at night, he said, "and I have yet to find one who does not want to work at night." Most are "healthy, earnest women" who need the work to support themselves and their families. They "wish to earn their living and provide for others in their own way." The Factory Investigating Commission did not find a single woman who worked at night who wanted to ban the practice.

"All this agitation is caused by paid social workers who have not a dollar invested in any business and whose income is secure whether the law is constitutional or unconstitutional," Ommen explained.

The Brandeis/Goldmark brief, though "as large as a telephone directory," really proved nothing beyond the fact that it can be injurious for anyone, man or woman, to work, day or night. Where would state overreach stop? If the state could prohibit night work and the courts approved, it could go on to other, even more extreme measures, such as banning work during the warm months of July and August. The court needed to call a halt now, Ommen insisted.

APPELLATE DIVISION: THE NIGHT-WORK BAN IS JUSTIFIED

The appellate division rendered its opinion on July 10, 1914. It reversed the trial court and held that the ban was constitutional. Presiding justice George L. Ingraham wrote the majority opinion. Three of his colleagues agreed; one dissented.[19]

Ingraham reviewed the law and the *Williams* decision. Since that decision was rendered, however, there had been "considerable investigation and discussion" leading to support for laws "conserving both the morals and physical condition of women." New York had lots of laws protecting women. Justice Ingraham contended that their well-being had "a direct bearing upon the welfare of the State and of future generations."

The amicus brief from Brandeis and Goldmark showed "the necessity of healthful rest."[20]

The Factory Investigating Commission report was "startling both in regard to the effect on the physical well-being of the night-workers and the moral effect upon the women who are employed in factories at night."[21] These conditions were not known to the judges who had rendered the *Williams* decision in 1907. Now, the courts had the evidence they needed for a better-informed decision. In recent years, moreover, several other states had enacted laws prohibiting or regulating women's night work in factories. The US Supreme Court had approved them, particularly in *Muller v. Oregon*. Ingraham approvingly quoted that opinion at length.

Constitutions must be interpreted in the light of changing needs, the judge said. People have a right to contract for their labor, but the State has "the right to pass laws to protect the race."[22] The law was declared constitutional.

Justice John Clark issued a short dissent. He agreed with Justice Ingraham but thought the *Williams* precedent must stand until the court of appeals overturned it. Schweinler appealed to the court of appeals.

THE DEFENDANT'S CASE:
WOMEN HAVE A RIGHT TO WORK IN FACTORIES AT NIGHT

Alfred Ommen prepared the appellant's spirited case.[23] The law was discriminatory; men could work nights in factories, but women could not. The 1907 *Williams* decision, quoted at length by Ommen, should have settled the issue. The law under consideration was essentially the same as what the court had invalidated in *Williams* but in "the new dress" of claiming to protect female health and morals. Since the *Williams* decision, though, "the demagogue has been in the land" and "the paid social worker" has held sway. The Factory Investigating Commission did not even consult women workers and pushed a great array of "so-called social welfare legislation" through the legislature. Ommen quoted a carefully selected excerpt from New York's Republican US senator Elihu Root's speech before the American Bar Association in 1914. Thousands of regulatory laws were being passed by state legislatures each year, the senator lamented, in disregard of "the practical knowledge of the people, who will be most affected by them."[24] The Supreme Court had approved a law regulating women's working hours, not one banning night hours, in *Muller v. Oregon*. But it has also struck down other state labor laws, a precedent the court of appeals should follow here.

The Brandeis/Goldmark brief was flawed, Ommen insisted. The evidence had been selected and organized to buttress a preconceived position. It mostly covered conditions elsewhere in the nation and in Europe, not New York. It was outdated. Working conditions had improved in the past few years. He quoted a 1914 magazine article by Ida Tarbell, a leading progressive muckraker who had exposed bad working conditions but now was narrating about improvements. May Cashel had testified to the pleasant conditions at Schweinler Press. She did not want to lose her job. It was ridiculous to claim that children's welfare depended on whether mothers worked at night. Some light factory work "is naturally women's work and they are best fitted for it." If the law stands, factory owners will replace women with men and "hundreds of women will be driven on the streets." Women workers, "in a class by themselves," will become "economically worthless."[25]

The appellate division's mistaken opinion had been driven by "flimsy testimony" in the FIC's "half baked . . . valueless investigation," Ommen argued. The commission admitted that a major rationale was to make it easier for the state to enforce the statutory limit on women's maximum work hours. The sort of fine work May Cashel was doing was so light that women can "do it cleaner" than men. In fact, "it never was a man's work." The court should recognize that.[26]

Moving to a broader argument, Ommen denied that women should be regarded as wards of the state. Women as a group should not be regarded as "a plaything for legislatures." Women can take care of themselves. The state cannot "put woman on a pedestal [so] that every comfort and convenience and joy will be hers." Ommen asked, "Why not leave her alone to earn her living when she can [and] let her have her hopes and ambitions"? His long brief concluded with a short recapitulation of legal points about constitutional protections for liberty of contract and due process of law and court decisions that circumscribed state legislation.[27]

THE STATE'S CASE: NEW YORK MUST PROTECT WOMEN

The court of appeals considered the Brandeis/Goldmark brief as part of the record that came from the appellate division. District Attorney Charles Whitman's brief, drafted by assistant DA William A. DeFord, was less dramatic than Ommen's, clinging closely to the evidence. The brief began with several pages quoting the Factory Investigating Commission about the dangers to women's health from night work. The FIC had said that women who worked at night suffered from "lowered vitality, if not actual disease, such as loss of appetite, headache, anemia," and other ailments.[28] DeFord included a summary of the information on the bookbinding trade from Mary van Kleeck's 1913 book, which the FIC had incorporated into its report. The FIC had assembled the evidence, made the case, and drafted the bill. The legislature had carefully considered the report and passed the law. The record of thorough investigation and enactment of appropriate legislation was obvious and convincing, DeFord's brief argued.

The law was a proper exercise of the state's police power. He cited several state and US Supreme Court decisions, including *Muller v. Oregon*, supporting state labor regulations and setting forth the underlying idea that state requirements must change with the times and according to evidence of actual conditions.[29]

It was sufficient if a statute "may be reasonably said to promote or *tend to promote*, the health and morality of women, or to protect them from physical injuries and moral dangers, real or *anticipated*" (emphasis in original). If there is "a reasonable relation" between the night-work ban and the health and "moral being" of women, then the law must stand. In support of that connection, DeFord cited the Brandeis/Goldmark brief. That document demonstrated that "sleep is physiologically indispensable," "night sleep is the natural sleep," and night work injures women's health more than men's because of the "structural and functional differentiation between the sexes." It had the added benefit of strengthening enforcement of another law, the prohibition of women working in factories for more than ten hours in any day.[30]

DeFord then tried to dispose of the argument that the *Williams* decision should hold sway here. The law invalidated in that decision was vague as to purpose. The one under consideration now clearly states its purpose: to protect the health and morals of females by providing an adequate period of rest at night. Moreover, the Brandeis/Goldmark document presents a great deal of information to establish a "clearer and more reasonable relation" between prohibiting night work and women's welfare than the court had available when it decided *Williams* in 1907. In fact, the court would almost certainly have gone the other way in the *Williams* case if it had had such extensive evidence before it then. The FIC and the Brandeis/Goldmark brief provided a "scientific foundation for the proposition that night work injures the health and morals of women." The reasoning in the *Williams* decision "is erroneous today." The court should sustain the appellate division's decision and uphold the night-work ban.[31]

A FLOOD OF LEGAL BRIEFS

Schweinler's legal contentions and the state's case had been well developed and documented. Usually, that would have been the end of the documentation. This case was exceptional because of its importance. It generated additional legal briefs both in support and opposition to the law.

Charles Whitman was elected governor in November 1914. That left his position as New York County DA vacant, and he appointed one of his deputies, Charles Perkins, to the position. Once in office, Perkins quickly filed a brief in his own name, prepared, like Whitman's, by assistant DA William DeFord. It made essentially the same points as DeFord's earlier brief: the statute is a legitimate exercise of police power and does not violate the state or federal constitutions. The law should stand because it has "a *real or substantial relation* to their [women's] health and morals" (emphasis in original).[32]

State attorney general Egburt Woodbury filed a lengthy brief in support of the law. It went over the legal precedents and the FIC evidence in detail. It emphasized that "worldwide common knowledge of present years, and the results of scientific investigations available since the decision in the Williams case, maintain and prove that night work in factories tends seriously to the injury of the health and morals of women." Woodbury added his own take on the argument about women's health: it was "the right and duty of the State to protect the health of its children before conception or birth . . . by guarding the health of the prospective mother."[33]

The Factory Investigating Commission submitted its own, long amicus brief, signed by its chairman, state senator Robert F. Wagner, and two counsels to the commission. It summarized its investigations of women and night work and quoted extensively from its own reports as well as the Brandeis/Goldmark brief. The commission's recommendation, enacted into law by the legislature, "amplifies and authoritatively confirms all previous information and statistics gathered in the worldwide movement to protect working women from the dangers of night work." In the commission's hearings and meetings, the only objections to proscribing night work by women had come from the printing industry. That was no surprise; they were the worst offenders in employing women for very long hours and violating the legal ten-hours-per-day limit. The "increased strain resulting from monotonous work and speeding-up" in factories further stressed women. The claim in Ommen's brief that the law would deprive thousands of women of their livelihood was "reckless and misleading." Women would just get more opportunities to work during the day, when it was legally permissible. The law helped factory inspectors enforce hours limitations. The legislature, armed with facts from "an official investigation," had enacted a good law. [34]

The Association of Ice Cream Manufacturers submitted a short brief. It mostly followed the points in Ommen's brief for Schweinler: the Brandeis/Goldmark brief was outdated, the FIC investigation partial and selective, and *Lochner* and *Williams* were controlling precedents. This was just an unconstitutional labor law disguised as a protection of women's health and morals.[35]

As the court of appeals judges looked through their high pile of briefs, the one that stood out for its strident tone was another one from Alfred Ommen, responding to the attorney general, the New York County DA, and the FIC. The brief practically sizzled with indignation. It was a last-ditch effort to stem the tide of evidence supporting the law:[36]

This law was essentially the same as the one invalidated in *Williams* despite its pretense of guarding women's health and morals. May Cashel's work was not unhealthy. The FIC found what it set out to find and it was no surprise that the legislature passed the law it recommended since its chair was senate majority leader and its vice-chair was speaker of the assembly. The Democratic majority in the legislature was voted out in 1914, Ommen noted.[37]

"There is no public sentiment in favor of this law." Nothing in the FIC's report showed any public support. At the commission's hearing on the proposed bill, only a few people spoke in favor. The whole thing is the product of "outsiders who look upon it as a personal conquest" and do not care about "its sad effects."[38]

The FIC's investigation of night work in one upstate twine factory proved nothing. If the investigators had visited one hundred women in their homes on Fifth Avenue and asked about their medical histories, they would have found plenty of complaints about backaches, headaches, and other ailments. They were not the result of factory work.[39]

This is class legislation, Ommen insisted. If men can work in factories at night but women cannot, "you are restricting her right of contract and making her a ward of the State." He repeated the claim that upholding the law would cost thousands of women their jobs, particularly in the printing industry, which he called the third largest industry in the state.[40]

Ommen took a parting shot at the FIC's report, which infringed the constitutional guarantee of liberty of contract: "If such a report had been submitted to the people of this country one hundred years ago, when men and women valued their liberty and the right to work, there would have been a revolution."[41]

THE COURT OF APPEALS UPHOLDS THE LAW

By early 1915, the case had become famous. Commentators felt the court could go either way. It could cite long-standing conservative legal precedent to invalidate the law, or it could refer to the new evidence of the impact of night work to support it. The court delivered its opinion on March 26, 1915. Judge Frank H. Hiscock wrote the opinion, upholding the night-work prohibition. Four judges concurred. Chief Judge Willard Bartlett concurred in part. One judge abstained.[42]

Hiscock recalled years later that the court's decision had not been easy. "The wisdom of this statute was earnestly debated and disputed even by some who were the supposed beneficiaries of it," he recalled. "The Court, however, held that disregarding the question of wisdom, which was not for its decision," the legislature had before it enough information to hold that "such night work might be injurious" and therefore "the interest of public health and welfare" justified its passage.[43]

Hiscock's opinion reflected the court's careful judicial reasoning and apparent lack of enthusiasm. The central question was whether night work by women in factories is so injurious to their health that the legislature was justified in banning it. Protection of women's health is "a subject of special concern to the state." Woman is equal to man in "many spheres of activity," but "as regards bodily strength and endurance she is inferior and . . . her health in the field of physical labor must be specially guarded by the state." The US Supreme Court had recognized this in its *Muller v. Oregon* decision.[44]

The Factory Investigating Commission made a strong case. Its recommendations were "based upon and supported by quite an extensive investigation by the commission of actual factory conditions in this state where women performed night work, by many opinions of medical and other experts, and examination of other industrial investigations and legislation adopted in other jurisdictions in obedience we must assume to public opinion, forbidding such night work." The evidence was persuasive though not definitive. But the preponderance of evidence was enough, said the judge, citing several previous opinions that held that legislatures can act even when not everyone agrees on the issues or what should be done. "If the statute upon its face appears to be reasonable and just and appropriate" and "its natural consequences will be in the direction of betterment of public health and welfare," the state "for its protection and advantage" may enact it. Hiscock went on to explain that it is "the duty of the courts to pronounce it constitutional even though they should doubt its wisdom."[45]

The *Williams* decision was not really a deterrent because of the "evidence of the extent to which during the intervening years the opinion and belief have spread and strengthened that such night work is injurious to women." Several other states and European nations had demonstrated this through their own legislation protecting women. Moreover, the law is "based upon and sustained by an investigation by the legislature deliberately and carefully made through an agency of its own creation," the Factory Investigating Commission.[46]

The night-work prohibition was indeed sweeping, with no loopholes or exceptions, as some critics had noted. But that was the choice the legislature had made. The law certainly constituted a "forward step in protective regulation," but one "within the power possessed by the legislature." The court concluded that "the statute is constitutional as a police regulation in the interest of public health and general welfare of the people of the state."[47]

The law's proponents cheered the decision as a victory for women and for the right of legislatures to protect them. Schweinler appealed to the US Supreme Court, but the judges refused to hear his appeal. The *Schweinler* decision is often cited by historians as a triumph for Progressivism for its acknowledgment by the courts that legislatures have broad power to enact labor laws.

But was it good for women?

Alfred Ommen interpreted the decision not as a defeat for his client, Schweinler, but rather for women. "A little group of serious thinkers" and "uplifters" had misled the court to into rendering a decision that was actually a setback for women. "Woman's best friend is man," he explained. Men had "found her a ward of the State and emancipated her so that she had industrial and economic liberty" to work at night if she wished. The work women did in the printing industry was no more than "folding and inserting" and not at all harmful to their health. The *Schweinler* decision "has turned the hands of the clock back fifty years" and relegated women to second-class citizenship.[48]

The *Schweinler* case was an excellent example of courts struggling to balance people's individual rights with the state's power to regulate and protect them. Night-work laws remained controversial. According to the historian Nancy Woloch, "whatever reformers' rationales, night work bans marked a tipping point between protection and restriction, or rather a sharp slide into restriction. For several groups of women workers, night work bans clearly inflicted hardships."[49]

Few states followed New York in banning night work by women in factories. But several states aligned with New York in passing maximum-hours laws for women, and some enacted minimum-wage laws. Most historians have hailed such legislation as appropriate and beneficial. Others, though, contend that "Kelley and female protectionists had made a Faustian bargain. These laws rested on the idea that women were dependent, not only on men, but on the state."[50]

Women gained the right to vote in New York in 1917 and at the national level three years later. The definitions of what women wanted for themselves in the workplace and what the state determined they needed began to shift. By the 1920s, with the rise of the National Women's Party, there was a push for equality, including a proposed amendment to the Constitution guaranteeing women equal rights. That was not fully consistent with laws like the night ban law in New York that treated them separately. Gradually, restrictions on where and when women could work and minimum-wage laws designed to protect them gave way to laws that treated all workers equally.[51]

Chapter 11

WORKERS' COMPENSATION DENIED

Figure 11.1. Crystal Eastman investigated working conditions and industrial accidents. Her publications raised public awareness of the need for a program to support injured workers. Eastman helped lead the development of New York's first workers' compensation law. *Source:* Bain News Service. Library of Congress Prints & Photographs Collection.

Can the state require employers to compensate workers for on-the-job accidents? Common-law practice and judicial decisions in the early twentieth century said no. Progressives changed that with the enactment of the state's first employers' liability act in 1910. The court of appeals found the new law unconstitutional the next year.

WORKPLACE ACCIDENTS TAKE A TOLL

By the early twentieth century, much of New York's economy had shifted from agriculture and small shops and workshops to larger scale companies such as railroads; steel production; product manufacturing; and building, tunnel, subway, and bridge construction. The work could be dangerous. Modern industry relied on high-speed, fast-paced machinery that could injure or kill in an instant. Exposed gears, drive shafts, and belts in factories; shaky scaffolds on construction sites; and railroad derailments, collisions, brake failures, and boiler explosions all took their toll on workers. The New York Department of Labor in 1907 reported 14,298 workers "temporarily injured," 4,786 "seriously or permanently injured," and 344 killed.[1] The vast majority were men, who constituted the bulk of the industrial workforce.

A few companies adequately compensated workers for their injuries or their families in case of death. Some workmen belonged to voluntary "mutual benefit societies" into which they and their employers paid and from which small payments were made to workers involved in accidents. Workers usually found purchasing accident insurance prohibitively expensive. Most employers were self-insured or carried liability insurance. If injured workers were dissatisfied with reimbursement offered by employers or insurance companies, which often was limited, they could sue the employer for negligence or the insurance company in court. But that meant the expense of hiring a lawyer and the delay and uncertainty of a jury trial. It was an uphill battle to prove employer fault (for instance, demonstrating that the employer had not exercised "due care," to cite one of the common criteria used in the courts). Litigation often resulted in a small settlement or none at all.

New York and other states did not have employer liability or workers' compensation laws yet. A federal employers' liability law, enacted in 1908, covered interstate railroad workers only, and its effectiveness was limited because the injured worker had to prove that the railroad was at least partially negligent in causing the injury. Liability in New York and other states was mostly governed by common law, the body of unwritten law based on judicial decisions and legal precedents established by the courts, sometimes called judge-made law. Under that body of precedents, three doctrines usually blocked employee recovery in courts: (1) the "assumption of risk" rule (the worker knowingly and willingly assumed the risks associated with the work and therefore was not entitle to compensation if injured), (2) the "contributory negligence" rule (plaintiffs were barred from recovery if they were in any way negligent in causing the accident), and (3) the "fellow servant" rule (no liability attached to the employer if the injury could be shown to have been caused directly or indirectly by an employee's coworker).[2]

New York passed a factory act in 1886 to regulate working conditions for women and children and to enforce state safety requirements and later enacted other safety regulations for dangerous factory work. But enforcement was spotty—the state's factory-inspection force was small, inspectors were friendly and lenient with factory owners, regulations were rarely enforced, and fines were light. A 1902 law declared employers liable for injuries caused by defects in machinery, and a 1906 law pertaining to railroads narrowed the fellow-servant loophole to exclude incidents when superintendents' or supervisors' orders led to employee injuries. But decisions by state courts effectively abrogated most of their provisions. Neither law changed the system substantially. Business influence in the legislature stifled further reform for several years.[3]

Gradually, though, public demand grew for a better system. An enlightened, progressive state like New York should not turn a blind eye to the human consequences of industrial development. Labor unions grew in strength and wanted safer working conditions and compensation for injured members. Corporations were frustrated by the vagaries of jury trials for negligence; the companies usually won, but when they lost awards for injuries or death could be burdensome. New organizations, including the National Civic Federation (established 1900) and the American Association for Labor Legislation (1906), backed by influential and wealthy community leaders, encouraged scientific study of laborers' needs and uniform labor legislation in the states. Dealing with employers' liability became one of their top priorities.[4]

A study of industrial working conditions in the Pittsburgh region in 1907–8 dramatically highlighted the issue. Crystal Eastman, an extraordinarily talented attorney and Progressive activist, carried out the project. The study was funded by the Russell Sage Foundation in New York, which supported improving conditions for working-class people. Eastman's work graphically recorded the maiming and killing of dozens of workers (many in the railroad and steel industries) over a one-year period. Many of the accidents were not due to the workman's actions or to errors by others; they just were inherent in industrial production. She documented the suffering of the injured and the devastation to widows and children of men who were killed. Striking photographs showed maimed men and families left devastated by the loss of husbands and fathers. Recovery of compensation in courts was very rare; the amounts awarded low. Eastman made clear that the conditions she described existed not just in Pittsburgh but also in New York and elsewhere in the nation.[5]

There had to be a better way. The federal liability act was an inadequate model, and the states had not yet enacted such laws. Eastman cited what she regarded as the best model: the English Workmen's Compensation Act, enacted in 1897 and updated since then, under which companies paid for employees' injuries. Hers was a fresh recommendation of a proposal first advanced to the legislature by the Social Reform Club of New York back in 1898. The proposal died in the state legislature then, but a decade of experience had proven the English system workable. The book sparked broad public discussion of the issue and the need for better public policies to address it. Other studies buttressed Eastman's analysis.

A STATE COMMISSION RECOMMENDS A BOLD NEW DEPARTURE

Charles Evans Hughes, a progressive Republican elected governor in 1906, highlighted the problem of industrial accidents in his 1907 and 1908 addresses to the legislature. By that time, there was an emerging consensus that something needed to be done. Workers wanted to be insured against accidents, employers wanted a better system of dealing with accidents and avoiding the vagaries of litigation, and insurance companies favored building more predictability into the system.[6] Other challenges, including banking and insurance reform and public utility regulation, described in chapters 7 and 8, forced Hughes to postpone action on the liability issue until 1909. In that year, to gather more information about industrial accidents and build public support for action, he persuaded the legislature to appoint a commission to study the issue.

The governor and both houses of the legislature appointed members. One of the senate appointees was Senator J. Mayhew Wainwright from

Westchester County, a Hughes ally, who became chair. The governor appointed, among others, Henry Seager, a Columbia University professor and a leading advocate for industrial reform; John Mitchell, vice president of the American Federation of Labor; Crystal Eastman, who was serving as secretary of the American Association for Labor Legislation and finishing her Pittsburgh study; and business leaders. The energetic commission held hearings (which garnered media attention) and distributed questionnaires to several organizations, judges, and labor experts. Several of its members also spoke at association meetings. The New York State Labor Department assisted the work. It soon became apparent that the commission would recommend legislation shifting responsibility for workers' accident-related injuries or deaths to employers.[7]

Support from the legal community would be crucial for enacting legislation and sustaining it in the courts afterward. But many lawyers were skeptical about state intrusion into industry-labor relations. Others made a living from representing injured employees—or the companies where they worked—in accident-related lawsuits. The Wainwright Commission sent a questionnaire to the New York State Bar Association, which appointed a committee whose cautious report only summarized pros and cons of the existing system and did not recommend any action. The association invited Eastman and Wainwright to speak at its January 1910 meeting.[8]

Eastman gave a stellar address. Citing evidence from her Pittsburgh study and the Wainwright Commission's investigations, she argued that the burden of injuries fell heavily on workmen and their families, the widows and families of men killed on the job were often reduced to desperate financial straits, the fellow-servant and assumption-of-risk doctrines were unfair and outdated, and an employers' liability law would increase safety precautions on the job. A liability law undoubtedly would increase insurance rates, but New York industry could bear the cost since it was in a "flourishing condition," and other states could be expected to follow New York's lead in enacting similar laws.[9]

The assembled attorneys listened politely, applauded Eastman's speech, asked her a few questions, and voted to print and distribute five thousand copies of her talk. Chairman Wainwright followed with a short appeal asking the association's support for the concept of employers' liability and assistance in framing the bill. But the lawyers would go no further than passing a cautious resolution pledging to cooperate with the commission.[10]

The commission concluded its work and issued its report on March 19, 1910. There was no acknowledgment of its actual author. But its assembly of evidence, analysis, conclusions, and recommendations bears a strong resemblance to Crystal Eastman's *Work-Accidents and the Law*, which was published about the same time. It is reasonable to conclude that she was a principal author of the commission report. "[An] astounding number of workers" are injured each year, said the report. "There is general dissatisfaction with the present system of employers' liability," which is "intolerable."[11] Four objections to the status quo emerged during the commission's investigation:

1. That only a small proportion of the workmen injured by accidents of employment get substantial compensation, and therefore, as a rule, they and their dependents are forced to a lower standard of living and often become burdens upon the State through public and private charity.

2. That the system is wasteful, being costly to employers and the State, and of small benefit to victims of accidents.

3. That the system is slow in operation, involving of necessity great delay in the settlement of cases.

4. That the operation of the law breeds antagonism between employers and employees.

The report discussed each of these defects in detail. It presented an array of statistics on accidents. It described the frustrations of employees who had to resort to court after being injured on the job and the dissatisfactions of employers who had to defend themselves there. Looking for models, it found few in the United States but several in Europe. It endorsed the English 1897 workmen's compensation law as a model (just as Eastman had in her study). That law had largely negated the age-old assumption-of-risk, contributory negligence, and fellow-servant doctrines. It required employers to make payments for employee injuries and deaths. The law originally pertained only to hazardous occupations, but it worked so well, the commission's report explained, that it was broadened to include just about all industries in 1906. The commission recommended a bill that was largely modeled on the English law, modified for New York state. It would apply to hazardous callings only (just as the English law had at first), but for them the requirements would be compulsory. Other companies could opt into the system if they wished.[12]

Business organizations balked at the law's compulsory features, and labor groups complained the proposed schedule of benefits was too low. Some union leaders supported it, but others lacked confidence in a new state program or preferred as an alternative changing the current laws to make it easier to sue employers for negligence. The liability bill was debated and modified. No one seemed enthusiastic about the bill, but there was no organized opposition. Support grew during the spring. With Governor Hughes's strong endorsement, it passed the legislature in June.

A BOLD NEW STATE POLICY

The new law was formally entitled "An Act to Amend the Labor Law in Relation to Workmen's Compensation in Certain Dangerous Employments."[13] It was restricted to jobs that entailed "extraordinary risks to the life and limb," defined in eight categories:[14]

1. Erection or demolition of bridges or buildings requiring iron or steel frame work

2. Operation of elevators, elevating machines, and hoisting derricks

3. Work on scaffolds twenty or more feet above the ground

4. Work on "wires, cables, switchboards or apparatus charged with electric currents"

5. Work necessitating dangerous proximity to dynamite, gunpowder, and other explosives

6. Construction and repair on railroads and operation of railroads

7. Construction of tunnels and subways

8. "All work carried on under compressed air"

The employer was made responsible for accidents to employees other than those caused through willful disregard of safety rules, intoxication, and so on. The old common-law loopholes—the injured employee's assumption of risk, contributory negligence, and negligence of fellow employees—were no longer to be considered factors. The law set out a "scale of compensation" that an employer must pay: for a dependent widow or next of kin, twelve hundred times the workman's daily salary up to a three-thousand-dollar limit; if he leaves no dependents, up to one hundred dollars for "medical attendance" and funeral expenses; for "total or partial incapacity," 50 percent of salary (but no more than ten dollars per week) for the duration of the incapacity (but no longer than eight years).[15] If a worker accepted these amounts, he could not also sue the employer for negligence in court; conversely, if he sued, he would be barred from collecting under the law.

It was mandatory for the designated industries but optional for other companies. If they voluntarily joined, the scale of payments would be the same as for the designated industries.

The new law was a significant new departure for public policy. As a state Department of Labor bulletin noted, it was "vastly different" from previous laws because it was based on "the principle of compulsory compensation by employers of workmen accidently injured while in their employ. This act is all the more notable because it is the first state law in the country to apply this principle."[16]

Was this new law, a dramatic departure from the past, constitutional?

It overturned long-standing common-law precedent. It also seemed, to critics at least, out of sync with the US Constitution's Fourteenth Amendment, which declared that no person should be deprived of life, liberty, or property without due process of law. The state constitution had a similar provision. As noted in several previous chapters, conservative-minded judges had ruled that provision applied to corporations as well as individuals and used it to strike down regulatory legislation. The liability law might also contravene the state constitution's guarantee of the right to a jury trial.

The Wainwright commission had circulated questionnaires, not about a specific piece of legislation but instead about the operation of the present system and the general concept of making employers liable. As noted above, the state bar association had been noncommittal. Chief Judge Edgar Cullen, on behalf of the court of appeals, declined to comment on the grounds that the issue might come before his court at some point (which it did). Other judges emphasized that the current system was not working well, and several noted it burdened both companies and their employees but avoided specific recommendations.

One state supreme court justice, Cuthbert W. Pound, in Lockport, was more forthcoming. "The present law does not operate efficiently to do justice," he said. Employees were often injured as the result of unsafe working conditions or the carelessness of their fellow workers. The fellow-servant notion was "a rule of convenience merely, based on no conclusive reasoning," and it is "unfair to place the entire burden where it falls with the most crushing force," the injured worker. Trial by juries took too long and put too much burden on the courts. It ought to be easier for injured employees particularly in hazardous industries, where there are many accidents, to get compensation. More employers would need to carry substantial insurance to pay for the results of accidents, but that would mean the insurance companies would push them toward ensuring safer workplaces. Insurance costs would be passed on to the consumer in the form of higher product costs.[17] Pound's endorsement turned out to be significant because, as it turned out, the first challenge to the new law would arise from Buffalo, in his region, and he would get to write an opinion confirming the law.

The commission's counsel, Joseph W. Cotton, reviewed state and federal court decisions and in a detailed appendix to the report concluded the proposed law was well within the legislature's power. The report's text declared that its constitutionality was "clear beyond reasonable question."[18]

Governor Hughes signed the bill on June 25. In a public statement, he praised the bill but, surprisingly, equivocated about its constitutionality. That "should be left to the determination of the courts. In this way only can there be an authoritative determination with respect to the measures that are within the limits of legislative power and a suitable shaping, in light of judicial decisions, of the policy of the State with respect to compensation for industrial accidents."[19]

If the governor who had urged the legislature to pass the bill and just signed it was not sure that it was constitutional, then who could be? Hughes's passing the buck to the courts was something of a green light for litigation to challenge the law.

INJURED WORKER EARL IVES: THE LAW IS CONSTITUTIONAL

The law went into effect on September 1, 1910. Nine days later, on September 10, Earl Ives, a South Buffalo Railway Company switchman, standing on a freight car, signaled the engineer to take up slack in the line of cars. The engineer did just that, but in the process Ives fell, sprained an ankle, and was "otherwise bruised and injured" and thereby "totally disabled" for four weeks, in the words of his attorney, Buffalo attorney Thomas W. Burke.[20] The railroad refused to pay Ives's claim of forty dollars while he was recovering from the accident, contending that the liability law was unconstitutional.

The South Buffalo Railway was a short line, connecting mainline railroads running through Buffalo with the Lackawanna Steel Company and moving freight within that sprawling plant. It seems possible that the big railroads encouraged the South Buffalo to dig in on Ives's claim as a way of testing and possibly invalidating the new law before their own employees could proceed under it. George W. Smith, manager at Lackawanna Steel, was a member of the Wainwright Commission (appointed by the governor) and the only member to dissent from the report (the issue needed more study, he said). Lackawanna Steel and the South Buffalo Railway were separate companies, but it would be plausible to suggest that the railroad's challenge to the law may have been done with Smith's knowledge.

Ives went to court to collect his claim. The state supreme court in Erie County backed his claim and the constitutionality of the law. Justice Cuthbert W. Pound, who, as noted above, had responded to the 1909 questionnaire from the Wainwright Commission with a letter endorsing the concepts in the proposed legislation, wrote persuasively that the law was constitutional and rightly shifted responsibilities for injuries from the worker to the employer. "The common law imposed upon the employee entire responsibility for injuries arising out of the necessary risks or dangers of the employment," wrote the judge. "The statute before us merely shifts such liability upon the employer."[21] Pound cited the US Supreme Court's 1898 decision in *Holden v. Hardy* upholding a Utah law limiting miners' working hours. He referenced the dissenting opinions in the Supreme Court's 1905 *Lochner v. New York* decision, where the majority overturned a New York law regulating bakers' hours but a minority of judges supported it. He also referred to a number of other court decisions cited in the Wainwright Commission's report in support of its recommendations. The appellate division upheld Judge Pound's decision. The company then appealed to the court of appeals in what had become a highly publicized test case.

Ives's attorney, Thomas W. Burke, cited the Wainwright Commission report and Justice Pound's state supreme court opinion in support of the act. State and federal courts have held that railroads are liable for some injuries to passengers and bystanders, so they should also be responsible for employees' on-the-job injuries. Burke cited other decisions in favor of regulatory legislation. He denied the railroad's assertion that the Employers' Liability Act contravened operating authority granted by the legislature in the railroad's operating charter. The law is not a violation of the due-process clause of either the state or federal constitutions. In fact, "the whole question of the relationship between employer and employee in regard to injuries is within the regulation and power of the Legislature." He cited federal maritime law making ship owners liable for crew injuries at sea and US Supreme Court decisions approving state laws that weakened the fellow-servant rule.[22]

Long years of experience have shown that the current system puts too much burden on the employee; by this law, the legislature "has imposed upon the employer part of the risk of personal injury to the employee, without negligence of the employer, incident to the business." The constitutional right to a jury trial is not abrogated. An injured employee could still sue for negligence. "An action for compensation is not a personal injury action sounding in tort, but is an action for breach of an implied contract" requiring the employer to provide safe working conditions.[23]

LIABILITY LAW'S CHAMPIONS: THE LAW IS CONSTITUTIONAL

Neither the attorney general (New York's law office) nor the labor department (which administered the liability law) submitted a brief in the case. In those days, state agencies often did not weigh in on cases challenging the constitutionality of state laws. But the Wainwright Commission was still in operation (its focus had shifted to workplace accidents and unemployment), and it submitted a brief as "intervenor" through its counsel, Joseph Cotton.

The document went over the history of the commission's deliberations, the evidence it found, the conclusion it reached (the old system was "out of joint"), what it recommended, and the provisions of the law.[24] Cotton dealt with four constitutional questions:

1. *Constitutional guarantees against deprivation of liberty and property without due process.* The law has "a legitimate and proper end, beneficial to the State." It sweeps away the employee negligence and fellow-servant rules and rightly shifts the burden to the employer, but that is consistent

with the long-standing common-law assumption that "an employer must provide for his men a reasonably safe place to work and safe tools for work." Cotton continued that "it may please the appellant to say that it is not the employer's fault; nevertheless, it is his responsibility."[25] Other provisions of the labor law already impose responsibilities on employers. The liability law is in line with that of other enlightened nations. Courts have not ruled (yet) on the liability law per se, but they have sustained laws placing safety requirements on employers.

2. *Equal protection under the laws.* The law dealt only with specified dangerous trades, but that is perfectly within the powers of the legislature. The legislature has previously passed laws regulating hazardous work, including erection of buildings, operation of elevators, electric work, explosives, and construction of tunnels and subways. Cotton cited a number of laws in other states that were struck down by the courts only because they were not confined to dangerous trades.

3. *Right to a trial by jury.* Actually, "either party in an action under the New Act can have a jury trial as to all the issues of fact in the case."[26] But the legislature had determined that the basic question—the employer's underlying responsibility—is not appropriate for a jury

4. *Limits to the amount of recovery for damages resulting in death.* The constitution states that "the right of action now existing to recover damages for injuries resulting in death shall never be abrogated; and the amount recoverable shall not be subject to any statutory limitation." Cotton contended that constitutional guarantee remained intact for instances where there was clearly employer negligence. The new law "gave defendants an additional right of action without interfering with the old one."[27]

The National Civic Federation also submitted an amicus brief. The federation, "composed of employers and employed, capitalists, labor unions, non-union men, and professional men," had approved the legislation "with substantial unanimity." The legislature can change the common law, which formerly burdened employees, and can select the objects of regulation, such as dangerous trades. Supreme Court decisions have supported Congress's broad regulatory authority, and, by analogy, the court of appeals should do likewise for the state's authority in this case. This really is an "extension" of the common law, well within the legislature's authority to interpret and expand it. "It surely will not be contended that it is competent to legislate for the protection of property, and not for the protection of life and limb." Under the law, "the risk of the business is assumed by the employer to an extent limited by the statute." It really does not limit freedom of contract. It will cut down frivolous lawsuits by "ambulance chasers"—attorneys who encourage lawsuits after accidents in order that the lawyers may profit. The New York State Bar Association and the American Bar Association have both condemned this practice.[28]

Looking at precedent, the National Civic Federation brief cited *Lochner v. New York*. The court of appeals had been right in upholding a state law in that case, the brief implied. The US Supreme Court overturned the court of appeals' decision in 1905, but, the brief noted, there were three dissents (agreeing with the New York court), and the four judges in the majority have now left the court. In any case, *Lochner* applied only to "the actual facts of that particular litigation," the hours of bakers. The principle has been established that "individual freedom of contract must yield to this larger consideration of the general welfare." Thus, they argued, the court should validate the liability law.[29]

SOUTH BUFFALO RAILWAY: THE LAW IS UNCONSTITUTIONAL

The South Buffalo Railway Company hired a team of three stellar attorneys. Louis Marshall, a distinguished constitutional lawyer, had already argued dozens of cases before the court of appeals. Charles Sears would later serve on the state supreme court, appellate division, and court of appeals. Louis Babcock was an accomplished litigator. They assembled a 137-page brief, which is a masterpiece of arguments against the liability law and against state regulation generally.

The brief began by suggesting that Ives was responsible for his own injury. He had signaled the engineer to move the train but then had been negligent "in failing to take precautions to prevent his [own] fall."[30] It then turned to condemning the law:

- *The law is based on the English Workmen's Compensation Act, but English courts have limited its application there.* The law "is borrowed almost literally" from the 1897 English Workmen's Compensation Act. The brief went into cases in English courts where judges had limited employers' liability where employee contributory negligence or willful misconduct had been a factor in accidents. If New York adopted the English law, then it should follow the English courts in restricting it, the reasoning in the brief went. Later, though, the brief circled back to the issue of foreign laws with a new twist: what works in Europe won't necessarily work in our country.[31]

- *The law is the entering wedge for broader coverage.* The Wainwright Commission and the law itself do not provide the criteria for "dangerous" trades. The brief quoted from speeches by Wainwright Commission members Crystal Eastman, Henry Seager, and John Mitchell at a 1910 national conference in Chicago on employers' liability policy. All three, in unguarded comments, indicated that the law was limited to "dangerous trades" mainly to get it passed by the legislature. Eastman said the limitation was "*a purely utilitarian opportunist reason. . . . We are quite frank in saying that we thought we could get this bill passed if we did not make it hit the manufacturer to begin with. We intend that it shall cover him in time, and just as soon as we can make it cover him*" (emphasis in original).[32]

- *The law does not increase workplace safety and in fact could make work more dangerous.* The law does not impose safety obligations on the employer, an act that might be construed as a reasonable exercise of the state's police power. In fact, "by encouraging, as it does, the relaxation of the obligation of care heretofore imposed on the workman, [it] will inevitably increase accidents." The employer could be entirely innocent and faultless, but the law "imposes on him the burden of his workman's negligence."[33]

- *It is "within the boundaries of socialism" and sets a dangerous precedent.* Not only does it "arbitrarily declare that the innocent employer shall compensate his guilty workman for the consequences" for his actions, it also "directs the amount of money which shall be taken out of the pockets of the employer and placed into those of the workman or his dependents" when an accident occurs. "A new era is ushered in by this legislation, potent with mischief, destructive of all ideas of liberty and property heretofore prevailing in this country; an era where majorities, unless restrained by the mandate of the Constitution, and by the independence of the judiciary, will be apt to resort to measures that are nothing short of confiscatory." The brief cited several court of appeals and US Supreme Court decisions protecting individual liberty against restrictive legislation.[34]

- *It cannot be justified under the state's police power.* Here the brief cited multiple court of appeals decisions curtailing the state's power, including *In the Matter of Jacobs* (1885), negating a law forbidding manufacture of tobacco products in tenements; *Wright v. Hart* (1905), striking down a law regulating sale of bulk goods; and *People v. Williams* (1907), invalidating a law restricting the hours of women's work. It also cited several US Supreme Court decisions, including one of conservatives' all-time favorites, *Lochner v. New York* (1905), declaring a New York law regulating bakers' hours unconstitutional. Many of these laws were "less subversive of the fundamental rights of citizens" than the liability law under consideration, which "takes the money of one person and gives it to another simply because the latter needs it." Approving the law would signal "the abandonment of the democratic, competitive individualistic system under which the country has thus far prospered."[35]

- *Justice Pound's state supreme court decision is mistaken.* In his decision approving the law, Pound cited cases that are not controlling or that actually back the railroad's case. For instance, Pound cited a US Supreme Court judge's opinion in a case involving a shipowner's liability for a seaman's injury, but much of the decision was "obiter"—a legal term meaning a judge's incidental expression of opinion, not essential to the decision and not establishing precedent. In other decisions, the same federal judge actually limited shipowners' liability. Pound cited another Supreme Court decision upholding a state's police power to hold railroads responsible for injuries to passengers. But, the trio of South Buffalo Railroad attorneys claimed, the state could impose that obligation because a railroad was a chartered "public service corporation" with safety responsibilities spelled out under its state charter. Pound cited Supreme Court opinions upholding states' power to protect workers' health and safety, but, said the railroad's brief, they were off point because the liability act does not actually protect workers.[36]

- *The act violates the US Constitution's guarantee of equal protection of the laws.* The law advances no justification or criteria for singling out the eight categories of "dangerous" trades. It omits some obviously risky ones such as mining.[37]

- *It violates the constitutional guarantee to trial by jury.* Under the law, the worker may go to court if he chooses (but thereby forfeits the right to collect under the liability law), but the employer has no comparable right to go to court.[38]

COURT'S RULING:
THE LAW IS "PLAINLY REVOLUTIONARY" AND UNCONSTITUTIONAL

The court of appeals ended the suspense by striking down the law in a unanimous decision on March 24, 1911, *Ives v. South Buffalo Railway Co.*[39] The opinion was written by Judge William Werner, at that time the court's most prominent advocate of limiting government regulation. The decision was ambiguous, the tone almost apologetic. The judge acknowledged the need for the law and the legislature's right to change common-law precedents. But he felt obligated to rule that the law foundered when it was measured against constitutional due-process protections.

THE LAW IS REVOLUTIONARY

"The statute, judged by our common-law standards, is plainly revolutionary," said the judge. It reverses the common-law assumptions and provides that "the employer is responsible to the employee for every accident in the course of the employment," even where the employer is not at fault. "The radical character of this legislation is at once revealed by contrasting it with the rule of the common law, under which the employer is liable for injuries to his employee only when the employer is guilty of some act or acts of negligence which caused the occurrence out of which the injuries arise, and then only when the employee is shown to be free from any negligence which contributes to the occurrence."[40]

THE LAW IS THE RESULT OF CAREFUL, DETAILED STUDY AND ADDRESSES A RECOGNIZED SOCIAL NEED

Werner summarized and quoted from the Wainwright Commission at length, noting its thorough investigation and documentation with "a most voluminous array of statistical tables, extracts from the works of philosophical writers and the industrial laws of many countries, all of which are designed to show that our own system of dealing with industrial accidents is economically, morally and legally unsound." He summarized the commission's rationale for the law. Werner acknowledged that public opinion supported the commission's recommendations.[41]

BUT UNDER OUR CONSTITUTIONAL SYSTEM, MASSIVE EVIDENCE AND PUBLIC OPINION ARE NOT ENOUGH

Having praised the commission, Judge Werner turned to its limitations. "Under our form of government, however, courts must regard all economic, philosophical and moral theories, attractive and desirable though they may be, as subordinate to the primary question whether they can be moulded into statutes without infringing upon the letter or spirit of our written constitutions," said Werner. The commission had endorsed the English liability law passed by Parliament, but here in the United States the constitution, not the legislature, holds sway, the judge noted. "In our country the Federal and State Constitutions are the charters which demark the extent and the limitations of legislative power; and while it is true that the rigidity of a written constitution may at times prove to be a hindrance to the march of progress, yet more often its stability protects the people against the frequent and violent fluctuations of that which, for want of a better name, we call public opinion."[42]

SOME PROVISIONS OF THE LAW ARE CLEARLY WITHIN LEGISLATIVE AUTHORITY

Werner reversed emphasis again, explaining that "we desire to present no purely technical or hypercritical obstacles to any plan for the beneficent reformation of a branch of our jurisprudence in which, it may be conceded, reform is a consummation devoutly to be wished. In this spirit we have called attention to those features of the new statute which might be upheld as consonant with legislative authority under our constitutional limitations."[43]

The fellow-servant and contributory negligence doctrines are "subjects clearly and fully within the scope of legislative power" and "may be regulated or even abolished." The fellow-servant rule was essentially an invention of the courts anyway, a rule "of judicial origin engrafted upon the common law for the protection of the master against the consequences of negligence in which he has no part." It made sense in an era of "simple industrial conditions." But "by degrees it was extended until it became evident that under the enormous expansion and infinite complexity of our modern industrial conditions the rule gave opportunity, in many instances, for harsh and technical defenses." It has already been curtailed by provisions of the labor law and court decisions.[44]

The doctrine of contributory negligence holds that "one who is himself to blame for his injuries should not be permitted to entail the consequences upon another who has not been negligent at all, or whose negligence would not have caused the injury if the one injured had been free from fault." It is a sound doctrine, though inconsistently applied in practice, and, the judge acknowledged reluctantly, the legislature has the right to negate it. Assumption of risk had already been restricted by labor-law provisions and court decisions, so the new compensation law's abolition of it just extended that trend. The legislature also has the right to restrict the law to selected categories of dangerous work: "all of the occupations enumerated in the statute are more or less inherently dangerous to a degree which justifies such legislative regulation as is properly within the scope of the police power."[45]

Werner then turned again from the positive to what he called three "fatal objections." Much of the rest of the opinion seemed to undercut what he had said earlier about the legislature's authority.

FATAL OBJECTION #1: VIOLATION OF DUE PROCESS

The law violates the state and federal constitutions' guarantees against deprivation of life, liberty, or property without due process of law. That was a familiar blow to regulatory legislation, as previous chapters have discussed. Werner illustrated it with carefully selected previous court of appeals decisions. But he offered his own, unusually sweeping, definition of those rights: "every man's right to life, liberty and property is to be disposed of in accordance with those ancient and fundamental principles which were in existence when our Constitutions were adopted. . . . One of the inalienable rights of every citizen is to hold and enjoy his property until it is taken from him by due process of law."

Shifting liability responsibility to the employer, forcing him to automatically pay for employees' injuries or process, "is a liability unknown to the common law and we think it plainly constitutes a deprivation of liberty and property under the Federal and State Constitutions." The Wainwright Commission set forth "cogent sociological and economic reasons" for this new policy, and Werner acknowledged "the strength of this appeal to a recognized and widely prevalent sentiment." But it takes more than "commendable impulses of benevolence or charity" and popular support to justify a law like this one. "This power must be exercised within the constitutional limitations which prescribe the law of the land." The fundamental right to due process "can be changed by the people [through amending the Constitution] but not by legislatures."[46]

FATAL OBJECTION #2: THE SLIPPERY SLOPE

Werner's next point, another one common in opposing new regulations in those days, was that the law, if sustained, could function as the leading edge of more intrusive legislation to come. "If such economic and sociologic arguments as are here advanced in support of this statute can be allowed to subvert the fundamental idea of property, then there is no private right entirely safe, because there is no limitation upon the absolute discretion of legislatures, and the guarantees of the Constitution are a mere waste of words." For instance, "if the legislature can say to an employer, 'you must compensate your employee for an injury not caused by you or by your fault,' why can it not go further and say to the man of wealth, 'you have more property than you need and your neighbor is so poor that he can barely subsist; in the interest of natural justice you must divide with your neighbor so that he and his dependents shall not become a charge upon the State?'" Why not impose on employers "a special tax for the support of hospitals and other charitable institutions, upon the theory that they are devoted largely to the alleviation of ills primarily due to his business. In its final and simple analysis that is taking the property of A and giving it to B, and that cannot be done under our Constitutions." Werner cited several court opinions reining in legislative power.[47]

FATAL OBJECTION #3: THE LAW EXCEEDS THE STATE'S POLICE POWER

Werner denied the law could be justified as an exercise of the state's inherent "police power." That term, which has emerged in several of the previous cases in the book, lacked a precise definition. Werner offered his own: "it embraces the whole system by which the state seeks to preserve the public order, to prevent offenses against the law, to insure to citizens in their intercourse with each other the enjoyment of their own so far as is reasonably consistent with a like enjoyment of rights by others." But he also offered his own limiting criteria:

> Its operation tends in some degree to prevent some offense or evil, or to preserve public health, morals, safety and welfare. If it discloses no such purpose, but is clearly calculated to invade the liberty and property of private citizens, it is plainly the duty of the courts to declare it invalid, for legislative assumption of the right to direct the channel into which the private energies of the citizen may flow, or legislative attempt to abridge or hamper the right of the citizen to pursue, unmolested and without unreasonable regulation, any lawful calling or avocation which he may choose, has always been condemned under our form of government.

This liability law fails the test, he said. It applies to dangerous industries, as the commission emphasized, but it "does nothing to conserve the health, safety or morals of the employees." It does not force the employer to improve workplace safety. The ease with which the commission had "brushed aside" constitutional limitations was "startling." The law "does not stop at reversing the common law; it attempts to reverse the very provisions of the Constitution," which are beyond the reach of the legislature. The judge offered a long list of examples of New York and federal court decisions invalidating regulatory legislation. He cited some that approved but interpreted these as applying only or mainly to the specific laws at issue rather than establishing broader principles.[48]

Judge Werner concluded by noting "the absence of any sound legal theory upon which this legislation can be sustained." He stated, "The liability sought to be imposed upon the employers enumerated in the statute before us is a taking of property without due process of law, and the statute is therefore void."[49]

Chief Judge Edgar Cullen weighed in with a concurring opinion, which Judge Willard Bartlett endorsed. Employers must be held accountable and pay for accidents only when they are "in some respect at fault." Endorsing the law would set a bad precedent. "It might as well be argued in support of a law requiring a man to pay his neighbor's debts." The chief judge briefly suggested that such a law might apply to companies incorporated *after* the law passed; it might then be considered a condition of their incorporation. But he closed with an assault on the notion of employers' liability:

> Individual citizens, following the ordinary vocations of life, asking no favors of the government, whether a corporate or other franchise, but only the protection of life and property, which every government owes to its citizens, and guilty of no fault, cannot be compelled to contribute to the indemnity of other citizens who, by misfortune or the fault of themselves or others, have suffered injuries, except by the exercise of the power of taxation imposed on all, at least all of the same class, for the maintenance of public charity.[50]

New York's breakthrough workers' compensation was gone by court action. The court's decision was "nothing less than a public misfortune," said a *New York Times* editorial. The court's "admirable tone" expressed support for the law's objectives, but "there does not seem to be any escape" from the court's invalidating it as a violation of due process.[51]

But the story was not over by any means. By coincidence, the day after the court's *Ives* decision, March 25, a fire at the Triangle Shirtwaist Factory in New York City claimed 146 lives, many of them young women. With the law invalidated, families of the deceased could not collect the death benefits the law had prescribed. The tragedy intensified loud public criticism of the court's decision. What followed was another investigatory commission, a battery of factory safety legislation, and a determination to reenact employers' liability, this time with the sanction of a constitutional amendment. That was accomplished in 1913, as discussed in the next chapter, giving New York its permanent workers' compensation system.

Chapter 12

WORKERS' COMPENSATION AFFIRMED

Figure 12.1. Martin H. Glynn, New York governor from 1913–14, secured the passage of the state's second workers' compensation law, which was sustained by the courts. *Source:* Bain News Service. Library of Congress Prints & Photographs Collection.

In 1911, the New York Court of Appeals decided that the state's workers' compensation law, passed in 1910, was unconstitutional. Proponents worked to enact an amendment to the state constitution and then pass a new law to authorize the program. Railroads challenged the new law in court. The court of appeals and the US Supreme Court both validated the law.

CHANGING THE STATE CONSTITUTION TO SUPPORT REFORM

A law to require employers to pay compensation for industrial accidents suffered by their workers passed the legislature in 1910, only to be overturned as unconstitutional by the court of appeals a year later, in *Ives v. South Buffalo Railway Co.* in March 1911, as related in the previous chapter.[1]

That left New York without a public policy or program for dealing with workers injured on the job. There were a number of industrial safety provisions on the statute books, and the state Department of Labor stepped up its enforcement work. Still, that department reported that there were 25,390 injuries in factories, including 353 fatal ones, for the period from October 1, 1909, to September 30, 1910.[2] The ramshackle system of liability insurance and litigation described in chapter 11, which made it very difficult for injured workers to be reimbursed for their injuries, was a continuing burden. There had to be a better way. Workers' compensation advocates saw *Ives* as a temporary setback, not a defeat.[3] The decision was widely denounced as obstructionist. Former president Theodore Roosevelt, plotting a return to the presidency, which he had occupied 1901–9, led critics in condemning the decision. He called for curtailing state courts' powers by enabling voters to recall judicial decisions where courts had declared laws unconstitutional and determine their constitutionality by popular vote. That radical proposal went nowhere, but the negative reaction to the *Ives* decision did encourage advocates to try again with a new law that would stand the constitutional test.

The commission, which had been established by the legislature back in 1909 under state senator J. Mayhew Wainwright to study employers' liability and which had written the 1910 law, was still operating, studying industrial accidents and other labor issues. The commission reviewed the court of appeals' decision, noting that the judges expressed agreement with the goals of workers' compensation but could not approve it because it was not authorized by the state and federal constitutions. The commission recommended a state constitutional amendment to take care of the court's objections there. Of course, that would leave the US Constitution unaffected, but the commission felt it would give the court of appeals confidence to support a new law.[4] The New York State Bar Association endorsed that strategy. Amending the constitution would be an important first step forward. The bar association could endorse that initial step and reserve judgment on whatever actual legislative proposals might emerge. Labor leaders who had been lukewarm about the first employers' liability law changed their views and advocated a replacement.

Amending the state constitution required approval by the legislature over two yearly sessions and then approval by the voters at the polls. That process took over two years.

The interests of labor organizations, whose influence and leadership were growing, had to be reconciled with industry's views. Republicans under progressive governor Charles Evans Hughes had pushed through the 1910 law. A bribery scandal involving Republican legislative leaders that year had weakened the party's appeal, and their chief vote-getter, Hughes, resigned to accept a US Supreme Court position in the fall. After he left, Republicans, under the leadership of state chairman William Barnes, became more conservative and attuned to businesses' conservative views on limiting state government. Democrats triumphed in the fall elections. Their interests increasingly aligned with organized labor. Democrats favored a broad authorizing amendment, but Republicans wanted something more circumspect. Wrangling over the amendment's wording took until 1912. That legislative session and the next one approved the amendment.[5] It was overwhelmingly approved by the voters on November 4, 1913. What it authorized was sweeping and unprecedented.

"Nothing contained in this Constitution shall be construed to limit the power of the legislature to enact laws" in these areas:[6]

"for the protection of the lives, health, or safety of employees;"

- This clause, well beyond workers' compensation, was included as partial justification for other labor legislation, particularly what was being developed by the Factory Investigating Commission, discussed below.

"or for the payment, either by employers, or by employers and employees or otherwise, either directly or through a State or other system of insurance or otherwise, of compensation for injuries to employees or for death of employees resulting from such injuries without regard to fault as a cause thereof,"

- There are two key phrases here: (1) "State or other system," which opened the way for a state commission and system where employers paid in and the system paid out for injuries or deaths, and (2) "without regard to fault as a cause," which swept aside the old common-law barrier that held that an employee could be held responsible, and the employer blameless, if it could be shown that the employee had in some way contributed to their own accident.

"except where the injury is occasioned by the willful intention of the injured employee to bring about the injury or death of himself or of another, or where the injury results solely from the intoxication of the injured employee while on duty;"

- There is no compensation when the employee deliberately causes the accident or is drunk on the job.

"or for the adjustment, determination and settlement, with or without trial by jury, of issues which may arise under such legislation;"

- This vague clause left the door open to a possible jury trial, a nod to the state and federal constitutions' right to a trial by jury.

"or to provide that the right of such compensation, and the remedy therefor shall be exclusive of all other rights and remedies for injuries to employees or for death resulting from such injuries;"

- The law could provide that if an employee collected under the new system, they could not also pursue damages in court.

"or to provide that the amount of such compensation for death shall not exceed a fixed or determinable sum; provided that all moneys paid by an employer to his employees or their legal representatives, by reason of the enactment of any of the laws herein authorized, shall be held to be a proper charge in the cost of operating the business of the employer."

Workers' compensation, supported by new constitutional authority, would henceforth be a routine part of doing business in New York State.

POLITICS AND WORKERS' COMPENSATION

As the constitutional amendment was under development, the tide turned in favor of a new compensation system. The discussion shifted to more talk about *workmen's compensation* and less about *employers' liability*, a subtle shift of phrase toward accentuating what workers were rightfully entitled to and away from the notion of employers' blame. Labor unions demanded a system, administered by the state, where reimbursement for accidents would be more or less routine and predictable. Employers reexamined their positions as courts seemed increasingly likely to grant workers sizeable damages in liability suits for accidents and, partly as a result, the cost of accident liability insurance rose.

New York's 1910 law had been a pioneer among the states, but by 1913 twenty-one other states (in addition to the federal government) had adopted workers' compensation laws, which were mostly being sustained by the courts. Things were becoming so routine and settled that in 1914 the American Association for Labor Legislation, an industry-labor group that promoted labor reform and had supported New York's 1910 law, issued a publication on standards for workers' compensation laws based mostly on state practices. New York had been alone on the frontier of state compensation laws in 1910; now it could follow precedents and standards. A new proposal would seem less leading-edge and experimental and more like just going where the other states were going. That made it more palatable to skeptics and conservatives.[7]

Another powerful source of support occurred on March 25, 1911, the day after the *Ives* decision, when a tragic fire swept through the Triangle Shirtwaist Factory in New York City, killing 146 workers, many of whom were young women. Locked factory doors and inadequate fire escapes contributed to the toll. New York County district attorney Charles Whitman indicted the owners for manslaughter, but they were acquitted at trial. Three years later, they settled twenty-three civil suits against them by victims' families for seventy-five dollars each. It was a stark reminder of the need for more factory safety requirements and workers' compensation. New York City tightened its factory fire code and expanded inspections. The state legislature established a factory investigating commission, headed by senate president pro tempore Robert Wagner and assembly majority leader Alfred E. Smith, which inspected factories, held hearings, assembled thirteen reports, and called a good deal of media attention to factory working conditions. Over the next few years, the legislature passed a battery of factory safety legislation recommended by the commission, including requirements for fire alarms and sprinklers, improved access and egress, fireproofing of buildings, and better lighting and ventilation. The tragic fire and its aftermath had moved the state dramatically behind worker welfare and safety. Workers' compensation began to seem like just another, very desirable, part of state government's expanding pattern of protecting the state's working people.[8]

It took until December 1914 to get a new compensation law formulated and passed. Discussions among Democratic leaders, labor interests, and reform groups, such as the National Civic Federation, stalled over a number of issues. Should there be a state workers' compensation fund to supplement (or in a sense compete with) industrial self-insurance or private liability insurance? Which industries should be declared hazardous ones and covered by a new program? How should benefits for injuries and death from accidents be calculated?

In 1912, the Democrats dropped their lackadaisical governor John A. Dix, elected in 1910, in favor of New York congressman William Sulzer, a progressive ally of labor. Sulzer won handily. The state legislature, under the leadership of Democrats Robert Wagner in the senate and Al Smith in the assembly, was already building an energetic track record of formulating legislation in the wake of the Triangle fire, based on the Factory Investigating Commission's investigation.

Getting to a consensus on a compensation bill proved beyond difficult. The legislature passed a compromise compensation law in February 1913, only to have it vetoed by Governor Sulzer because, he said, organized labor did not support it. Sulzer had begun feuding with Democrats in the legislature over political patronage and other issues. He fought with Charles F. Murphy, head of Tammany Hall, the powerful New York City Democratic organization, accusing Murphy of political bossism. Assemblyman James Foley, Murphy's son-in-law, had introduced the compensation bill that Sulzer vetoed; that led to the accusation that the governor had ignored the bill's merits in order to take an indirect swipe at Murphy. The governor was a fighter, a self-proclaimed tribune of the people against political bosses and domineering businesses. Sulzer, though, had his own flaws and problems. In August, he was impeached by the assembly for not reporting all the funds received for his campaign and diverting some of those funds to personal use. He was tried, convicted, and removed from office in October.[9]

Lieutenant Governor Martin H. Glynn succeeded Sulzer. A former congressman and state comptroller, and also the publisher of the Albany *Times Union*, he was a modest but strong leader. He exerted a calming influence after the Sulzer impeachment drama. The new governor urged his fellow Democrats to come together and pass a workers' compensation bill and also a bill to expand the direct primary for nominating political candidates, another source of contention and indecision over several years. In the November elections (the same one where the constitutional amendment was approved), voters, weary of the Democrats wrangling among themselves and stalling on the compensation and direct primary issues, gave the Republicans a majority in the assembly. That would mean a divided legislature in 1914, making labor reform legislation much harder.

Glynn called a special session of the legislature in December 1913 and urged action. Put your differences aside, come together, act now or the opportunity will be gone, he counseled. A new workers' compensation bill came out of hurried sessions where organized labor's influence was particularly strong. The law passed in a rush on December 12 by a vote of thirty-five to zero in the senate and by unanimous vote under a rapid roll call in the assembly. The *New York Times* reported that it passed virtually without debate and that few lawmakers had adequate knowledge of just what was in the bill. But by then, politicians were eager to align behind workers' compensation or, at least, recognized it was politically risky to oppose it. The legislature also passed a direct-primary bill and other reform measures the governor had demanded and then adjourned. Governor Glynn signed the workers' compensation bill on December 16.[10]

A POWERFUL STATE PROGRAM

The new law tracked closely with the just-passed constitutional amendment. It created a powerful new commission that blended quasi legislative, executive, and judicial powers, another example of the administrative state, described in chapters 7 and 8, that was taking root in New York State during the Progressive Era. It set up a state fund that could pay people for their injuries, something radically different from anything New York had seen before.

The law had several features:[11]

1. *Broad application.* The previous liability law applied to only eight categories of dangerous occupations. The new one applied to forty-two categories of work, practically everything except agriculture, domestic labor, and public employment. For several categories, the wording was expansive, covering "operation, including construction and repair." Group 1 included a list of types of railroads, and, apparently to be on the safe side, group 2 covered "construction and operation of railways not included in Group 1." Group 10 covered longshore work, including the loading and unloading of cargoes, an important provision, as it turned out, because, as noted below, a constitutional test case would involve an accident incurred while unloading a vessel. Group 21 covered iron and steel manufacturing. Group 38 was "manufacture of men's or women's clothing, white wear, shirts, collars, corsets, hats, caps, fur or robes," a reminder of the lives lost in the 1911 Triangle fire.

2. *Compensation required.* All employers subject to the law were required to pay compensation for disability or death of their employees "resulting from an accidental personal injury sustained by the employee arising out of and in the course of his employment, without regard to fault" of either the employer or employee. The only exceptions were accidents due to the willful intention of an employee or intoxication; there was to be no compensation in those cases.

3. *Basis for compensation.* The 1910 law had specified rates for injuries and death from accidents. The new one made weekly wages the basis for compensation. Injuries were required to be reported within ten days to the commission. "Temporary partial disability" payments for injuries where there was no permanent damage were prorated according to salary for the period of the disability. Total permanent disability, defined in detail in the law, would give the employee two-thirds of their salary. Examples of "permanent partial disability" yielded certain payments—for example,

loss of a thumb, the equivalent of sixty weeks of salary; loss of the first finger, forty-six weeks; loss of a hand, 240 weeks; loss of a leg, 288 weeks. All claims had to be sent to the commission, which would review them, determine their validity (including requiring a medical examination if necessary) and the amount of compensation, and ensure that payment was made to the worker. "The commission shall have full power and authority to determine all questions in relation to the payment of claims for compensation under the provisions of this chapter," read one section, giving the commission great power.

4. *Death benefits.* The law provided for "reasonable funeral expenses, not exceeding $100." If there is "a surviving wife (or dependent husband)," the survivor got 30 percent of the salary. If a widow remarried, she got two years' worth of benefits, and then they stopped. There was also a schedule for payments for dependent children.

5. *"Security for compensation."* Employers could secure compensation for their employees in any of three ways: (1) furnishing proof to the commission of ability to pay (the commission could require deposit of securities to document that proof), (2) carrying insurance through an authorized stock corporation or mutual association, or (3) paying into a new workers' compensation fund established by the law and administered by the commission. This fund was a major and unprecedented provision of the law. Employers who elected either of the first two options were required to make payments through the commission. The amount required to be paid into the fund would be determined by the commission based on its assessment of how hazardous the work was in each of the forty-two categories. There was a powerful incentive to choose option 3, the new fund: paying into the fund meant that the fund would pay for injuries or deaths sustained by employees.

6. *A powerful new commission.* The new law would be administered by a five-person commission, appointed by the governor and confirmed by the senate. A 1914 amend-

ment required that no more than three members could be from the same party, ensuring a measure of bipartisanship. The commission administered the law, operated the state compensation fund, and reviewed and decided on all claims. It was authorized to establish regional offices, issue subpoenas, call witnesses, and investigate accidents if it chose. The state attorney general was empowered to enforce commission decisions and defend it in court, a feature that had been lacking in the first compensation law.

Governor Glynn's appointments to the commission included John Mitchell and J. Mayhew Wainwright, both veteran advocates who had served on the state commission that recommended the first workers' compensation law back in 1910. The Workmen's Compensation Commission got down to work in March 1914. Its first report noted that it needed to do "much pioneer work" to set up the compensation fund, establish rules and procedures, set up district offices, classify the hazard level of the employment categories covered by the fund, and review claims. New York's industrial landscape was huge—about two million workers in upwards of 180,000 industrial establishments, many of them "vast industries highly organized, using tremendous machines"—with an aggregate payroll of a billion dollars. But New York now had some models to follow. Ohio loaned the commission one of its compensation program administrators to help the New Yorkers get started, and the commission adopted some Massachusetts regulations with little change. The state compensation fund proved very popular due to lower costs than insurance competitors, employers relieved of liability, and claims settled quickly and fairly; 5,011 policies were in force by July 1, when the fund officially began. The first accident claims began in July, and soon the commissioners were swamped with them. Claims were processed expeditiously; payments began to flow. The commission documented "substantial accomplishment and notable progress" in its first report to the legislature.[12]

The commission made sure the press got information on its work of assisting the injured and bereft. One highly publicized award enabled a widow to pay the mortgage and thereby save the home where she had lived with her husband before his accidental death at Edison Illuminating Company.[13] Governor Glynn, campaigning for election to the governorship in his own right in the fall of 1914, touted the direct primary and workers' compensation as his major accomplishments. On September 23, during a campaign trip, he sat in on a commission meeting that awarded a widow with a child death benefits for her husband, who had died after falling through the hatchway of a cargo ship in New York Harbor. "Of all the things that I have even begun in public, the thing that I am proudest of is the Workmen's Compensation act, which gives some measure of recompense to our workmen who are injured while earning their daily bread," he told news reporters. This decision was a good example of the program's human face. "What would have become of that woman if she had not received that award?" the governor asked.[14]

Despite Governor Glynn's leadership in shepherding the workers' compensation and direct-primary bills through the legislature, voters were disillusioned with the Democrats over the Sulzer debacle and perceptions of "boss rule" by New York City's Democratic organization, Tammany Hall. Glynn was the state's first Catholic governor, and anti-Catholic prejudice was also a factor. His supporters' campaign slogan—"We Can Win with Martin H. Glynn!"—proved to be wishful thinking. Glynn was defeated by New York County district attorney Charles Whitman in 1914. Republicans retained control of the assembly and gained a majority in the senate.

Republicans considered repealing a number of progressive labor reforms but were headed off by the new governor. Charles Whitman was a conservative—his campaign slogan was "competency, efficiency, and economy"—but as New York County DA he had prosecuted the owners of the Triangle Factory for manslaughter. Whitman had lost that case and had concluded that industrial reform was an idea whose time had come. He discouraged his party's leaders from pushing repeal legislation and vetoed a number of bills that did reach his desk.[15]

Citing the need to streamline the state's labor programs, though, Whitman and Republican leaders consolidated the Labor Department with the Workmen's Compensation Commission under a new Industrial Commission. The Workmen's Compensation Commission was abolished, its functions transferred to a new bureau of the Industrial Commission. That commission was empowered to enact rules and regulations to carry out the labor law's sweeping safety, health, and hours provisions, including the new ones enacted as a result of the Factory Investigating Commission's work. But also, in deference to the Republicans' business supporters who railed against too much state interference, in certain circumstances the commission could "modify the law in order to avoid imposing unnecessary hardships upon certain industries."[16] The Industrial

Commission was another example of the emerging concept of the administrative state. As a study of state government a few years later noted, the commission was noteworthy because it "combined in one department all the functions of the state government so far as they affect industrial relations, labor standards and workmen's compensation. It was also noteworthy because of the wide powers given the Commission in the interpretation of the Labor Law through the making of rules and regulations." Creation of the commission was acknowledgment that "the fixing of employment standards by statute is too inflexible, and that it is best done on the basis of current investigation by experts which provides a ready means of amendment and variation as conditions change. The combination of the administration of labor and workmen's compensation laws makes possible the maximum degree of co-ordination of the two and the application of accident experience to preventive standards. The power conferred upon such a department is therefore very great."[17]

The Industrial Commission was chaired by labor leader John Mitchell, who had served on the Workmen's Compensation Commission. To reduce the state's administrative staff and costs and speed resolution of claims, the compensation law was amended to allow direct settlement of claims by the employer and employee and payments of compensation directly by the employer, instead of indirectly via the commission, and was refined in other ways. The state insurance fund stayed robust and was "an aggressive competitor" with insurance companies for business. The Industrial Commission stepped up enforcement of industrial safety regulations. It operated regional employment offices. It set up a new Industrial Council, chaired by the durable, ever-helpful J. Mayhew Wainwright, to promote industry-labor relations. The next year, 1916, the number of "hazardous" trades was expanded. The workers' compensation program had found a comfortable administrative home alongside other, supportive labor regulations.[18]

COURT OF APPEALS, 1915: THE WORKMEN'S COMPENSATION LAW IS "FUNDAMENTALLY FAIR" AND CONSTITUTIONAL

Workers' compensation had made it through New York's political turbulence in the governorship and legislature. It had gone from being an independent entity to being part of a larger agency, where some of its powers were curtailed but where there were compensatory benefits of compatibility with other labor functions.

Things were more or less on an even keel. But was the compensation law constitutional? That question, as always, fell to the quieter venues of the third branch of state government, the courts.

The 1913 state constitutional amendment' s wording—"Nothing contained in this Constitution shall be construed to limit the power of the legislature to enact laws" for workmen's compensation—seemed to supersede and override other provisions of the state constitution. But would the courts really consider it strong enough to overcome the court of appeals' reasoning in the 1911 *Ives* decision? That decision had cited long-standing constitutional provisions against infringing on personal liberty, taking property without due process of law, and blocking the right to a trial by jury. Even if the state constitution had been changed, the US Constitution had not. The outcome of a contest in the courts was by no means certain.

There were a number of appeals of commission decisions to the courts, mostly about interpretations of the law, during its first year. A test case that would determine its constitutionality soon made an appearance. Christen Jensen, a stevedore, died in an accident on August 5, 1914, while driving an electric truck unloading freight on a gangway between the steamship *El Oriente*, owned by the Southern Pacific Company, and a pier in New York City. His widow received a death benefit award from the workmen's compensation fund.

The company went to court, objecting to the award. It contended that the law was unconstitutional on two bases. One, it violated the US Constitution's clause that assigned all interstate commerce and admiralty issues to the federal government (the company's main business was interstate railroads, and its ships plied between New York and Galveston, Texas). Jensen's widow should have filed under the federal employers' liability law rather than the state law. Two, it contravened the Fourteenth Amendment's proscription of taking property without due process of law and the similar clause in the state constitution.

In the 1911 *Ives* case, the state attorney general had not defended the state. The 1913 law included a specific provision that the attorney general must represent the commission in litigation. Attorney General Egburt Woodbury defended the law for the state, emphasizing that the statute was well within the state's police powers, that the 1913 amendment to the state constitution sanctioned the new law, and that it did not violate the US Constitution. The state supreme court and appellate division affirmed the commission's constitutional validity and its decision in this case.

The company appealed to the court of appeals, which rendered a unanimous opinion validating the law on July 13, 1915, in *Matter of Jensen v. Southern Pacific Co.*[19]

The opinion was written by Judge Nathan Miller, a Republican who had a brief tenure on the court (1913–15) and went on to serve an equally brief term as governor (1921–23). Willard J. Bartlett, who replaced Edgar Cullen as chief judge in 1914, was more liberal on regulatory matters than Cullen. Other judges who had joined the court in the previous few years were also more open to supporting state regulations than their predecessors had been.

Judge William Werner, author of the 1911 opinion *Ives v. South Buffalo Railway Co.*, which had struck down the previous workmen's compensation law, had been defeated when he ran for chief judge against Bartlett in 1913, in part because the *Ives* decision was so unpopular. He was still on the court but is noted in the *Jensen* opinion as "not sitting" for this one, meaning he did not participate, but no explanation is given.

The court's opinion was extensive:

- *This is not interstate commerce.* The accident occurred while Jensen was unloading a ship anchored in a New York river via a gangway "connecting the vessel with the pier" in New York. That made it an intrastate issue, the judges reasoned. State law governs here in the absence of specific congressional legislation asserting federal authority. "The legislature evidently intended to regulate, as far as it had the power, all employments within the state of the kinds enumerated." The parent company is an interstate railroad company, but the 1908 federal employers' liability act does not apply because "as far as this case is concerned the appellant is a carrier by water" rather than interstate commerce within the meaning of the Interstate Commerce Commission act.[20]

- *This is not "taking property without due process of law."* The company relied heavily on the *Ives* decision. The amendment to the state constitution approved in 1913 "amply sustains the act" from the vantage point of that document, said the court. But what about the Fourteenth Amendment to the US Constitution? Not a deterrent either, said the court. The 1910 law that *Ives* struck down placed the burden on individual employers, whereas the 1913 law "protects both employer and employee, the former from wasteful suits and extravagant verdicts, the latter from the expense, uncertainties and delays of litigation in all cases and from the certainty of defeat if unable to establish a case of actionable negligence." The first act burdened individual employers, whereas "this act does in fact as well as in theory distribute the burden equitably over the industries affected. It allows compensation only for loss of earning power, but by the creation of a state insurance fund, or by the substitute methods provided, it insures the prompt receipt by the injured employee or his dependents of a certain sum undiminished by the expenses of litigation. The two acts are, therefore, so plainly dissimilar that the decision in the *Ives* case is not controlling in this." The judge cited recent US Supreme Court decisions sustaining a similar workmen's compensation law in Ohio and an Oklahoma legal requirement that banks pay into a fund to insure depositors against bank default; neither was a "taking" in the sense of the Fourteenth Amendment. New York's compensation law was not either.[21]

- *The law was well within the state's police power.* The situation before the 1910 law was wasteful due to uncertainty, the vagaries of litigation, and the fact that in most cases injured workmen wound up with little compensation. The new law was enlightened and practical: "This subject should be viewed in the light of modern conditions, not those under which the common-law doctrines were developed. With the change in industrial conditions, an opinion has gradually developed, which almost universally favors a more just and economical system of providing compensation for accidental injuries to employees as a substitute for wasteful and protracted damage suits, usually unjust in their results either to the employer or the employee, and sometimes to both."[22]

The 1913 law was a pragmatic compromise where "the state in the promotion of the general welfare [requires] both employer and employee to yield something toward the establishment of a principle and plan of compensation for their mutual protection and advantage." This is a good example of the application of the state's police power. "Its elasticity makes progress possible under a written constitution guaranteeing individual rights. The question is often one of degree. The act now before us seems to be fundamentally fair to both employer and employee."[23]

That was a strong endorsement of the constitutionality of the workmen's compensation law by a unanimous decision of the state's highest court.

The Southern Pacific appealed the *Jensen* decision to the US Supreme Court, which invalidated it on the grounds that the case actually was about interstate commerce and fell within federal maritime law. The ship was in navigable waters, its work part of interstate commerce, and the obligations of the Southern Pacific Company were governed by the rules of the federal maritime law. Jensen should have applied under the federal employers' liability law; the New York Workmen's Compensation Act was inapplicable. But the court did not question the constitutional validity of the workmen's compensation law itself. That left the court of appeals' pronouncement on the constitutionality of the law intact.[24]

US SUPREME COURT, 1917:
THE NEW YORK WORKMEN'S COMPENSATION LAW IS
"A JUST SETTLEMENT OF A DIFFICULT PROBLEM" AND CONSTITUTIONAL

Another case proceeded parallel to the *Jensen* case. On September 12, 1914, about a month after Christen Jensen's death, Jacob White, a watchman for the New York Central railroad, was killed while on duty guarding tools and materials assembled for use in building a new station and tracks. His widow, Sarah White, applied for and received payment from the workmen's compensation fund. The railroad went to court, claiming that White had been engaged in interstate commerce—the station and trackage would be part of the interstate rail network. Sarah White should have filed under the federal employers' liability act and was ineligible for an award under the New York compensation law—essentially the same point that the Southern Pacific made in *Jensen*. Moreover, the law was unconstitutional, a violation of the Fourteenth Amendment to the US Constitution. The New York Appellate Division of the Supreme Court, Third Department, ruled against the railroad. Guarding materials for construction of structures within New York was not interstate commerce, and the law was constitutional, said the court. The railroad appealed to the court of appeals, which affirmed the lower court's ruling without issuing an opinion.[25]

The railroad appealed to the US Supreme Court. The case was argued before the court on March 1, 1916, but for reasons not evident from the case materials was reargued on November 17 and finally decided on March 6, 1917, a couple of months before the high court ruled on *Jensen*. The high court was conservative in those days, fond of using the Fourteenth Amendment's "due process" and "liberty of contract" notions to upend state regulatory laws. But in this case the court unanimously confirmed the workmen's compensation law and the court of appeals' decision. Its opinion resonated with that court's 1915 *Jensen* decision and with the 1910 Wainwright Commission report, discussed in chapter 11, which had provided the justification for New York's first workers' compensation law.[26]

Justice Mahlon Pitney, writing for the court, began with asserting that the interstate commerce claim was "without basis in fact."[27] Guarding construction materials could not be stretched to encompass interstate commerce. Pitney reviewed the *Ives* decision (which had invalidated the state's original workmen's compensation law), the subsequent constitutional amendment, and the provisions of the current law. He summarized the points made for and against the law. He then turned to the constitutional issues:

- *State legislatures have the right to contravene the common law.* The traditional notion that an employer was not responsible if a fellow employee directly or indirectly contributed to the accident was "the product of . . . judicial conception." That rule, as well as the "assumption of risk" concept—employees knowingly assumed risks when they took jobs—and the "contributory negligence" rule—an employee was not entitled to payment if it could be demonstrated that his actions led to an accident—were "subject to change in the exercise of the sovereign authority of the state. . . . Subject to legislative change." Liability for death is "a modern statutory innovation." Pitney cited eleven Supreme Court decisions where the court had upheld state laws departing from common law rules guiding employers' liability for workers' accidents.[28]

- *The law is reasonable and just.* This is a modest law, said Justice Pitney. It "sets aside one body of rules only to establish another" and "is intended as a just settlement of a difficult problem." It is acceptable to ask employers "to contribute a reasonable amount, and according to a reasonable and definite scale" to a system that consistently provides compensation for disability or death on the job. It is reasonable to ask employees to exchange a system where they assume the entire risk of injury and where after an accident "a right to recover an amount [was] more or less speculative upon proving facts of negligence that were often difficult to prove" for one where they can be "sure of a definite and easily ascertained compensation." There was no evidence that the New York system was "arbitrary and unreasonable."[29]

- *It does not undermine freedom of contract.* "It is said [by the railroad's counsel], the statute strikes at the fundamentals of constitutional freedom of contract," the judge noted. Counsel cited two 1915 Supreme Court decisions, *Coppage v. Kansas*, striking down a Kansas law that restricted an employee's freedom of contract, and *Truax v. Raich*, nullifying an Arizona law that required employers to hire at least 80 percent native-born people as a violation of the equal protection clause of the Fourteenth Amendment. The New York workmen's compensation law was unlike either of those invalidated state laws. It was "a reasonable exercise of the police power of the state," not an interference with contract, covering "compensation for human life or limb lost or disability" through accidents, and "the public has a direct interest in this as affecting the common welfare."[30]

- *The law is fair and just in other ways.* Pitney dismissed the criticism that the law did not improve safety; other laws do that, he noted. The denial of trial by jury "is not inconsistent with 'due process.'" The law excludes farm laborers and domestic servants, but that is reasonable based on the state's assessment of risks inherent in these occupations. It is a system of "compulsory compensation," but companies are not coerced into joining the state-administered compensation fund. They may take out a policy with an authorized insurance company or association or deposit securities with the commission, which the railroad had done in this case.[31]

As the Progressive Era closed, workers' compensation was solidly embedded as an important part of the state's labor code. New York's program got stronger—more people covered, more-liberal benefits—over the next few decades and today is one of the strongest in the nation. The New York court cases cited above helped anchor and legitimize the notion of accident compensation a century ago by ratifying it in the nation's most important state. The program, with changes over the years, continues today. "Workers' compensation was an idea whose time had come," notes legal historian G. Edward White.[32] It reflected acknowledgment of the progressives' push for an "increased role of state governments as caretakers of disadvantaged persons, and of organized labor." White concludes:

> Collectively, the reform signaled a recognition that workplace injuries had become so ubiquitous in certain industries, and the established doctrines of tort law had so regularly failed to address the problem in an adequate fashion, that the best policy was to remove workplace injuries from the tort system and address them through a system that emphasized a kind of bureaucratic justice. No single reform of the common law of torts had previously had a comparable effect in America, and none has since.

CONCLUSION

NEW YORK COURTS
"REASONABLY SUCCESSFUL AND SATISFACTORY"

The New York Court of Appeals' *Jensen v. Southern Pacific Co.* decision and the US Supreme Court's *New York Central Railroad v. White* decision (essentially confirming the court of appeals' *Jensen* decision), discussed in chapter 12, were greeted with resignation (by companies that had opposed the workmen's compensation law), relief (by its sponsors and advocates), and praise (by progressives and organized labor). The year after *Jensen*, the court chalked up another victory for the cause of the state protecting the people in a decision asserting the responsibility of an automobile manufacturer for a defective wheel that had broken, injuring the driver. The decision helped establish the principle of manufacturers' liability for their products.[1]

As the years went by in the new century and the work of the court of appeals continued at a brisk pace, it outgrew its cramped, inadequate space in the state capitol. In January 1917, the court moved to a new location, the renovated State Hall, a historic building that had formerly housed state offices, across the street from the capitol. The court's stately new quarters featured six tall columns, a massive rotunda, a large court-room with impressive oak paneling (dismantled from the court's capitol quarters and moved to the new building at Chief Judge Cullen's insistence), a judges' library and judges' conference room, and commodious new offices for the judges. Court of Appeals Hall, as it was named, was an impressive edifice befitting the nation's most important state court. "From now on and judging from the splendid character of the building itself, we trust for centuries it is to be devoted to a purpose, the noblest purpose to which a building or a life can be devoted, the administration of justice," said Governor Charles S. Whitman at the dedication of the building on January 8, 1917.[2] The building continues in use today.

New Yorkers might grumble about the courts' delay, expenses, or some decisions. But, on balance, the court of appeals was reasonably supportive of progressive reforms though sometimes slow to endorse them. It validated regulation of bakers' hours. The court rejected limitations on women's working hours, then accepted them when more evidence of need was presented. It rejected workers' compensation, then endorsed it after the state constitution was amended to clearly sanction it. It backed state public health measures such as smallpox vaccination for school students.

There was no public outcry for change. The 1915 Constitutional Convention made limited recommendations for changing the court system's organization and policies, but it was moot because the proposed constitution was rejected by the voters at the polls.

The legislature in 1921 established a "Judiciary Constitutional Convention" to recommend any needed changes to the "Judiciary" article of the state constitution. It was called a constitutional convention, but it was in fact just a commission charged to report to the legislature, which would have the power to adopt or reject its recommendations. The convention held public hearings, analyzed several issues, and reported to the legislature in January 1922.

The group concluded that "the judicial system of the State of New York had proved reasonably successful and satisfactory as a whole in practical experience." Complaints about "the uncertainty, delay and expense of the law" were due not to courts or judges but instead to "litigants and the profession itself, to constant tinkering with our procedure," and to the legislature's failure to enact "scientific and accurate remedial legislation." In fact, the legislature was itself a main cause of delays and congestion in the courts. It was too hurried and distracted to attend to the consequences of the laws it was passing. During the previous six years, the legislature had passed 4,450 new laws, an average of 742 each session. Many wound up before the court for interpretation, clarification, or rejection. The convention did not advance a particular recommendation to meet this problem but called the legislature's attention to it.[3]

The convention's report expressed concern at the erosion of judicial power through the rise of more and more state departments, boards, and commissions—"the constant extension of the functions of government, with the subsequent multiplication of public officials and of interference with the conduct of private individuals." It continued that "extensive legislative, executive and judicial powers are being vested and combined in administrative bodies in distinct and reckless disregard of the sound principle of the separation of governmental powers." Issues formerly decided by courts and juries are now "being entrusted to bureaucratic discretion," and "arbitrary methods and untrained judgment are being constantly substituted." The whole thing was "a menace to the inalienable personal and property rights of all our citizens and to all our ideas of the due and fair administration of justice according to law." The convention advocated amending the constitution's judiciary article to "guarantee to all affected or aggrieved an ultimate hearing in a real court of justice whenever interference with or violation of private rights is threatened."[4]

That was an attack on a central tenet of progressive reform and the administrative state, manifested in New York by such entities as the Public Service Commissions, the Workmen's Compensation Commission, and the Industrial Commission, all of which the courts had approved. Opening such a wide door to appeals would have thrown much of the state's regulatory and labor oversight programming into chaos. The legislature accepted some of the commission's recommendations but ignored that one.

The legislature, hearing no public clamor for change and uninterested in changing a judicial system that worked tolerably well, left the judicial system mostly intact as the Progressive Era gave way to the 1920s. The courts in the next era continued to consider important public policy issues, but they were mostly different in nature. The courts effected what legal scholar William E. Nelson called "the legalist reformation." Courts undertook the task of "regulating the interactions of diverse groups," and "the movement was reform-oriented: its goal was social change and the expansion of existing hierarchies to include people who had previously been made subordinate." But it also adhered to the rule of law, which "not only served as an established cultural norm but also offered greater promise of social change than any other political or philosophical alternative."[5]

Historians debate the role of the courts in the progressive period, though without focusing particularly on New York. Many historians portray the courts as obstructionists and stumbling blocks to needed reforms. But others contend that, overall, and with some inconsistencies, state courts approved more substantial legislation than they struck down.[6] Others go further, explaining that while courts are often seen as enemies of reform, in fact they were progressive and liberal in upholding most important reform laws.[7] Still others acknowledge that the courts did indeed invalidate a good deal of reform legislation but that they were motivated by fidelity to the constitution and concern for property rights and individual and economic freedom. Those are issues and concerns that continue today.[8]

The New York Court of Appeals does not fit neatly into any of these patterns. Its record in the progressive period might be called pragmatic. Judge and legal scholar Richard Posner maintains that the word that best describes the average American judge at all levels of our judicial hierarchies over time is *pragmatist*. Judges cannot decide difficult cases just by reference to universal principles or authoritative past decisions. They decide with reference to probable social and economic consequences and their instincts about those consequences. A good deal of their work boils down to common sense and reasonableness. Precedents count, but more as guides than as dictatorial sources. "A pragmatist judge always tries to do the best he can do for the present and the future, unchecked by any felt *duty* to secure consistency in principle with what other officials have done in the past," Posner writes. "The pragmatist judge . . . wants to come up with the best decision having in mind present and future needs, and so does not regard the maintenance of consistency with past decisions as an end in itself but only as a means for bringing about the best results in the present case."[9]

That is a useful way to view the philosophy of the New York Court of Appeals in the Progressive Era. The court operated amid tension among contending values of personal liberty, corporate responsibility, and state regulation. It balanced precedent with an obligation to keep the law fresh and responsive. It determined when to defer to the legislature, when to overrule it, and when to give it guidance. The court operated in the context of the progressive movement, sometimes resisting it, other times aligning with it.

Judge Cuthbert Pound set forth the reasons for the court's rocky journey but relative success in this time period.[10] Courts, he explained, are responsible for constantly stating and restating the law. They love and respect precedent. "Judges love to quote 'authorities' even when they are merely illustrative or advisory and not controlling." But judges are also realists. They recognize the need for social and economic change, government reforms, and courts keeping up to date. "Courts cannot long ignore the will of the people. It is futile for judges to think that the attempts to supply an urgent need of social welfare can be permanently denied by a judicial ruling. Sometimes, the courts say 'stop' but just as often their real message is 'go slow.'" They may seem unpredictable, holding fast to constitutional doctrine in one case, stretching the law in another, and in other cases going still further and enunciating a new common-law doctrine. It is all part of making our system of government work even if it seems inconsistent to the public and occasionally frustrates politicians. "After all," Pound concluded, "the courts exist not to make the way of officialdom easy but to uphold constitutional rights as they see them."

NOTES

NOTES TO THE INTRODUCTION

1. Stewart E. Sterk, "The New York Court of Appeals: 150 Years of Leading Decisions," *Syracuse Law Review* 48, no. 4 (1998): 1392.

2. Theodore Roosevelt, "The Man with the Muck-Rake," speech delivered April 14, 1906, quoted in Michael McGerr, *A Fierce Discontent: The Rise and Fall of the Progressive Movement in America, 1870–1920* (New York: Free Press, 2003), 176.

3. Charles Evans Hughes, *Public Papers of Charles E. Hughes*, vol. 1 (Albany: J. B. Lyon, 1908), 7, quoted in Robert F. Wesser, *Charles Evans Hughes: Politics and Reform in New York, 1905–1910* (Ithaca, NY: Cornell University Press, 1967), 109.

4. McGerr, *Fierce Discontent*, 153.

5. Robert D. Putnam, *The Upswing: How America Came Together a Century Ago and How We Can Do It Again* (New York: Simon and Schuster, 2020), 50, 76, 285.

6. G. Edward White, *Law in American History, Volume II: From Reconstruction through the 1920s* (New York: Oxford University Press, 2016), 355, 359.

7. Elihu Root, "Judicial Decisions and Public Feeling," *New York State Bar Association Proceedings of the Thirty-Fifth Annual Meeting Held at New York, January 19–20, 1912* [. . .] (Albany: Argus, 1912), 151–52. Root was secretary of war (1899–1904), secretary of state (1905–09), and US senator from New York (1909–15).

8. Root, 152.

9. Root, 152.

10. Root, 153–54, 162.

11. People v. Lochner, 177 N.Y. 145, 157 (1904).

12. Alton B. Parker, "American Constitutional Government," *Constitutional Review* 79 (1922): 86.

13. Alton B. Parker, "The Citizen and the Constitution," *Yale Law Journal* 23 (1914): 631, 632, 634.

14. *The Fourth Constitution of New York, 1894* (1894), article VI, http://www.nycourts.gov/history/legal-history-new-york/documents/publications_1894-ny-constitution.pdf; Peter J. Galie, *Ordered Liberty: A Constitutional History of New York* (New York: Fordham University Press, 1996), 170–71; Francis Bergan, *The History of the New York Court of Appeals, 1847–1932* (New York: Columbia University Press, 1985), 199–223; Mark Bloustein, *A Short History of the New York State Court System* (1987), http://www.nycourts.gov/history/legal-history-new-york/documents/History_Short-History-NY-Courts.pdf.

15. *Fourth Constitution*, article VI, §1.

16. *Fourth Constitution*, article VI, §9.

17. "New York State Judges' Biographies by Court," Historical Society of the New York Courts, accessed Oct. 17, 2021, https://history.nycourts.gov/biographies.

18. Judith S. Kaye, "State Courts at the Dawn of a New Century: Common Law Courts Reading Statutes and Constitutions," *New York University Law Review* 70, no. 1 (April 1995): 29, 4, 7, 9, 33–34.

CHAPTER 1

1. New York's Progressive movement is covered in Richard L. McCormick, *From Realignment to Reform: Political Change in New York State, 1893–1910* (Ithaca, NY: Cornell University Press, 1981); Robert F. Wesser, *Charles Evans Hughes: Politics and Reform in New York, 1905–1910* (Ithaca, NY: Cornell University Press, 1967); Wesser, *A Response to Progressivism: The Democratic Party and New York Politics, 1902–1918* (New York: New York University Press, 1986); and Terry Golway, *Machine Made: Tammany Hall and the Creation of Modern American Politics* (New York: Liveright, 2014).

2. Literature on the role of courts in the Progressive Era includes Melvin I. Urofsky, "State Courts and Protective Legislation during the Progressive Era: A Reevaluation," *Journal of American History* 72, no. 1 (June 1985): 63–91; Felice Batlan, "A Reevaluation of the New York Court of Appeals: The Home, the Market, and Labor, 1885–1905," *Law and Social Inquiry* 27, no. 3 (2002): 489–528; Paul Kens, "The Constitution and Business Regulation in the Progressive Era: Recent Developments and New Opportunities," *American Journal of Legal History* 56, no. 1 (March 2016): 97–103; and David E. Bernstein, *Rehabilitating Lochner: Defending Individual Rights against Progressive Reform* (Chicago: University of Chicago Press, 2011).

3. Ernst Freund, *The Police Power, Public Policy and Constitutional Rights* (Chicago: Callaghan, 1904), 3.

4. Freund, 3.

5. People ex rel. Durham Realty Corp. v. LaFetra, 230 N.Y. 429, 442 (1921).

6. Cuthbert W. Pound, "Jurisprudence: Science or Superstition," *American Bar Association Journal* 18, no. 5 (May 1932): 312.

7. Kermit L. Hall, editor-in-chief, *The Oxford Companion to American Law* (New York: Oxford University Press, 2002), 125–30.

8. Peter Strauss, "Due Process," *Wex*, Legal Information Institute, accessed July 31, 2021, https://www.law.cornell.edu/wex/due_process; Adam Winkler, *We the Corporations: How American Businesses Won Their Civil Rights* (New York: Liveright, 2018), 113–228.

9. Lawrence M. Friedman, *A History of American Law*, 4th ed. (New York: Simon and Schuster, 2019), 326–30, 502–7.

10. In the Matter of the Application of Peter Jacobs, 98 N.Y. 98, 105, 112 (1885).

11. People v. Marx, 99 N.Y. 377, 386 (1885).

12. Edward S. Corwin, "The Extension of Judicial Review in New York: 1783–1905," *Michigan Law Review* 15, no. 4 (Feb. 1917): 296.

13. People ex rel. Nechamcus v. Warden of the City Prison, 144 N.Y. 529, 536 (1895).

14. *Id.* at 540, 542, 543. Peckham was appointed to the US Supreme Court in 1896 and used similar wording in writing the majority opinion in *Lochner v. New York* (1905), discussed in chapter 3.

15. People v. Havnor, 149 N.Y. 195, 199 (1896).

16. *Id.* at 206, 209. Havnor appealed to the US Supreme Court, which sustained the court of appeals.

17. Oliver Wendell Holmes Jr., *The Common Law* (London: Macmillan, 1892); Holmes, "The Path of the Law," *Harvard Law Review* 10 (1897): 1–20; Stephen Budiansky, *Oliver Wendell Holmes: A Life in War, Law and Ideas* (New York: W. W. Norton, 2019), 234–45.

18. Sheldon M. Novick, "Justice Holmes' Philosophy," *Washington University Law Review* 70 (1992): 737; see also Hall, *American Law*, 447–48.

19. Roscoe Pound, "The Spirit of the Common Law," *Green Bag* 18 (1906): 19–20.

20. R. Pound, "The Need of a Sociological Jurisprudence," *Green Bag* 19 (1907): 611.

21. Melvin I. Urofsky, *Louis D. Brandeis: A Life* (New York: Pantheon Books, 2009), 202–6, 431–33.

22. Louis D. Brandeis, "Living Law," *Illinois Law Review* 10, no. 7 (Feb. 1916): 464.

23. William B. Hornblower, "A Century of 'Judge-Made' Law," *Columbia Law Review* 7, no. 7 (Nov. 1907): 458.

24. Hornblower, "Century," 461.

25. Hornblower, "Century," 466.

26. Hornblower, "Century," 473.

27. Andrew L. Kaufman, *Cardozo* (Cambridge, MA: Harvard University Press, 1998), 200.

28. Benjamin N. Cardozo, *The Nature of the Judicial Process: The Storrs Lectures Delivered at Yale University* (New Haven, CT: Yale University Press, 1922), 165. See in particular Cardozo's first lecture, "Introduction: The Method of Philosophy," 9–50; Kaufman, 199–222.

29. Cardozo, 67.

30. Cardozo, 10.

31. Cuthbert W. Pound, "Jurisprudence: Science or Superstition," *American Bar Association Journal* 18 (1932): 313.

32. Cuthbert W. Pound, "Constitutional Aspects of American Administrative Law," *American Bar Association Journal* 9, no. 7 (July 1923): 409.

33. Kaufman, *Cardozo*, 130–33.

34. George W. Wingate, "The Honorable Edgar Montgomery Cullen," *Bench and Bar* 7, no. 1 (Nov. 1913): 94–95.

35. Bohmer v. Hoffen, 161 N.Y. 390, 399–400 (1900).

36. Wright v. Hart, 182 N.Y. 330, 336, 335 (1905).

37. *Id.* at 335, 341.

38. *Id.* at 352–53.

39. Klein v. Maravelas, 219 N.Y. 383, 385–387 (1916).

40. People ex rel. Armstrong v. Warden, 183 N.Y. 223, 226 (1905).

41. Fisher Co. v. Woods, 187 N.Y. 90, 94 (1907).

42. People ex rel. Wineburgh Advertising Co. v. Murphy, 195 N.Y. 126, 131 (1909).

43. *Id.* at 133.

44. People v. Klinck Packing Co., 214 N.Y. 121, 126 (1915).

45. *Id.* at 134.

46. *Id.* at 138.

47. *Id.* at 140.

48. Cuthbert W. Pound, "Defective Law—Its Cause and Remedy," *New York State Bar Association Bulletin* 1, no. 13 (1929): 286.

49. Theodore Roosevelt, *A Charter of Democracy: Address by Hon. Theodore Roosevelt [. . .] before the Ohio Constitutional Convention February 21, 1912* (Washington, DC: Government Printing Office, 1912), 13; Roosevelt, "Judges and Progress," *Outlook* 100 (Jan. 6, 1912): 40–48.

50. "Gaynor Raps Courts Hostile to Progress," *New York Times*, May 8, 1912.

51. "Report of the Sub-Committee Appointed to Investigate the Causes underlying the Dissatisfaction with Our Judicial System to the Bar Association of the State of New York," in New York State Bar Association, *Proceedings of the Thirty-Sixth Annual Meeting Held at Utica, January 24–25, 1913 [. . .]* (Albany: Argus, 1913), 223–24, 225, 226.

52. "Report of the Sub-Committee," 205.

53. William B. Hornblower, "The Independence of the Judiciary, the Safeguard of Free Institutions," *Yale Law Journal* 22, no. 1 (Nov. 1912): 6.

54. Hornblower, "Independence," 9.

55. C. W. Pound, "Constitutional Aspects of American Administrative Law," 410, 411, 414 (italics in the original).

56. Edgar M. Cullen, "Some Observations upon Unjustifiable Criticisms of Our Judges," *Bench and Bar* 7 (1914): 98, 101, 102.

57. Cuthbert W. Pound, "Some Recent Phases of the Evolution of Case Law," *Yale Law Journal* 31, no. 4 (1922): 363, 365, 365–66.

58. Cuthbert W. Pound, "The Relation of the Practicing Lawyer to the Efficient Administration of Justice," *Cornell Law Quarterly* 9, no. 3 (1925): 242.

59. Edgar M. Cullen, "The Decline of Personal Liberty in America," *American Law Review* 48 (1914): 346, 364, 345.

60. Cullen, "Decline," 363.

61. Frank H. Hiscock, "Progressiveness of New York Law," *Cornell Law Quarterly* 9 (1924): 374, 377, 382, 384.

62. Alton B. Parker, "The Congestion of Law," *Commonwealth Law Review* 4, no. 2 (1906): 69, 72, 73, 74.

63. Alton B. Parker, "President's Annual Address," *American Lawyer* 15, no. 10 (Oct. 1907): 477.

64. Parker, "President's Annual Address," 470.

CHAPTER 2

1. Jim Boles, "Abandoned History: Franklin Mills Wheat Products, Lockport's Early Health Food," *Lockport Union-Sun and Journal*, Nov. 9, 2016, https://www.lockportjournal.com/news/lifestyles/abandoned-history-franklin-mills-wheat-products-lockport-s-early-health/article_20eb42f3-74a8-5938-a9b9-0b6ca19da1e3.html.

2. Samantha Barbas, "From Privacy to Publicity: The Tort of Appropriation in the Age of Mass Consumption," *Buffalo Law Review* 61 (2013): 1143.

3. Milton E. Gibbs, "Complaint," April 15, 1900, 2–4. Supreme Court, State of New York, County of Monroe, *Abigail M. Roberson against Rochester Folding Box Company and the Franklin Mills Company*. Copy in New York State Court of Appeals Records, *Cases and Briefs on Appeal* for *Abigail M. Roberson, an Infant, by Her Guardian Ad Litem, Margaret E. Bell, Plaintiff*, against *The Rochester Folding Box Company and The Franklin Mills Company*, 171 N.Y. 538, New York State Archives, Albany.

4. Robert E. Mensel, " 'Kodakers Lying in Wait': Amateur Photography and the Right of Privacy in New York, 1885–1915," *American Quarterly* 43, no.

1 (March 1991): 24–25; Samantha Barbas, "Saving Privacy from History," *DePaul Law Review* 61 (2012): 973–89.

5. Jessica Lake, *The Face That Launched a Thousand Lawsuits: The American Women Who Forged a Right to Privacy* (New Haven, CT: Yale University Press, 2016), 1–87.

6. Sarah E. Igo, *The Known Citizen: A History of Privacy in Modern America* (Cambridge, MA: Harvard University Press, 2018), 1–30.

7. Edwin L. Godkin, "The Rights of the Citizen to His Own Reputation," *Scribner's Magazine* 8 (July 1890): 65–66.

8. Dorothy J. Glancy, "Privacy and the Other Miss M," *Northern Illinois University Law Review* 10 (1990): 401–40.

9. Schuyler v. Curtis, 147 N.Y. 434, 443 (1895). Judge John C. Gray wrote a dissenting opinion supporting the lower courts' views on the need for courts to protect individuals' privacy, presaging the dissent he would write in the *Roberson* decision seven years later.

10. Samuel D. Warren and Louis D. Brandeis, "The Right to Privacy," *Harvard Law Review* 4, no. 5 (Dec. 15, 1890): 193–220.

11. Thomas M. Cooley, *A Treatise on the Law of Torts, or The Wrongs Which Arise Independent of Contract*, 2nd ed. (Chicago: Callaghan, 1888), 29.

12. Warren and Brandeis, "The Right to Privacy," 195–96.

13. Warren and Brandeis, 205–6.

14. Warren and Brandeis, 214–18.

15. Melvin I. Urofsky, *Louis D. Brandeis: A Life* (New York: Pantheon Books, 2009), 98–102.

16. Roberson v. Rochester Folding-Box Co., 32 Misc. 344, 346 (N.Y. Sup. Ct. Monroe Cy. 1900).

17. *Id.* at 346–47.

18. *Id.* at 348, 350, 351.

19. Roberson v. Rochester Folding-Box Co., 64 A.D. 30, 31, 33 (N.Y. App. Div. 1901).

20. *Id.* at 33–34.

21. *Id.* at 35.

22. Milton E. Gibbs, "Brief of Respondent" (1902), 7, 13, 30, 37. In *Cases and Briefs on File* for Roberson v. Rochester Folding-Box Co., 171 N.Y. 538 (1902), New York State Court of Appeals Records.

23. Elbridge L. Adams, "Appellants' Brief" (1902), 4, 7, 16, 17, 27, 35, 36, 52. In *Cases and Briefs on File* for Roberson v. Rochester Folding-Box Co.

24. Roberson v. Rochester Folding-Box Co., 171 N.Y. 538 (1902).

25. *Id.* at 544.

26. *Id.* at 550.

27. *Id.* at 551.

28. *Id.* at 543.

29. *Id.* at 547.

30. *Id.* at 556, 555.

31. John C. Gray, "Some Definitions and Questions in Jurisprudence," *Harvard Law Review* 6, no. 1 (1892): 26.

32. Gray, 33.

33. Roberson v. Rochester Folding-Box Co., 171 N.Y. 538, 559–60 (1902).

34. *Id.* at 560.

35. *Id.* at 561–62.

36. *Id.* at 563, 564.

37. *Id.* at 566.

38. "The Right of Privacy," *New York Times*, Aug. 23, 1902.

39. Denis O'Brien, "The Right of Privacy," *Columbia Law Review* 2, no. 7 (Nov. 1902): 438, 439, 440, 442, 444.

40. O'Brien, 445.

41. N.Y. Laws of 1903, ch. 132, §1.

42. Jennifer E. Rothman, "The Right of Publicity: Privacy Reimagined for New York?," *Cardozo Arts and Entertainment Law Journal* 36, no. 3 (2018): 573–84.

43. Elbridge L. Adams, "The Right of Privacy, and Its Relation to the Law of Libel," *American Law Review* 39 (1905): 55, 57.

44. Rhodes v. Sperry Hutchinson Co., 193 N.Y. 223, 227, 231, 232 (1908).

45. Sperry & Hutchinson Co. v. Rhodes, 220 U.S. 502 (1911).

46. "Parker Taken to Task by an Indignant Woman," *New York Times*, July 24, 1904.

47. William L. Prosser, "Privacy," *California Law Review* 48, no. 3 (1960): 383–423.

48. Stuart Banner, *American Property: A History of How, Why, and What We Own* (Cambridge, MA: Harvard University Press, 2011), 131–61; Edward H. Rosenthal and Barry Werbin, "A Historical Retrospective on New York's Right of Privacy Law: 115 Years of Court of Appeals Jurisprudence," *NYSBA Entertainment, Arts and Sports Law Journal* (Fall/Winter 2018): 35–39; William S. Gyves, "The Right to Privacy One Hundred Years Later: New York Stands Firm as the World and Law around It Change," *St. John's Law Review* 64, no. 2 (1990): 315–34.

CHAPTER 3

This chapter is an expanded version of "The *Lochner* Case: New Yorkers in Conflict," *New York State Bar Association Journal* 89, no. 2 (Feb. 2017): 26–31.

1. William H. Rehnquist, *The Supreme Court: How It Was, How It Is* (New York: William Morrow, 1987), 205.

2. Quoted in David E. Bernstein, "Lochner v. New York: A Centennial Retrospective," *Washington University Law Quarterly* 83, no. 5 (2005): 1470n12.

3. N.Y. Laws of 1895, ch. 518, §2.

4. Paul Kens, *Lochner v. New York: Economic Regulation on Trial* (Lawrence: University Press of Kansas, 1998), 1–66. Kens's book provides comprehensive coverage of the case.

5. Adam Winkler, *We the Corporations: How American Businesses Won Their Civil Rights* (New York: Liveright, 2018), 113–228.

6. People v. Lochner, 73 A.D. 120, 122, 124 (N.Y. App. Div. 4th Dep't 1902).

7. "Appellant's Points" (1902), 1–18. Copy in *Cases and Briefs on File* for People v. Lochner, 175 N.Y. 145, New York State Court of Appeals Records, New York State Archives, Albany.

8. "Respondent's Points" (1902), 1–17. Copy in *Cases and Briefs on File* for People v. Lochner, 175 N.Y. 145.

9. Robert M. Mandelbaum, "Alton Brooks Parker: Biography," Historical Society of the New York Courts, accessed July 31, 2021, https://history.nycourts.gov/biography/alton-brooks-parker; Leslie H. Southwick, *Presidential Also-Rans and Running Mates, 1788 through 1996*, 2nd ed. (Jefferson, NC: McFarland, 1998), 439–44.

10. Roberson v. Rochester Folding-Box Co., 175 N.Y. 315 (1902).

11. National Protective Association v. Cumming, 170 N.Y. 315, 331 (1902).

12. John D. Park & Sons Co. v. National Wholesale Druggists' Association, 175 N.Y. 1, 21–22 (1903).

13. People ex rel. Rodgers v. Coler, 166 N.Y. 1, 25 (1901).

14. *Id.* at 27.

15. "Due Process of Law," *New York Times*, July 5, 1903.

16. Alton B. Parker, "Due Process of Law," *American Lawyer* 11 (1903): pt. 1, 333–36; pt. 2, 388–91; pt. 3, 431–34.

17. People v. Lochner, 175 N.Y. 145 (1904).

18. *Id.* at 149, 152, 154.

19. *Id.* at 150.

20. *Id.* at 156.

21. *Id.* at 158.

22. *Id.* at 161, 162.

23. *Id.* at 166, 163.

24. *Id.* at 177–78, 182, 180, 179.

25. *Id.* at 187, 189, 188.

26. "Made the 10-Hour Law, Then Had It Unmade," *New York Times*, April 19, 1905.

27. Kens, *Lochner v. New York*, 110–28.

28. "Peckham Honored," *New York Tribune*, Dec. 19, 1909.

29. "Justices Good Timber," *Washington Post*, Feb. 16, 1908.

30. United States v. Trans-Missouri Freight Association, 166 U.S. 290 (1897).

31. Bernard Schwartz, *A History of the Supreme Court* (New York: Oxford University Press, 1993), 179.

32. People v. Budd, 117 N.Y. 1, 45, 69, 71 (1889).

33. Allgeyer v. Louisiana, 165 U.S. 578, 589 (1897).

34. Holden v. Hardy, 169 U.S. 366 (1898).

35. James W. Ely Jr., "Rufus W. Peckham and Economic Liberty," *Vanderbilt Law Review* 62, no. 2 (2009): 591–612.

36. Lochner v. New York, 198 U.S. 45, 57, 53, 57 (1905).

37. *Id.* at 75.

38. Matthew S. Bewig, "Lochner v. the Journeymen Bakers of New York: The Journeymen Bakers, Their Hours of Labor, and the Constitution: A Case Study in the Social History of Legal Thought," *American Journal of Legal History* 38, no. 4 (Oct. 1994): 417.

39. Sidney G. Tarrow, "Lochner versus New York: A Political Analysis," *Labor History* 5, no. 3 (1964): 300.

40. *State of New York Department of Labor Bulletin* 7, no. 2 (June 1905): 131–32.

41. People v. Charles Schweinler Press, 214 N.Y. 395, 412, 411 (1915).

42. Victoria F. Nourse, "A Tale of Two *Lochners*: The Untold History of Substantive Due Process and the Idea of Fundamental Rights," *California Law Review* 97 (June 2009): 751–99.

43. Paul A. Freund, "Charles Evans Hughes as Chief Justice," *Harvard Law Review* 81, no. 1 (Nov. 1967): 13.

44. Morehead v. New York ex rel. Tipaldo, 298 U.S. 587, 610 (1936).

45. Quoted in Schwartz, *A History of the Supreme Court*, 231.

46. Burt Solomon, *FDR v. The Constitution: The Court-Packing Fight and the Triumph of Democracy* (New York: Walker, 2009), 165.

47. West Coast Hotel Co. v. Parrish, 300 U.S. 379 (1937).

48. *Id.* at 392.

49. *Id.* at 398.

50. *Id.* at 391–93.

51. Paul Kens, "*Lochner v. New York*: Tradition or Change in Constitutional Law?," *NYU Journal of Law and Liberty* 1, no. 1 (2005): 404–31; Bernstein, "Lochner v. New York," 1469–527.

52. Ted Stewart, *Supreme Power: Seven Pivotal Supreme Court Decisions That Had a Major Impact on America* (Salt Lake City: Shadow Mountain Publishing, 2017), 96.

53. Cass R. Sunstein, "Lochner's Legacy," *Columbia Law Review* 87 (June 1987): 873–919; Howard Gillman, *The Constitution Besieged: The Rise and Demise of Lochner Era Police Powers Jurisprudence* (Durham, NC: Duke University Press, 1995).

CHAPTER 4

1. Herbert J. Bass, *"I Am a Democrat": The Political Career of David Bennett Hill* (Syracuse, NY: Syracuse University Press, 1961), 1–253. Ironically, as senator, in a tiff with President Cleveland over political power in New York, Hill blocked the president's nomination of New York judge Wheeler Peckham to the US Supreme Court in 1894. The next year, he reluctantly acceded to Cleveland's nomination of another New York judge, Wheeler Peckham's brother, Rufus Peckham, to the court. Peckham took his seat in 1896. Nine years later, Peckham wrote the court's decision in *Lochner v. New York*, which overturned Chief Judge Parker's opinion in *People v. Lochner.*

2. Robert M. Mandelbaum, "Alton Brooks Parker: Biography," Historical Society of the New York Courts, accessed July 31, 2021, https://history.nycourts.gov/biography/alton-brooks-parker; Leslie H. Southwick, "A Judge Runs for President: Alton Parker's Road to Oblivion," *Green Bag* 5 (Autumn 2001): 37–50; Southwick, *Presidential Also-Rans and Running Mates, 1788 through 1996* (Jefferson, NC: McFarland, 2008), 439–44. There is no published biography of Parker.

3. Theodore Roosevelt, *Theodore Roosevelt: An Autobiography* (New York: Charles Scribner's Sons, 1913), 269.

4. Susan Berfield, *The Hour of Fate: Theodore Roosevelt, J. P. Morgan, and the Battle to Transform American Capitalism* (New York: Bloomsbury, 2020), 258.

5. John D. Park & Sons Co. v. National Wholesale Druggists' Association, 175 N.Y. 1, 21, 22 (1903).

6. National Protective Association v. Cumming, 170 N.Y. 315, 331 (1902).

7. Roberson v. Rochester Folding-Box Co., 171 N.Y. 538 (1902).

8. People v. Lochner, 177 N.Y. 145 (1904).

9. Alton B. Parker, "Due Process of Law," *American Lawyer* 11 (1903): 333–37, 388–91, 431–34.

10. "Judge Parker Speaks," *New York Times*, July 5, 1903.

11. Quoted in Richard B. Doss, "Democrats in the Doldrums: Virginia and the Democratic National Convention of 1904," *Journal of Southern History* 20, no. 4 (Nov. 1954): 514.

12. "Pen Portrait of a Possible President; Judge Alton B. Parker, a Man of Method and Enormous Capacity for Work—His Early Career and Daily Routine," *New York Times*, April 3, 1904.

13. "Cincinnatus at the Plow," *Boston Daily Globe*, July 4, 1904; "Judge Parker Pitches Hay for Two Hours," *New York Times*, July 5, 1904.

14. "Littleton Presents the Claims of Parker; Hails Him as a Democrat Worthy of the Nomination," *New York Times*, July 9, 1904.

15. "Parker Nominated on First Ballot; Received 667 Votes to 204 Cast for Hearst," *New York Times*, July 10, 1904; J. Rogers Hollingsworth, *The Whirligig of*

Politics: *The Democracy of Cleveland and Bryan* (Chicago: University of Chicago Press, 1963), 207–22.

16. "Convention Accepts Parker's Declaration for Gold Standard," *St. Louis Post-Dispatch*, July 10, 1904; Southwick, "A Judge Runs for President," 44–45.

17. Democratic National Committee, *The Campaign Text Book of the Democratic Party of the United States, 1904* (New York: Democratic National Committee, 1904), 16, 81, 17.

18. Democratic National Committee, *Campaign Text Book*, 22.

19. "Parker Accepts for Single Term; Qualifying Declaration Electrifies Audience," *New York Times*, Aug. 11, 1904.

20. Champ Clark, "Notification Address of Hon. Champ Clark, of Missouri, Delivered at Esopus, Aug. 10th, 1904," in Democratic National Committee, *Campaign Text Book*, 30.

21. Alton B. Parker, "Address of Acceptance of Alton Brooks Parker, at Esopus, New York, August 10, 1904," in Democratic National Committee, *Campaign Text Book*, 33, 35.

22. Parker, "Address," 37.

23. Parker, "Address," 39, 40.

24. Quoted in Lewis L. Gould, *The Presidency of Theodore Roosevelt* (Lawrence: University Press of Kansas, 1991), 139.

25. "Parker's Letter of Acceptance Issued," *New York Times*, Sept. 26, 1904.

26. "Parker, the Orator, Cheered by Throngs," *New York Times*, Nov. 3, 1904.

27. "Parker in First Campaign Speech," *Chicago Tribune*, Oct. 16, 1904.

28. "The Issue," cartoon in *American Monthly Review of Reviews* 30, no. 3 (Sept.1904): 266.

29. Gould, *Presidency of Theodore Roosevelt*, 139–44; H. W. Brands, *T. R.: The Last Romantic* (New York: Basic Books, 1997), 507–12.

30. Grover Cleveland, "The Presidential Candidates: Parker," *McClure's Magazine* 24, no. 1 (Nov. 1904): 5, 8.

31. James Creelman, "Alton B. Parker: A Character Sketch," *American Monthly Review of Reviews* 30 (Aug. 1904): 170–71.

32. "Campaign Work Keeps Parker Another Day," *New York Times*, Sept. 24, 1904.

33. Southwick, "A Judge Runs for President," 46.

34. Berfield, *The Hour of Fate*, 260–69.

35. Edmund Morris, *Theodore Rex* (New York: Random House, 2001), 351–63.

36. "Government Controlled by Trusts, Says Parker; Charges Corporate Interests with Buying Federal Protection," *New York Times*, Oct. 25, 1904; "Roosevelt Speaks; Cortelyou Charges Called Monstrous; Declares Parker Has Accused Him of Complicity in Blackmail of Corporations," *New York Times*, Nov. 5, 1904; "Connecticut Turns Out to Meet Parker; Frantic Applause for Judge's Attack on Trusts," *New York Times*, Nov. 5, 1904.

37. "Mayor Cites Jefferson in Denouncing Greed," *New York Times*, April 14, 1905.

38. "Parker on Corporate Corruption of Parties," *New York Times*, Sept. 18, 1905.

39. "Parker in Courts' Defense," *Washington Post*, Sept. 1, 1910.

40. "Assailed as Usurper," *Washington Post*, Sept. 30, 1910.

41. "Parker Hails Rival, Lauds Bryan for Services to the Democratic Party," *Washington Post*, June 26, 1912.

42. "Parker Flays Sulzer," *New York Times*, Oct. 11, 1913.

43. Alton B. Parker, "The Congestion of the Law," *Commonwealth Law Review* 4, no. 2 (1906): 69–78.

44. Alton B. Parker, "President's Annual Address," *American Lawyer* 15, no. 10 (Oct. 1907): 470.

45. Alton B. Parker, "The Citizen and the Constitution," *Yale Law Journal* 23, no. 8 (June 1914): 636.

46. "Don't Need Big Armies," *Washington Post*, July 23, 1914.

47. Loewe v. Lawlor, 208 U.S. 274 (1908).

48. "Clergy Criticized by Alton B. Parker," *San Francisco Chronicle*, Jan. 30, 1920; "Committee of 150 Appointed to Hunt Disloyalty in U.S.," *New York Tribune*, March 11, 1920.

CHAPTER 5

1. "History of Smallpox," Centers for Disease Control and Prevention, accessed July 31, 2021, https://www.cdc.gov/smallpox/history/history.html.

2. Quoted in James Colgrove, *State of Immunity: The Politics of Vaccination in Twentieth-Century America* (Berkeley: University of California Press, 2006), 27–28; Colgrove (pp. 17–32) is the source for this and the next paragraph.

3. Quoted in Colgrove, 32.

4. Michael Willrich, *Pox: An American History* (New York: Penguin Press, 2011), 1–14, 211–45.

5. Willrich, 12.

6. Montague R. Leverson, "Vaccination: Should It Be Enforced by Law?" *Medico-Legal Journal* 14, no. 3, pt. 1 (1896): 270–78; Leverson, *Medico-Legal Journal* 14, no. 4, pt. 2 (1896): 421–41.

7. Colgrove, *State of Immunity*, 33–38.

8. Ernst Freund, *The Police Power: Public Policy and Constitutional Rights* (Chicago: University of Chicago Press, 1904), 116.

9. Bruce W. Dearstyne, *The Spirit of New York: Defining Events in the Empire State's History* (Albany: State University of New York Press, 2015), 131–52.

10. N.Y. Laws of 1893, ch. 661, §200.

11. In re Walters, 32 N.Y.S. 322, 322, 323, 322 (N.Y. Sup. Ct. 2nd Dep't 1895).

12. In re Walters, 32 N.Y.S. 333 (N.Y. App. Div. 1895); "Vaccination of School Children," *Journal of the American Medical Association* 25 (1895), 505.

13. "Malodorous Newtown Creek," *New York Times*, Aug. 25, 1894.

14. "Affidavit of Robert A. Gunn, Read in Favor of the Motion," in *In the Matter of the Application of Edmund C. Viemeister for a Peremptory Writ of Mandamus [. . .]*, New York Supreme Court, Kings County (July 1, 1902), 7, 9. Copy in *Cases and Briefs on Appeal* for Matter of Viemeister, 179 N.Y. 253 (1904), New York State Court of Appeals Records, New York State Archives, Albany.

15. "Affidavit of Montague R. Leverson, Read in Favor of the Motion," in *Application of Edmund C. Viemeister* (July 2, 1902), 17, 16.

16. "Affidavit of Edward B. Foote, Read in Favor of the Motion" and "Reporter's Sworn Statement," in *Application of Edmund C. Viemeister* (July 2, 1902), 18–22.

17. "Affidavit of F. H. Lutze, Read in Favor of the Motion," in *Application of Edmund C. Viemeister* (July 2, 1902), 24.

18. "Affidavit of Samuel H. Hendrickson, Read in Opposition to the Motion," in *Application of Edmund C. Viemeister* (June 26, 1902), 26–29.

19. Viemeister v. White, 88 A.D. 44, 45–47, 49–50 (N.Y. App. Div. 2nd Dep't 1903).

20. "Appellant's Brief," in *Application of Edmund C. Viemeister* (May 1904), 2, 5.

21. "Appellant's Brief," 7, 8, 9, 11, 16.

22. "Respondents' Points," in *Application of Edmund C. Viemeister* (May 23, 1904), 7.

23. Matter of Viemeister, 179 N.Y. 235 (1904).

24. *Id.* at 238.

25. People v. Arensberg, 105 N.Y. 123, 127 (1887).

26. People v. Adirondack Railway Co., 160 N.Y. 225, 236 (1899).

27. Matter of Viemeister, 239.

28. *Id.* at 239–41.

29. "Vaccination in the Public Schools," *New York State Journal of Medicine* 5, no. 1 (Jan. 1905): 60.

30. Sanford T. Church, "The Present Status of the Law Relating to the Vaccination of School Children," in *Twenty-Fifth Annual Report of the State Department of Health, New York, for the Year Ending December 31, 1904* (Albany: Brandow Printing, 1906), 722.

31. Jacobson v. Massachusetts, 197 U.S. 11, 35, 34 (1905).

32. *Fifth Annual Report of the Education Department for the School Year Ending July 31, 1908* (Albany: New York State Education Department, 1909), 11.

33. "Vaccination Law Defied by Parents," *New York Times*, Jan. 10, 1911.

34. "Call Vaccination a Medical Sham," *New York Times*, Feb. 6, 1911.

35. *Ninth Annual Report of the Education Department* (Albany: New York State Education Department, 1913), 52.

36. People v. Ekerold, 211 N.Y. 386, 394 (1914).

37. James A. Loyster, *Vaccination Results in New York State in 1914* (Cazenovia, NY: printed by the author, 1915); Colgrove, *State of Immunity*, 65–67.

38. Loyster, *Vaccination Results*, 10, 16.

39. Loyster, 36, 38, 39.

40. "Compulsory Vaccination," *New York State Journal of Medicine* 15, no. 3 (March 1915): 85.

41. Quoted in "A History of New York State's Health Commissioners," New York State Department of Health, accessed July 31, 2021, https://www.health.ny.gov/commissioner/previous.

42. Howard Markel, "The Extraordinary Dr Biggs," *JAMA* 305, no. 23 (June 25, 2011), https://pubmed.ncbi.nlm.nih.gov/21673303.

43. Hermann M. Biggs, "Arguments in Favor of the Jones-Tallett Amendment to the Public Health Law in Relation to Vaccination. Given before the Public Health Committee of the Senate and Assembly.," Feb. 10, 1915, in *New York State Journal of Medicine* 15, no. 3 (March 1915): 89–90.

44. The cities were Albany, Buffalo, New York City, Rochester, Schenectady, Syracuse, Troy, Utica, and Yonkers. Department of Commerce, Bureau of the Census, "Statistics for New York," in *Thirteenth Census of the United States, Taken in the Year 1910* (Washington, DC: Government Printing Office, 1912), 568–69.

45. N.Y. Laws of 1915, ch. 133, §310.

46. Colgrove, *State of Immunity*, 70–74; *Forty-Second Annual Report of the State Department of Health for the Year Ending December 31, 1921* (Albany: J. B. Lyon, 1922), 81.

47. *Fifty-Fifth Annual Report of the Department of Health for the Year Ending December 31, 1934* (Albany: New York State Department of Health, 1935), 67.

48. Centers for Disease Control and Prevention, "Ten Great Public Health Achievements—United States, 1900–1999," *Morbidity and Mortality Weekly Report* 48, no. 12 (April 2, 1999): 244–48.

49. New York State Public Health Law §2164, accessed July 31, 2021, https://www.health.ny.gov/prevention/immunization/schools/docs/phl_title_vi.pdf.

50. Linda Poon, "How Mandatory Vaccination Fueled the Anti-Vaxxer Movement," *Bloomberg CityLab*, April 24, 2019, https://www.bloomberg.com/news/articles/2019-04-24/america-s-long-history-with-the-anti-vaxxers.

51. Erwin Chemerinsky and Michele Bratcher Goodwin, "Compulsory Vaccination Laws Are Constitutional," *Northwestern University Law Review* 110 (2016): 589–615; James G. Hodge Jr. and Lawrence O. Gostin, "School Vaccination Requirements: Historical, Social, and Legal Perspectives," *Kentucky Law Journal* 90, no. 4 (2002): 831–90.

52. F.F. v. State of New York, 2019 NY Slip Op 29261, 65 Misc. 3d 616, 626 (N.Y. Sup. Ct., Albany Cy. 2019).

CHAPTER 6

1. Douglas O. Linder, "The Trials of Harry Thaw for the Murder of Stanford White," *Famous Trials* (blog), ed. Douglas O. Linder, accessed Oct. 22, 2021, https://www.famous-trials.com/thaw/405-home. Paula Uruburu covers Evelyn Nesbit Thaw's life and the Thaw trials in detail in her book *American Eve: Evelyn Nesbit, Stanford White, the Birth of the "It" Girl, and the Crime of the Century* (New York: Riverhead Books, 2008).

2. Thomas Maeder, *Crime and Madness: The Origins and Evolution of the Insanity Defense* (New York: Harper and Row, 1985), 1–35.

3. William H. Silvernail, *The Penal Code of the State of New York* (Albany: W. C. Little, 1900), 9–11.

4. Richard Noll, "The Rise and Fall of American Madness," interview, *Harvard University Press Blog*, Jan. 30, 1912, accessed July 31, 2021, https://harvardpress.typepad.com/hup_publicity/2012/01/the-rise-and-fall-of-american-madness.html; James C. Mohr, *Doctors and the Law: Medical Jurisprudence in Nineteenth-Century America* (New York: Oxford, 1993).

5. Mark Twain, "A New Crime," in *The Writings of Mark Twain*, vol. 19 (New York: Harper & Bros., 1909), 24, quoted in Maeder, *Crime and Madness*, 54.

6. William C. Clark, "Insanity as a Defense in Homicide Cases in New York," *Bench and Bar* 50 (1907): 50–59.

7. People v. Taylor, 138 N.Y. 398, 407 (1893).

8. Donald F. Paine, "Murder in the Churchyard," *Tennessee Bar Journal* 43, no. 6 (2007): 14, 16, quoted in Russell D. Covey, "Temporary Insanity: The Strange Life and Times of the Perfect Defense," *Boston University Law Review* 91 (2011): 1616.

9. Lawrence M. Friedman, *Crime without Punishment: Aspects of the History of Homicide* (New York: Cambridge University Press, 2018), 20–59.

10. "People v. Cole," Historical Society of the New York Courts, accessed July 31, 2021, http://www.nycourts.gov/history/legal-history-new-york/legal-history-eras-04/history-new-york-legal-eras-people-cole.html.

11. Thomas J. Kernan, "The Jurisprudence of Lawlessness," *Green Bag* 18, no. 11 (1906): 588.

12. Analysis of the trial is provided in Uruburu, *American Eve*, 305–55; Simon Baatz, *The Girl on the Velvet Swing: Sex, Murder, and Madness at the Dawn of the Twentieth Century* (New York: Little, Brown, 2018), 130–84; Richard O'Connor, *Courtroom Warrior: The Combative Career of William Travers Jerome*

(New York: Little, Brown, 1963), 207–36; Cait Murphy, *Scoundrels in Law: The Trials of Hummel and Howe* (New York: Harper Collins, 2010), 240–61; Martha Merrill Umphrey, "Media Melodrama! Sensationalism in the 1907 Trial of Harry Thaw," *New York Law School Law Review* 43 (1999): 715–39.

13. "Jerome Stirs a Foe," *Washington Post*, Feb. 13, 1907.

14. "Fight to Prove Thaw Insane," *New York Times*, Feb. 28, 1907; O'Connor, *Courtroom Warrior*, 230–32.

15. "Jerome Scores on Thaw Expert," *New York Times*, March 2, 1907.

16. "Shift by Jerome Gives Thaw Hope," *New York Times*, March 5, 1907.

17. "Seven Experts All in Harmony," *San Francisco Chronicle*, March 22, 1907.

18. "Attacks Trial Experts," *New York Tribune*, March 3, 1907.

19. "Back to Thaw in Final Test," *Boston Daily Globe*, April 3, 1907.

20. "Agree Thaw Is Sane," *Washington Post*, April 5, 1907; "Report of the Lunacy Commission: Harry Thaw Trial, April 4, 1907, Submitted to Justice Fitzgerald by Chairman McClure," *Famous Trials*, https://www.famous-trials.com/thaw/429-report.

21. "Summation of Delphin Delmas for the Defense: Harry Thaw Trial, April 1907," *Famous Trials*, accessed July 30, 2021, https://www.famous-trials.com/thaw/424-summation; Baatz, *Girl on the Velvet Swing*, 174.

22. "Summation of William T. Jerome, D.A.: Harry Thaw Trial (April 10, 1907)," *Famous Trials*, accessed July 30, 2021, https://www.famous-trials.com/thaw/428-jeromeclose; Baatz, *Girl on the Velvet Swing*, 174–75; O'Connor, *Courtroom Warrior*, 230–36.

23. Martha Merrill Umphrey, "The Dialogics of Legal Meaning: Spectacular Trials, the Unwritten Law, and Narratives of Criminal Responsibility," *Law and Society Review* 33, no. 2 (1999): 395.

24. Harry C. Brearley, "The Thaw Trial as Seen by a Juror," *The Brief* 7 (1907): 94–106.

25. Baatz, *Girl on the Velvet Swing*, 25.

26. O'Connor, *Courtroom Warrior*, 236–40.

27. "Thaw Trial Near End," *Baltimore Sun*, Jan. 28, 1908.

28. "Shielding Himself in Wife's Skirts," *Boston Daily Globe*, Jan. 31, 1908.

29. Martin W. Littleton, "Summing Up to the Court or Jury," *Bench and Bar* 8 (1919): 13.

30. "Insanity Plea Urged to Save Harry Thaw," *Atlanta Constitution*, Jan. 30, 1908; "Littleton Pleads Insanity for Thaw," *New York Times*, Jan. 30, 1908.

31. "Fishkill Correction [sic] Facility," New York Correction History Society, accessed July 30, 2021, http://www.correctionhistory.org/html/chronicl/docs2day/fishkill.html. Originally published in "Facility Profile: Albion," *DOCS|TODAY* (Dec. 1998).

32. "To Be Out within a Week," *Boston Daily Globe*, Feb. 3, 1908.

33. People ex rel. A. Russell Peabody v. Chanler, 133 A.D. 159 (N.Y. App. Div. 2nd Dep't 1909).

34. "Thaw Stays in Matteawan," *Washington Post*, Oct. 21, 1908.

35. People ex rel. A. Russell Peabody v. Chanler, 196 N.Y. 525 (1909).

36. Baatz, *Girl on the Velvet Swing*, 216–63.

37. "Justice Denied Though Demanded," *Lawyer & Banker and Bench & Bar Review* 2 (1909): 210–12.

38. Baatz, *Girl on the Velvet Swing*, 264–93.

39. "Thaw Victory Brief in Jury Trial Fight," *New York Times*, April 24, 1915.

40. People ex rel. Woodbury v. Hendrick, 215 N.Y. 339, 342, 343, 349 (1915).

41. "Fourteen Thaw Witnesses Say He Is Sane Now," *New York Times*, June 26, 1915; Baatz, *Girl on the Velvet Swing*, 294–328.

42. "Thaw Not Insane in Killing White," *New York Times*, June 30, 1915.

43. "Thaw Now Acts Sanely, Dr. Flint Admits to Court," *New York Tribune*, July 7, 1915.

44. "Thaw Bears Well Five-Hour Grilling," *New York Times*, July 9, 1915.

45. "Thaw Matches Wits against Lawyers," *New York Times*, July 10, 1915.

46. "Thaw Found Sane by a Jury," *New York Times*, July 15, 1915.

47. "Thaw Issues His Final Statement," *New York Times*, July 21, 1915.

48. "'Unwritten Law' Won Thaw Juror," *New York Times*, July 19, 1915; "Robinson Censured by Fellow Jurors," *New York Times*, July 20, 1915.

49. "Harry Thaw's Story (from His Book, *The Traitor*): One Night in New York: Harry's Account of the Murder of Stanford White," *Famous Trials*, accessed July 30, 2021, https://www.famous-trials.com/thaw/420-thetraitor; "Harry L. [sic] Thaw, 76, Is Dead in Florida," *New York Times*, Feb. 22, 1947.

50. Uruburu, *American Eve*, 366–72; Stephanie Savage, "Evelyn Nesbit and the Film(ed) Histories of the Thaw-White Scandal," *Film History* 8, no. 2 (1996): 159–75.

51. "Sent Thaw's $1,000 Back," *New York Times*, July 4, 1913.

52. Allan McLane Hamilton, "The Defense of Insanity in Criminal Cases and Medical Expert Testimony: An Expert's View," *American Lawyer* 15, no. 7 (July 1907): 311.

53. Frederick W. Griffin, "Insanity as a Defense to Crime: With Especial Reference to the Thaw Case," *Journal of the American Institute of Criminal Law and Criminology* 1, no. 2 (1910): 13.

54. N.Y. Laws of 1910, ch. 557.

55. "Regulation of Expert Testimony as to Insanity in Criminal Cases," *Yale Law Journal* 38 (Jan. 1929): 368–76.

56. Committee on the Criminal Insane, "Report of the Special Committee on the Commitment and Discharge of the Criminally Insane," in *New York State Bar Association Proceedings of the Thirty-Fifth Annual Meeting [. . .]* (Albany: Argus, 1912), 176, 177, 185; Maeder, *Crime and Madness*, 60–61.

57. Smith Ely Jelliffe, "The New York State Bar Association Questionnaire—Some Comments," *Journal of the American Institute of Criminal Law and Criminology* 4 (May 1913): 368–77.

58. Mohr, *Doctors and the Law*, 251–57.

59. Friedman, *Crime without Punishment*, 137–38.

60. "Criminal Law—New York Procedure for Determination of Sanity of Defendant—Desmond Act," *Columbia Law Review* 39, no. 7 (Nov. 1939): 1260–68.

61. Robert Allan Carter, *History of the Insanity Defense in New York State* (Albany: New York State Library, 1982), 12.

62. New York State Unified Court System, *Insanity (Lack of Criminal Responsibility by Reason of Mental Disease or Defect): Penal Law §40.15*, accessed July 30, 2021, https://www.nycourts.gov/judges/cji/1-General/Defenses/CJI2d.Insanity.pdf.

63. Kevin Davis, *The Brain Defense: Murder in Manhattan and the Dawn of Neuroscience in America's Courtrooms* (New York: Penguin Press, 2017), 23–30, 55–57, 299–301.

CHAPTER 7

An earlier version of this chapter appeared as an article in *New York History* (fall 2021).

1. William J. Novak, "Institutional Economics and the Progressive Movement for Social Control of American Business," *Business History Review* 93, no. 4 (Winter 2019): 656–96; Joseph D. Kearney and Thomas W. Merrill, "The Great Transformation of Regulated Industries Law," *Columbia Law Review* 98, no. 6 (Oct. 1998): 1323–409; Anne Fleming, "Anti-Competition Regulation," *Business History Review* 93, no. 4 (Winter 2019): 701–24; Herbert J. Hovenkamp, "Appraising the Progressive State," *Iowa Law Review* 102 (March 2017): 1063–112.

2. Lawrence M. Friedman, *A History of American Law*, 4th ed. (New York: Oxford University Press, 2019), 417–18; see also William J. Novak, "The Public Utility Idea and the Origins of Modern Business Regulation," in Naomi R. Lamoreaux and William J. Novak, eds., *Corporations and American Democracy* (Cambridge, MA: Harvard University Press, 2017), 139–76. The issue of "legislative delegation" to administrative agencies is discussed in Eric A. Posner and Adrian Vermeule, "Interring the Nondelegation Doctrine," *University of Chicago Law Review* 69 (2002): 1721–62; and Cass R. Sunstein, "The American Nondelegation Doctrine," *George Washington Law Review* 86, no. 5 (2018): 1181–208.

3. Greg A. Jarrell, "The Demand for State Regulation of the Electric Utility Industry," *Journal of Law and Economics* 21, no. 2 (Oct. 1978): 269–96; William J. Hausman and John L. Neufeld, "How Politics, Economics, and Institutions Shaped Electric Utility Regulation in the United States: 1879–2009," *Business History* 53, no. 5 (Aug. 2011): 723–46.

4. Thomas M. Cooley, *A Treatise on the Constitutional Limitations Which Rest Upon the Legislative Power of the States of the American Union*, 7th ed. (Boston: Little, Brown, 1903), 116.

5. Field v. Clark, 146 U.S. 694 (1892).

6. "Assembly Passes Gas Bills; Senate Waits," *New York Times*, May 4, 1905. See also Robert F. Wesser, *Charles Evans Hughes: Politics and Reform in New York, 1905–1910* (Ithaca, NY: Cornell University Press, 1967), 18–33; Richard L. McCormick, *From Realignment to Reform: Political Change in New York State, 1893–1910* (Ithaca, NY: Cornell University Press, 1981), 193–97.

7. N.Y. Laws of 1905, ch. 737, §9.

8. N.Y. Laws of 1905, ch. 737, §17.

9. "Hearing on Gas Bill," *New York Tribune*, Feb. 16, 1906; "Gas Cut to 80 Cents by State Board Order," *New York Times*, Feb. 24, 1906.

10. The case file for this case in the New York Court of Appeals records, *Cases and Briefs on Appeal* in the State Archives, includes more than one thousand pages of attorneys' briefs filed before the court of appeals. Some were revised versions of those filed with the appellate division; some were new, just for the court of appeals. For convenience, the briefs are all covered later in this chapter, beginning with note 18.

11. Trustees of Village of Saratoga Springs v. Saratoga Gas, Electric Light, Heat & Power Co., 122 A.D. 203 (N.Y. App. Div. 3rd Dep't 1907).

12. *Id.* at 205, 206.

13. *Id.* at 214.

14. *Id.* at 215.

15. *Id.* at 217–22.

16. *Id.* at 229, 231.

17. "Cheap Gas Is Killed; No Special Session," *New York Times*, April 5, 1905; "Brackett Turned Down; Wemple Is Nominated," *New York Times*, Oct. 6, 1906. Brackett's political career rebounded, and he served again in the senate, 1909–12.

18. "Brief on Behalf of the Saratoga Gas, Electric Light and Power Company, the Appellant" (Jan. 2, 1908), in *Cases and Briefs on Appeal* for Village of Saratoga Springs v. Saratoga G., etc., Co., 191 N.Y. 123, New York State Court of Appeals Records, New York State Archives, Albany.

19. "Brief on Behalf of Saratoga Gas," 42, 43, 44, 79.

20. "Brief for the Appellant on Special Points of Law" (Jan. 17, 1908), 32, in *Cases and Briefs on Appeal* for Village of Saratoga Springs v. Saratoga G., etc., Co.

21. "Special Points of Law," 37.

22. "Special Points of Law," 22, 24, 25.

23. "Special Points of Law," 86, 62.

24. "Special Points of Law," 33, 34, 35.

25. "Brief on Behalf of the Trustees of the Village of Saratoga Springs, Respondents" (1908), 138–57, in *Cases and Briefs on Appeal* for Village of Saratoga Springs v. Saratoga G., etc., Co.

26. "Brief of the Attorney General" (1908), 48, in *Cases and Briefs on Appeal* for Village of Saratoga Springs v. Saratoga G., etc., Co.

27. "Brief of the Attorney General," 8, 18, 11.

28. "Brief of the Attorney General," 37, 38, 39, 44.

29. "Brief for the Public Service Commission—Second District" (1908), 3, 9, in *Cases and Briefs on Appeal* for Village of Saratoga Springs v. Saratoga G., etc., Co.

30. "Brief for the Public Service Commission," 6–8.

31. "Brief for the Public Service Commission," 30.

32. "Supplementary Brief for Respondent" (Jan. 21, 1908), 2, 3, 10, 12, in *Cases and Briefs on Appeal* for Village of Saratoga Springs v. Saratoga G., etc., Co.

33. "Supplemental Brief for Appellant" (Jan. 1908), 2, 5, 8, 18–42, in *Cases and Briefs on Appeal* for Village of Saratoga Springs v. Saratoga G., etc., Co.

34. "Supplemental Brief for Appellant," 50–56.

35. "Edgar M. Cullen," Historical Society of the New York Courts, accessed Aug. 1, 2021, https://history.nycourts.gov/biography/edgar-m-cullen; George W. Wingate, "The Honorable Edgar Montgomery Cullen," *Bench and Bar* 7, no. 3 (1914): 94–95; Edgar M. Cullen, "The Decline of Personal Liberty in America," *American Law Review* 48 (1914): 345–64.

36. Village of Saratoga Springs v. Saratoga G., etc., Co., 191 N.Y. 123, 125–37 (1908).

37. *Id.* at 138.

38. *Id.* at 143.

39. *Id.* at 144–45, 147.

40. *Id.* at 149.

41. William Schuyler Jackson, *Annual Report of the Attorney General of the State of New York for the Year Ending December 31, 1908* (Albany: J. B. Lyon, 1909), 119.

42. David J. Danelski and Joseph S. Tulchin, eds., *The Autobiographical Notes of Charles Evans Hughes* (Cambridge, MA: Harvard University Press, 1973), 143–44.

43. Walter Carrington, "Delegation of Power to Boards and Commissions," *Virginia Law Register* 6, no. 11 (March 1921): 801–12.

44. Michael Ezra Fine, "Rethinking the Nondelegation Doctrine," *Boston University Law Review* 62 (1982): 257–69.

45. A. L. A. Schechter Poultry Corp. v. United States, 295 U.S. 495, 529–30 (1935). James A. Henretta, "Charles Evans Hughes and the Strange Death of Liberal America," *Law and History Review* 24, no. 1 (Spring 2006): 115–71, traces the evolution of Hughes's views on regulation.

46. Roscoe Pound, "Administrative Law and the Courts," *Boston Law Review* 24, no. 4 (1944): 201, 203, 204, 210, 219.

47. Alasdair S. Roberts, "Should We Defend the Administrative State?," *Public Administration Review* 80, no. 3 (May/June 2020): 391–401; Joseph Postell, "The Nondelegation Doctrine after *Gundy*," *New York University Journal of Law and Liberty* 13 (2020): 279–323.

CHAPTER 8

1. Robert F. Wesser, *Charles Evans Hughes: Politics and Reform in New York, 1905–1910* (Ithaca, NY: Cornell University Press, 1967), 70–101; Richard L. McCormick, *From Realignment to Reform: Political Change in New York State, 1893–1910* (Ithaca, NY: Cornell University Press, 1981), 219–27. The work of the Public Service Commission is summarized in Bruce W. Dearstyne, "Regulation in the Progressive Era: The New York Public Service Commission," *New York History* 58, no. 3 (July 1977): 330–47. Its work with railroads is covered in Dearstyne, *Railroads and Railroad Regulation in New York State, 1900–1913* (New York: Garland Press, 1986).

2. Charles Evans Hughes, "Message to the Legislature, January 2, 1907, Recommending the Passage of a Public-Service Commissions Law," in *Addresses and Papers of Charles Evans Hughes, Governor of New York, 1906–1908*, ed. Jacob Gould Schurman (New York: G. P. Putnam's Sons, 1908), 89–99.

3. David J. Danelski and Joseph S. Tulchin, eds., *The Autobiographical Notes of Charles Evans Hughes* (Cambridge, MA: Harvard University Press, 1973), 141. Wesser, 153–67, describes the legislative history of the proposal.

4. Dearstyne, *Railroads and Railroad Regulation*, 31–74.

5. Charles Evans Hughes, "Speech at the Banquet of the Utica Chamber of Commerce, April 1, 1907" and "Speech before the Elmira Chamber of Commerce, May 3, 1907," in Schurman, *Addresses and Papers*, 105, 141, 140.

6. N.Y. Laws of 1907, ch. 429.

7. Wesser, 168–69.

8. Frank W. Stevens, "The Work of the Public Service Commission, Second District, and Its Policies with relation to the Corporations under Its Supervision" (speech), in *Discussion of Present Day Problems* (pamphlet, Empire State Gas and Electric Association / Street Railway Association of the State of New York, Oct. 1, 1907), 11, 6.

9. Thomas M. Osborne, "The Public Service Commissions Law of New York State," *Proceedings of the American Political Science Association* 4 (1907): 300.

10. Martin S. Decker, "Practical versus Theoretical Railway Regulation," *Railway Age* 45 (May 1, 1908): 636–37.

11. New York State Public Service Commission, Second District, *First Annual Report of the Public Service Commission, Second District, for the Six Months ending December 31, 1907*, vol. 1 (Albany: J. B. Lyon, 1908), 43, 34–35.

12. "Regulation by Commission," *Railway Age* 45 (May 1, 1908): 622–23.

13. Harold J. Howland, "A Year of 'Government by Commission,'" *Outlook* 90 (October 31, 1908).

14. Dearstyne, *Railroads and Railroad Regulation*, 184–292.

15. Leon Leighton, "Review of the Public Service Commission and the Transit Commission in the New York Courts," *St. John's Law Review* 3 (1928): 43–102;

Charles Hyneman, "The Case Law of the New York Public Service Commission," *Columbia Law Review* 67 (1934): 67–105.

16. William M. Ivins and Herbert Delavan Mason, *The Control of Public Utilities, in the Form of an Annotation of the Public Services Commissions Law of the State of New York and Covering All Important American Cases [. . .]* (New York: Baker, Voorhis, 1908), 4–8.

17. People ex rel. Joline v. Willcox, 129 A.D. 267, 269, 273, 270, 271, 273 (N.Y. App. Div. 1st Dep't 1908).

18. People ex rel. C. P., etc., R. R. Co. v. Willcox, 194 N.Y. 383, 386 (1910).

19. Matter of Buffalo Frontier Terminal R. R. Co., 113 A.D. 503, 510, 509 (N.Y. App. Div. 4th Dep't 1909).

20. Adikes v. Long Island Railroad, 165 A.D. 221, 224 (N.Y. App. Div. 2d Dep't 1914).

21. Loomis v. Lehigh Valley R. R. Co., 208 N.Y. 312, 326, 327 (1913).

22. People ex rel. N.Y. Queens Gas Co. v. McCall, 219 N.Y. 84, 87–88 (1916).

23. People ex rel. South Shore Traction Co. v Willcox, 196 N.Y. 212, 217 (1909).

24. People ex rel. New York Edison Co. v. Willcox, 207 N.Y. 86, 93–94 (1912).

25. People ex rel. Long Island Railroad v. Public Service Commission, First District, 173 A.D. 780, 781, 782 (N.Y. App. Div. 1st Dep't 1916).The opinion was written by Judge Alfred Page, a former state senator who had been a sponsor of the PSC bill in the senate.

26. People v. New York Central & Hudson River Railroad Co., 138 A.D. 601, 602, 605 (N.Y. App. Div. 3rd Dep't 1910). The court was lenient, imposing only a $100 fine. The court of appeals confirmed the decision but without issuing an opinion (199 N.Y. 539 [1910]).

27. New York Central & Hudson River Railroad v. Smith, 62 Misc. 526 (N.Y. Sup. Ct. Putnam Special Term 1909).

28. City of Troy v. United Traction Co., 202 N.Y. 333, 340 (1911).

29. People ex rel. Dry Dock, East Broadway & Battery R. R. Co. v. Public Service Commission, 167 A.D. 286, 296, 308, 297 (N.Y. App. Div. 1st Dep't 1915).

30. People ex rel. D. H. Co. v. Stevens, 197 N.Y. 1, 9, 10, 12, 13 (1909).

31. People ex rel. Binghamton L., H. P. Co. v. Stevens, 203 N.Y. 7, 21 (1911).

32. Murphy v. New York Central Railroad Co., 225 N.Y. 548, 557, 555, 552 (1919).

33. People ex rel. New York Central & Hudson River R. R. Co. v. Public Service Commission, 215 N.Y. 241, 246, 248 (1915); People ex rel. New York, New Haven & Hartford R. R. Co. v. Public Service Commission, 215 N.Y. 689 (1915).

34. Dearstyne, *Railroads and Railroad Regulation*, 289–90.

35. "Hughes Sticks Questions to Chanler," *New York Times*, Oct. 15, 1908.

36. Frank W. Stevens, *The Beginnings of the New York Central Railroad: A History* (New York: G. P. Putnam, 1926).

37. Charles Evans Hughes, "Address before the New York State Bar Association, January 14, 1916: Some Aspects of the Development of American Law," in Jacob Gould Schurman, ed., *Addresses of Charles Evans Hughes, 1906–1916* (New York: G. P. Putnam's Sons, 1916), 332, 333, 336, 335–36, 347.

38. Hughes, "American Law," 353, 355, 357.

CHAPTER 9

1. William S. Pretzer and Thomas Tanselle, "Printing," in *The Encyclopedia of New York City*, 2nd ed., ed. Kenneth T. Jackson (New Haven, CT: Yale University Press, 2010), 1037–38.

2. "Legislation for Women in Industry," *American Labor Legislation Review* 6 (1916): 357–59.

3. "Information," Court of Special Sessions of the City of New York, 1st Division, People v. Williams (1907), 3, 5. Copy in *Cases and Briefs on Appeal* for People v. Williams, 189 N.Y. 131, New York State Court of Appeals Records, New York State Archives, Albany.

4. Michael McGerr, *A Fierce Discontent: The Rise and Fall of the Progressive Movement in America, 1870–1920* (New York: Free Press, 2003), 137.

5. New York State Department of Labor, *Eighteenth Annual Report on Factory Inspection for Twelve Months Ending September 30, 1903* (Albany: Oliver A. Quayle, 1904), xv.

6. New York State Department of Labor, *Fourth Annual Report of the Commissioner of Labor for the Twelve Months Ended September 30, 1904* (Albany: Brandow Printing, 1905), 42.

7. New York State Department of Labor, *Fifth Annual Report of the Commissioner of Labor for the Twelve Months Ended September 30, 1905* (Albany: Brandow Printing, 1906), 18–37.

8. Josephine C. Goldmark, "Workingwomen and the Laws: A Record of Neglect," *Annals of the American Academy of Political and Social Science* 28 (Sept. 1906): 64.

9. David E. Bernstein, *Rehabilitating* Lochner: *Defending Individual Rights against Progressive Reform* (Chicago: University of Chicago Press, 2011), 56–72.

10. Bernstein, 57.

11. Nancy Woloch, *A Class by Herself: Protective Laws for Women Workers, 1890s–1990s* (Princeton, NJ: Princeton University Press, 2015), 33–53.

12. Julie Novkov, *Constituting Workers, Protecting Women: Gender, Law, and Labor in the Progressive Era and New Deal Years* (Ann Arbor: University of Michigan Press, 2001), 86.

13. Novkov, 78–121.

14. New York State Department of Labor, *Sixth Annual Report of the Commissioner of Labor for the Twelve Months Ended September 30, 1906* (Albany: J. B. Lyon, 1907), I.59.

15. New York State Department of Labor, *Sixth Annual Report*, I.60.

16. "Decisions of New York Courts," *New York Labor Bulletin* 8, no. 3 (Sept. 1906): 339.

17. "Testimony," Court of Special Sessions of the City of New York, People v. Williams, 6–7.

18. "Labor Laws for Women," *New York Tribune*, April 4, 1906.

19. Opinion (Aug. 3, 1906), Court of Special Sessions of the City of New York, People v. Williams, 11.

20. Opinion, Court of Special Sessions, 16.

21. Opinion, 15.

22. Opinion, 17.

23. Opinion, 21.

24. Opinion, 18–19.

25. "Women's Work," *New York Times*, Aug. 5, 1906.

26. Quoted in Josephine Goldmark, *Impatient Crusader: Florence Kelley's Life Story* (Urbana: University of Illinois Press, 1953), 148.

27. Opinion, Sup. Ct. App. Div., 1st Dep't, *People v. Williams* (Dec. 3, 1906), 29. Copy in *Cases and Briefs on Appeal* for People v. Williams, 189 N.Y. 131.

28. Opinion, Sup. Ct. App. Div., 30, 33.

29. Opinion, Sup. Ct. App. Div., 36.

30. Brief of appellant (1907). Copy in *Cases and Briefs on Appeal* for People v. Williams, 189 N.Y. 131.

31. Brief of appellant, 4–5.

32. Brief of appellant, 5.

33. Brief of appellant, 5–6.

34. Brief of appellant, 7.

35. Brief of appellant, 8–9.

36. Brief of appellant, 10–11.

37. Henry B. Corey, *Law without Lawyers: A Compendium of Business and Domestic Law for Popular Use* (New York: A. L. Burt, 1885), 5.

38. Brief of respondent (1907). Copy in *Cases and Briefs on Appeal* for People v. Williams, 189 N.Y. 131.

39. Brief of respondent, 2–3.

40. Brief of respondent, 3.

41. Brief of respondent, 7, 9–10.

42. Brief of respondent, 10, 12.

43. People v. Williams, 189 N.Y. 131 (1907).

44. *Id.* at 134.

45. *Id.* at 135.

46. People v. Lochner, 177 N.Y. 145, 167 (1904).

47. *Williams*, 136, 137.

48. "Decisions of New York Courts," *New York Labor Bulletin* 9, no. 2 (June 1907): 177.

49. New York State Department of Labor, *Seventh Annual Report of the Commissioner of Labor for the Twelve Months Ended September 30, 1907* (Albany: J. B. Lyon, 1908), I.47–I.51.

50. Robert F. Wesser, *Charles Evans Hughes: Politics and Reform in New York, 1905–1910* (Ithaca, NY: Cornell University Press, 1967), 311–12.

51. Andrew A. Bruce, "Constitutional Law. (Police Power—Labor Law.) N. Y.," *Green Bag* 19, no. 10 (1907): 627.

52. Josephine Goldmark, *Fatigue and Efficiency: A Study in Industry* (New York: Russell Sage Foundation, 1912), 248, 251.

53. Ernest Bruncken, "The Elasticity of the Constitution," *Green Bag* 20 (1908): 19.

54. P. Tecumseh Sherman, "Factory Laws and the Courts," *New York Labor Bulletin* 9, no. 3 (Sept. 1907): 336.

55. Sherman, 337.

56. Sherman, 337, 338, 343, 343–44.

CHAPTER 10

1. Annelise Orleck, *Common Sense and a Little Fire: Women and Working-Class Politics in the United States, 1900–1965* (Chapel Hill: University of North Carolina Press, 1995), 53–86, 121–58.

2. Melvin I. Urofsky, *Louis D. Brandeis: A Life* (New York: Pantheon Books, 2009), 201–24; Nancy Woloch, *A Class by Herself: Protective Laws for Women Workers, 1890s–1990s* (Princeton, NJ: Princeton University Press, 2015), 54–84; David E. Bernstein, *Rehabilitating Lochner: Defending Individual Rights against Progressive Reform* (Chicago: University of Chicago Press, 2011), 57–72.

3. John Thomas McGuire, "Making the Case for Night Work Legislation in Progressive Era New York, 1911–1915," *Journal of the Gilded Age and Progressive Era* 5, no. 1 (Jan. 2006): 47–51; Josephine Goldmark, *Impatient Crusader: Florence Kelley's Life Story* (Urbana: University of Illinois Press, 1953), 50–65, 143–79.

4. Robert F. Wesser, *A Response to Progressivism: The Democratic Party and New York Politics, 1902–1918* (New York: New York University Press, 1986), 71–75; "Remembering the 1911 Triangle Factory Fire," Kheel Center, Cornell University, accessed July 31, 2021, https://trianglefire.ilr.cornell.edu.

5. *Second Report of the Factory Investigating Commission* (Albany: J. B. Lyon, 1913), 194, 202.

6. *Second Report*, 203, 205, 208; McGuire, "Night Work Legislation," 63–67.

7. N. Y. Laws of 1913, ch. 83.

8. *The Consumers' League of the City of New York: Report for the Year 1913* (New York: Consumers' League of the City of New York, 1914), 31.

9. "The Man Who Prints the Magazines," *McClure's Magazine* 41 (Sept. 1913): 112.

10. Nancy Woloch, *A Class by Herself*, 95–96.

11. "Test Woman's Right to Work at Night," *New York Times*, Feb. 20, 1914.

12. "Test Woman's Right."

13. "Woman Labor Law Upheld by Court," *New York Times*, April 28, 1914.

14. Louis D. Brandeis and Josephine Goldmark, *The People of the State of New York, against Charles Schweinler Press, a Corporation, Defendant: A Summary of "Facts of Knowledge" Submitted on Behalf of the People in Support of Its Brief on the Law* (1914). Copy in *Cases and Briefs on Appeal* for People v. Charles Schweinler Press, 214 N.Y. 402, New York State Court of Appeals Records, New York State Archives, Albany.

15. Brandeis and Goldmark, *"Facts of Knowledge,"* 8, 55–74, 110–11, 174, 213.

16. Brandeis and Goldmark, 512–29.

17. Josephine Goldmark, "Night Work of Women," *New York Times*, May 1, 1914.

18. Alfred Ommen, "Night Work Not Harmful," *New York Times*, May 3, 1914.

19. People v. Charles Schweinler Press, 163 A.D. 620 (N.Y. App. Div. 1st Dep't 1914).

20. *Id.* at 624–25.

21. *Id.* at 626.

22. *Id.* at 630.

23. "Appellant's Points" (1914). In *Cases and Briefs on Appeal* for People v. Charles Schweinler Press, Court of Appeals Records.

24. "Appellant's Points," 1–5.

25. "Appellant's Points," 16, 20, 19.

26. "Appellant's Points," 26–27, 29.

27. "Appellant's Points," 38.

28. "The People's (Respondent's) Brief on the Law" (1914), 6. In *Cases and Briefs on Appeal* for People v. Charles Schweinler Press, Court of Appeals Records.

29. "People's Brief," 17–27.

30. "People's Brief," 28, 30–31.

31. "People's Brief," 17, 45, 47.

32. "Supplement to the People's (Respondent's) Brief on the Law" (1915), 7. In *Cases and Briefs on Appeal* for People v. Charles Schweinler Press, Court of Appeals Records.

33. "Brief of the Attorney-General in Support of the Labor Law" (1915), 5, 40. In *Cases and Briefs on Appeal* for People v. Charles Schweinler Press, Court of Appeals Records.

34. "Brief Submitted on Behalf of the New York State Factory Investigating Commission as Amicus Curiae" (1915), 5, 7, 14, 30, 35, 49, 67. In *Cases and Briefs on Appeal* for People v. Charles Schweinler Press, Court of Appeals Records.

35. "Brief on Behalf of the Association of Ice Cream Manufacturers of New York State" (1914). In *Cases and Briefs on Appeal* for People v. Charles Schweinler Press, Court of Appeals Records.

36. "Appellant's Reply Brief" (1915). In *Cases and Briefs on Appeal* for People v. Charles Schweinler Press, Court of Appeals Records.

37. "Reply Brief," 1–6.

38. "Reply Brief," 7.

39. "Reply Brief," 9.

40. "Reply Brief," 10, 11, 15.

41. "Reply Brief," 12.

42. People v. Charles Schweinler Press, 214 N.Y. 395 (1915).

43. Frank Harris Hiscock, "Progressiveness of New York Law," *Cornell Law Quarterly* 9, no. 4 (1924): 383.

44. People v. Charles Schweinler Press, 214 N.Y. 395, 401 (1915).

45. *Id.* at 403, 406.

46. *Id.* at 411, 412–13.

47. *Id.* at 408, 409.

48. Alfred Ommen, "Women's Work," *New York Times*, April 15, 1915.

49. Woloch, *A Class by Herself*, 94.

50. Jill Lepore, *These Truths: A History of the United States* (New York: W. W. Norton, 2018), 382.

51. Woloch, *A Class by Herself*, 121–234.

CHAPTER 11

1. *Report to the Legislature of the State of New York by the Commission Appointed under Chapter 518 of the Laws of 1909 to Inquire into the Question of Employers' Liability and Other Matters: First Report* (Albany: J. B. Lyon, 1910), 5. Referred to hereafter as *Wainwright Commission First Report*, after its chairman, state senator J. Mayhew Wainwright.

2. John Fabian Witt, "The Transformation of Work and the Law of Workplace Accidents, 1842–1910," *Yale Law Journal* 107, no. 5 (March 1998): 1467–501; G. Edward White, *Law in American History, Volume II: From Reconstruction through the 1920s* (New York: Oxford University Press, 2016), 232–33, 256–58.

3. R. Rudy Higgens-Evenson, "From Industrial Police to Workmen's Compensation: Public Policy and Industrial Accidents in New York, 1880–1910," *Labor History* 39, no. 4 (1998): 365–80.

4. Robert F. Wesser, "Conflict and Compromise: The Workmen's Compensation Movement in New York, 1890s–1913," *Labor History* 12, no. 3 (1971): 345–48; Irwin Yellowitz, *Labor and the Progressive Movement in New York State 1897–1916* (Ithaca, NY: Cornell University Press, 1965), 108–21; Robert Asher, "Failure and Fulfillment: Agitation for Employers' Liability Legislation and the Origins of Workmen's Compensation in New York State, 1876–1910," *Labor History* 24, no. 2 (1983): 198–222.

5. Crystal Eastman, *Work-Accidents and the Law* (New York: Russell Sage Foundation, 1910). Eastman summarized her findings in a booklet, *Employers' Liability: A Criticism Based on Facts* (New York: American Association for Labor Legislation, 1909).

6. Robert F. Wesser, *Charles Evans Hughes: Politics and Reform in New York, 1905–1910* (Ithaca, NY: Cornell University Press, 1967), 313–19; "Pleads for Justice to Injured Workers," *New York Times*, Feb. 28, 1910; "Would Broaden Liability Law," *New York Times*, March 22, 1910.

7. Price V. Fishback and Shawn Everett Kantor, "The Adoption of Workers' Compensation in the United States, 1900–1930," *Journal of Law and Economics* 41, no. 2 (Oct. 1998): 305–41.

8. New York State Bar Association, *Proceedings of the Thirty-Third Annual Meeting Held at Rochester January 18, 20–21, 1910 [. . .]* (Albany: Argus, 1910), 428–58.

9. Crystal Eastman, "Employers' Liability," in New York State Bar Association, *Proceedings of the Thirty-Third Annual Meeting*, 482.

10. New York State Bar Association, *Proceedings of the Thirty-Third Annual Meeting*, 460–511.

11. *Wainwright Commission First Report*, 5, 19, 10.

12. *Wainwright Commission First Report*, 1–69.

13. N.Y. Laws of 1910, ch. 674. The law referred to "he," "workman," and "workmen," though it was meant to apply to all workers in the designated industries. The compensation law enacted in 1914, described in the next chapter, also used masculine references. Years later, the title and text of the law were changed to "workers" to make it gender neutral.

14. *Wainwright Commission First Report*, 51.

15. *Wainwright Commission First Report*, 54.

16. "Notes on the Labor Laws of 1910," *New York Labor Bulletin* 12, no. 2 (June 1910): 234.

17. *Wainwright Commission First Report*, 81–82. Pound would later join the court of appeals and serve as chief judge.

18. *Wainwright Commission First Report*, 262–71, 47.

19. Charles Evans Hughes, "Memoranda of Legislative Bills Approved," *Public Papers of Charles E. Hughes, Governor, 1910* (Albany: J. B. Lyon, 1910), 236.

20. "Papers on Appeal" (1911), 6. Copy in *Cases and Briefs on Appeal* for Ives v. South Buffalo Railway Co., 201 N.Y. 271, New York State Court of Appeals Records, New York State Archives, Albany.

21. "Papers on Appeal," 19.

22. "Brief on Behalf of Respondent" (1911), 28. Copy in *Cases and Briefs on Appeal* for Ives v. South Buffalo Railway Co., 201 N.Y. 271.

23. "Brief on Behalf of Respondent," 32, 43.

24. Joseph P. Cotton Jr., "Brief of Intervenor in Support of Judgment" (1911), 7. Copy in *Cases and Briefs on Appeal* for Ives v. South Buffalo Railway Co., 201 N.Y. 271.

25. Cotton, "Brief of Intervenor," 12, 16, 17.

26. Cotton, 39.

27. Cotton, 42.

28. "Brief on Behalf of the Civic Federation Filed by Everett P. Wheeler as Amicus Curiae, in Support of the Judgment" (Feb. 1, 1911), 2, 13, 15, 18, 21–22. Copy in *Cases and Briefs on Appeal* for Ives v. South Buffalo Railway Co., 201 N.Y. 271.

29. "Brief on Behalf of the Civic Federation," 29, 30.

30. "Appellant's Points" (1911), 6–7. Copy in *Cases and Briefs on Appeal* for Ives v. South Buffalo Railway Co., 201 N.Y. 271.

31. "Appellant's Points," 8, 13–23, 136.

32. "Appellant's Points," 27–28.

33. "Appellant's Points," 31–32.

34. "Appellant's Points," 33, 36, 37–41.

35. "Appellant's Points," 57, 67, 68.

36. "Appellant's Points," 75–108.

37. "Appellant's Points," 116–23.

38. "Appellant's Points," 128–36.

39. Ives v. South Buffalo Railway Co., 201 N.Y. 271 (1911).

40. *Id.* at 285.

41. *Id.* at 287.

42. *Id.* at 287.

43. *Id.* at 292.

44. *Id.* at 288–89.

45. *Id.* at 288, 291.

46. *Id.* at 293, 294, 300, 294.

47. *Id.* at 295–96.

48. *Id.* at 300, 301, 302, 304, 306–8.

49. *Id.* at 307, 317.

50. *Id.* at 318–20.

51. "Employers' Liability," *New York Times*, March 25, 1911.

CHAPTER 12

1. Ives v. South Buffalo Railway Co., 201 N.Y. 271 (1911).

2. New York State Department of Labor, *Annual Reports of Department Bureaus for the Twelve Months Ended September 30, 1910* (Albany: State Department of Labor, 1912), 13.

3. The compensation laws referred to "workman" and "workmen" though the laws were meant to apply to all workers in designated industries. Years later, the title and text of the law were changed to "workers" to make it gender neutral.

4. *Report to the Legislature of the State of New York by the Commission Appointed under Chapter 518 of the Laws of 1909 to Inquire into the Question of Employers' Liability and Other Matters: Fourth Report* (Albany: J. B. Lyon, 1911), 1–7.

5. "Bar Wants Action on Workmen's Bill," *New York Times*, Jan. 26, 1913; "Four Amendments before the Voters," *New York Times*, Oct. 26, 1913.

6. "The Constitution of the State of New York," in Edgar L. Murlin, *The New York Red Book* (Albany: J. B. Lyon, 1915), Article I, §19, pp. 237–38.

7. Lawrence M. Friedman, *A History of American Law*, 4th ed. (New York: Oxford University Press, 2019), 664–67; American Association for Labor Legislation, *Standards for Workmen's Compensation Laws* (New York: AALL, 1914), 3–12.

8. "Remembering the 1911 Triangle Factory Fire," Kheel Center, Cornell University, accessed July 30, 2021, https://trianglefire.ilr.cornell.edu; Richard A. Greenwald, *The Triangle Fire, the Protocols of Peace, and Industrial Democracy in Progressive Era New York* (Philadelphia: Temple University Press, 2005), 129–214.

9. Robert F. Wesser, "Conflict and Compromise: The Workmen's Compensation Movement in New York, 1890s–1913," *Labor History* 12, no. 3 (1971): 358–67; Matthew L. Lifflander, *The Impeachment of Governor Sulzer: A Story of American Politics* (Albany: State University of New York Press, 2012), 115–320; Terry Golway, *Machine Made: Tammany Hall and the Creation of Modern American Politics* (New York: Liveright, 2014), 211–12.

10. "All Glynn Bills Pass in a Rush," *New York Times*, Dec. 13, 1913; Wesser, "Conflict and Compromise," 368–72. The governor signed the law again on January 8, 1914, due to a technicality—the constitutional amendment that authorized it, approved in November 1913, did not actually take effect until January 1, 1914. The legislature passed an amended version of the law on March 16, 1914, providing that no more than three of the five commissioners may be of the same party, and the governor signed it.

11. N.Y. Laws of 1913, ch. 816.

12. State of New York, *Annual Report of the State Workmen's Compensation Commission, February 1, 1915* (transmitted to the legislature March 8, 1915; Albany: J. B. Lyon, 1915), 10, 9, 67, 80; "Accident Awards Begin," *New York Times*, July 20, 1914; "Accident Claims Swamp State Board," *New York Times*, July 29, 1914.

13. "Compensation Law Saves Her House," *New York Times*, Oct. 4, 1914.

14. "Glynn Sees Widow Get Labor Pension," *New York Times*, Sept. 24, 1914.

15. Bruce W. Dearstyne, *The Spirit of New York: Defining Events in the Empire State's History* (Albany: State University of New York Press, 2015), 185.

16. *Annual Report of the Industrial Commission for the Twelve Months Ended September 30, 1915* (transmitted to the legislature April 7, 1916; Albany: New York State Department of Labor, 1916), 10.

17. *Report of Reconstruction Commission to Governor Alfred E. Smith on Retrenchment and Reorganization in the State Government, October 10, 1919* (Albany: J. B. Lyon, 1919), 115.

18. *Annual Report of the Industrial Commission [. . .] 1915*, 9–32; *Annual Report of the Industrial Commission for the Nine Months Ended June 30, 1916* (transmitted to the legislature April 17, 1917; Albany: State Department of Labor, 1917), 15–19, 113–23. Years later, the compensation board returned to being an independent agency.

19. Matter of Jensen v. Southern Pacific Co., 215 N.Y. 514 (1915).

20. *Id.* at 516, 521, 522.

21. *Id.* at 523, 524, 525.

22. *Id.* at 528.

23. *Id.* at 528.

24. Southern Pacific Co. v. Jensen, 244 U.S. 205 (1917); James E. Brown, "The Jensen Case and the Doctrine of Local Concern," *Loyola Law Review* 1 (1941): 74–83.

25. Matter of White v. New York Central & Hudson River Railroad, 216 N.Y. 653 (1915).

26. New York Central Railroad Co. v. White, 243 U.S. 188 (1917). The Supreme Court validated workmen's compensation laws in Iowa and the state of Washington the same day. "Compensation Law Upheld," *New York Times*, March 7, 1917; Leon S. Senior, "A Study of Judicial Decisions in New York Workmen's Compensation Cases," *Proceedings of the Casualty Actuarial Society* 12 (1925): 73–96.

27. *New York Central R.R. Co. v. White*, 192.

28. *Id.* at 198, 200.

29. *Id.* at 201–5.

30. *Id.* at 206.

31. *Id.* at 208.

32. G. Edward White, *Law in American History, Volume II: From Reconstruction through the 1920s* (New York: Oxford University Press, 2016), 257–58.

CONCLUSION

1. MacPherson v. Buick Motor Co., 217 N.Y. 382 (1916); Andrew L. Kaufman, *Cardozo* (Cambridge, MA: Harvard University Press, 1998), 265–85; G.

Edward White, *Law in American History, Volume II: From Reconstruction through the 1920s* (New York: Oxford University Press, 2016), 259–66.

2. *Court of Appeals of the State of New York: Restoration and Renovation, 1842–2004* (pamphlet, 2004), 4, accessed July 30, 2021, https://www.nycourts.gov/ctapps/news/1230LB.pdf.

3. *State of New York Judiciary Constitutional Convention of 1921: Report to Legislature* (Albany: J. B. Lyon, 1922), 7–8.

4. *Judiciary Constitutional Convention*, 10–12; Peter J. Galie, *Ordered Liberty: A Constitutional History of New York* (New York: Fordham University Press, 1996), 214–16.

5. William E. Nelson, *The Legalist Reformation: Law, Politics, and Ideology in New York, 1920–1980* (Chapel Hill: University of North Carolina Press, 2001), 5, 7.

6. Kermit L. Hall, *The Magic Mirror: Law in American History* (New York: Oxford University Press, 1989), 227–46; Lawrence M. Friedman, *American Law in the 20th Century* (New Haven, CT: Yale University Press, 2002), 45–79.

7. Melvin I. Urofsky, "State Courts and Protective Legislation during the Progressive Era: A Reevaluation," *Journal of American History* 72, no. 1 (June 1985): 63–91; Felice Batlan, "A Reevaluation of the New York Court of Appeals: The Home, the Market, and Labor, 1885–1905," *Law and Social Inquiry* 27, no. 3 (2006): 489–528.

8. Paul Kens, "The Constitution and Business Regulation in the Progressive Era: Recent Developments and New Opportunities," *American Journal of Legal History* 56, no. 1 (2016): 97–103; David E. Bernstein, *Rehabilitating* Lochner: *Defending Individual Rights against Progressive Reform* (Chicago: University of Chicago Press, 2011); Howard Gillman, *The Constitution Besieged: The Rise and Demise of Lochner Era Police Powers Jurisprudence* (Durham, NC: Duke University Press, 1995).

9. Richard A. Posner, "Pragmatic Adjudication," *Cardozo Law Review* 18, no. 1 (1996): 4–5; Posner, *How Judges Think* (Cambridge, MA: Harvard University Press, 2008), 230–65.

10. Cuthbert W. Pound, "American Law Institute Speech of Judge Pound," *New York State Bar Association Bulletin* 5 (1933): 265–70.

SELECTED BIBLIOGRAPHY

Two sources are of outstanding importance for the book. The first is decisions of New York State courts, primarily the court of appeals, the state's highest court. Most of these are available online, e.g., in Casetext (http://www.casetext.com) and Casemine (http://www.casemine.com). The judges' opinions provide information about the issues and are essential to understanding how the courts dealt with them.

The second key source is the *New York State Court of Appeals Cases and Briefs on Appeal* held by the New York State Archives in Albany. The records and briefs in this series were submitted to the court of appeals upon appeal of a lower-court judgment. They contain defendants' and appellants' briefs and other materials. As the archives' finding aid for this series notes, "Together, these records document the legal history of a case, often including lower court transcripts, necessary formal applications, arguments for and against legal issues, testimony, and exhibits." Most have not been used by previous researchers.

This book uses multiple newspaper accounts, particularly the *New York Times*. Articles in scholarly and legal journals are another important source.

The Historical Society of the New York Courts (https://history.nycourts.gov) has a wealth of information online, including court histories and biographies of judges of the supreme court, appellate division, and court of appeals. There are also analytical essays on key cases.

Cornell Law School's Legal Information Institute (https://www.law.cornell.edu) has a slogan that "everyone should be able to read and understand the law." It is an invaluable source of information on legal concepts and key cases.

Many articles, books, and reports are available online. The following sources were particularly useful:

Google Books, https://books.google.com/
HathiTrust Digital Library, http://www.hathitrust.org
Internet Archive, https://archive.org
Online Books Page, http://onlinebooks.library.upenn.edu

Many books were also used in this research. The following were particularly important:

Baatz, Simon. *The Girl on the Velvet Swing: Sex, Murder, and Madness at the Dawn of the Twentieth Century*. New York: Little, Brown, 2018.

Baer, Judith A. *The Chains of Protection: The Judicial Response to Women's Labor Legislation*. Westport, CT: Greenwood Press, 1978.

———. *Ironic Freedom: Personal Choice, Public Policy, and the Paradox of Reform*. New York: Palgrave Macmillan, 2013.

Baker, Paul R. *Stanny: The Gilded Life of Stanford White*. New York: Free Press, 1989.

Banner, Stuart. *American Property: A History of How, Why, and What We Own*. Cambridge, MA: Harvard University Press, 2011.

Bass, Herbert J. *"I Am a Democrat": The Political Career of David Bennett Hill*. Syracuse, NY: Syracuse University Press, 1961.

Berfield, Susan. *The Hour of Fate: Theodore Roosevelt, J. P. Morgan, and the Battle to Transform American Capitalism*. New York: Bloomsbury, 2020.

Bergan, Francis. *The History of the New York Court of Appeals, 1847–1932*. New York: Columbia University Press, 1985.

Bergstrom, Randolph E. *Courting Danger: Injury and Law in New York City, 1870–1910*. Ithaca, NY: Cornell University Press, 1992.

Bernstein, David E. *Rehabilitating Lochner: Defending Individual Rights against Progressive Reform*. Chicago: University of Chicago Press, 2011.

Brands, H. W. *T. R.: The Last Romantic*. New York: Basic Books, 1997.

Budiansky, Stephen. *Oliver Wendell Holmes: A Life in War, Law, and Ideas*. New York: W. W. Norton, 2019.

Cardozo, Benjamin N. *The Nature of the Judicial Process*. New Haven, CT: Yale University Press, 1921.

Carter, Robert Allan. *History of the Insanity Defense in New York State*. Albany: New York State Library, 1982.

Chiles, Robert. *The Revolution of '28: Al Smith, American Progressivism, and the Coming of the New Deal*. Ithaca, NY: Cornell University Press, 2018.

Corey, Henry B. *Law without Lawyers: A Compendium of Business and Domestic Law for Popular Use*. New York: A. L. Burt, 1885.

Colgrove, James. *State of Immunity: The Politics of Vaccination in Twentieth-Century America*. Berkeley: University of California Press, 2006.

Cooley, Thomas M. *A Treatise on the Law of Torts; or, The Wrongs Which Arise Independent of Contract* (2nd ed.). Chicago: Callaghan, 1888.

Danelski, David J., and Joseph S. Tulchin, editors. *The Autobiographical Notes of Charles Evans Hughes*. Cambridge, MA: Harvard University Press, 1973.

Davis, Kevin. *The Brain Defense: Murder in Manhattan and the Dawn of Neuroscience in America's Courtrooms*. New York: Penguin Press, 2017.

Dearstyne, Bruce. *The Spirit of New York: Defining Events in the Empire State's History*. Albany: State University of New York Press, 2015.

————. *Railroads and Railroad Regulation in New York State, 1900–1913*. New York: Garland Publishing, 1986.

Democratic National Committee. *The Campaign Text Book of the Democratic Party of the United States, 1904*. New York: Democratic National Committee, 1904.

Eastman, Crystal. *Work-Accidents and the Law*. New York: Russell Sage Foundation, 1910.

Eisenstadt, Peter, editor-in-chief. *The Encyclopedia of New York State*. Syracuse, NY: Syracuse University Press, 2005.

Ellis, David M., James A. Frost, Harold C. Syrett, and Henry J. Carman. *A History of New York State*. Ithaca, NY: Cornell University Press, 1967.

Freund, Ernst. *The Police Power, Public Policy and Constitutional Rights*. Chicago: Callaghan, 1904.

Friedman, Lawrence M. *Crime without Punishment: Aspects of the History of Homicide*. New York: Cambridge University Press, 2018.

————. *A History of American Law* (4th ed.). New York: Oxford University Press, 2019.

Galie, Peter J. *Ordered Liberty: A Constitutional History of New York*. New York: Fordham University Press, 1996.

Gillman, Howard. *The Constitution Besieged: The Rise and Demise of Lochner Era Police Powers Jurisprudence*. Durham, NC: Duke University Press, 1995.

Goldmark, Josephine. *Fatigue and Efficiency: A Study in Industry*. New York: Russell Sage Foundation, 1912.

————. *Impatient Crusader: Florence Kelley's Life Story*. Urbana: University of Illinois Press, 1953.

Golway, Terry. *Machine Made: Tammany Hall and the Creation of Modern American Politics*. New York: Liveright, 2014.

Goodier, Susan, and Karen Pastorello. *Women Will Vote: Winning Suffrage in New York State*. Ithaca, NY: Cornell University Press, 2017.

Gould, Lewis L. *The Presidency of Theodore Roosevelt*. Lawrence: University Press of Kansas, 1991.

Greenwald, Richard. *The Triangle Fire, the Protocols of Peace, and Industrial Democracy in Progressive Era New York*. Philadelphia: Temple University Press, 2005.

Hall, Kermit L., editor. *The Oxford Companion to American Law*. New York: Oxford University Press, 2002.

Hollingsworth, J. Rogers. *The Whirligig of Politics: The Democracy of Cleveland and Bryan*. Chicago: University of Chicago Press, 1963.

Holmes, Oliver Wendell, Jr. *The Common Law*. London: Macmillan, 1882.

Igo, Sarah E. *The Known Citizen: A History of Privacy in Modern America*. Cambridge, MA: Harvard University Press, 2018.

Ivins, William M., and Herbert Delavan Mason. *The Control of Public Utilities in the Form of an Annotation of the Public Services Commissions Law of the*

State of New York and Covering All Important American Cases [. . .]. New York: Baker, Voorhis, 1908.

Jackson, Kenneth T., editor. *The Encyclopedia of New York City* (2nd ed.). New Haven, CT: Yale University Press, 2010.

Karsten, Peter. *Heart versus Head: Judge-Made Law in Nineteenth-Century America.* Chapel Hill: University of North Carolina Press, 1997.

Klein, Milton M., editor. *The Empire State: A History of New York.* Ithaca, NY: Cornell University Press, 2001.

Kolko, Gabriel. *The Triumph of Conservatism: A Reinterpretation of American History, 1900–1916.* New York: Free Press, 1977.

Lake, Jessica. *The Face That Launched a Thousand Lawsuits: The American Women Who Forged a Right to Privacy.* New Haven, CT: Yale University Press, 2016.

Lamoreaux, Naomi R., and William J. Novak, editors. *Corporations and American Democracy.* Cambridge, MA: Harvard University Press, 2017.

Lears. Jackson. *Rebirth of a Nation: The Making of Modern America, 1877–1920.* New York: HarperCollins, 2009.

Lepore, Jill. *These Truths: A History of the United States.* New York: W. W. Norton, 2018.

Lifflander, Matthew L. *The Impeachment of Governor Sulzer: A Story of American Politics.* Albany: State University of New York Press, 2012.

Lincoln, Charles Z. *The Constitutional History of New York, from the Beginning of the Colonial Period to the Year 1905, Showing the Origin, Development, and Judicial Construction of the Constitution.* 5 vols., Rochester, NY: Lawyers Co-operative Publishing, 1906.

Lizzi, Dominick C. *Governor Martin H. Glynn: Forgotten Hero.* Valatie, NY: Valatie Press, 2007.

Lowe, David Garrad. *Stanford White's New York.* New York: Doubleday, 1992.

Loyster, James A. *Vaccination Results in New York State in 1914.* Cazenovia, NY: printed by the author, 1914.

Maeder, Thomas. *Crime and Madness: The Origins and Evolution of the Insanity Defense.* New York: Harper and Row, 1985.

McCormick, Richard L. *From Realignment to Reform: Political Change in New York State, 1893–1910.* Ithaca, NY: Cornell University Press, 1981.

McGerr, Michael. *A Fierce Discontent: The Rise and Fall of the Progressive Movement in America, 1870–1920.* New York: Free Press, 2003.

Mohr, James C. *Doctors and the Law: Medical Jurisprudence in Nineteenth-Century America.* New York: Oxford University Press, 1993.

Morris, Edmund. *Theodore Rex.* New York: Random Books, 2001.

Murphy, Cait. *Scoundrels in Law: The Trials of Howe and Hummel.* New York: Harper Collins, 2010.

Nelson, William E. *The Legalist Reformation: Law, Politics, and Ideology in New York, 1920–1980.* Chapel Hill: University of North Carolina Press, 2001.

Noll, Richard. *American Madness: The Rise and Fall of Dementia Praecox*. Cambridge, MA: Harvard University Press, 2011.

Novkov, Julie. *Constituting Workers, Protecting Women: Gender, Law and Labor in the Progressive Era and the New Deal Years*. Ann Arbor: University of Michigan Press, 2011.

O'Connor, Richard. *Courtroom Warrior: The Combative Career of William Travers Jerome*. New York: Little, Brown, 1963.

Orleck, Annelise. *Common Sense and a Little Fire: Women and Working-Class Politics in the United States, 1900–1965*. Chapel Hill: University of North Carolina Press, 1995.

Posner, Richard A. *How Judges Think*. Cambridge, MA: Harvard University Press, 2010.

Putnam, Robert D. *The Upswing: How America Came Together a Century Ago and How We Can Do It Again*, with Shaylyn Romney Garrett. New York: Simon and Schuster, 2020.

Rehnquist, William H. *The Supreme Court: How It Was, How It Is*. New York: William Morrow, 1987.

Reitano, Joanne. *New York State: Peoples, Places and Priorities: A Concise History with Sources*. New York: Routledge, 2015.

Roosevelt, Theodore. *The Autobiography of Theodore Roosevelt*. New York: Scribner's, 1913.

Schurman, Jacob Gould, editor. *Addresses and Papers of Charles Evans Hughes, Governor of New York, 1906–1908*. New York: G. P. Putman's Sons, 1908.

———. *Addresses and Papers of Charles Evans Hughes, 1906–1916*. New York: G. P. Putnam's Sons, 1916.

Schwartz, Bernard. *A History of the Supreme Court*. New York: Oxford University Press, 1993.

Solomon, Burt. *FDR v. Constitution: The Court-Packing Fight and the Triumph of Democracy*. New York: Walker, 2009.

Southwick, Leslie H. *Presidential Also-Rans and Running Mates, 1788 through 1996*. Jefferson, NC: McFarland Publishing, 1998.

Stewart, Ted. *Supreme Power: Seven Pivotal Supreme Court Decisions That Had a Major Impact on America*. Salt Lake City: Shadow Mountain Publishing, 2017.

Urofsky, Melvin I. *Louis D. Brandeis: A Life*. New York: Pantheon Books, 2009.

Uruburu, Paula. *American Eve: Evelyn Nesbit, Stanford White, the Birth of the "It" Girl, and the Crime of the Century*. New York: Riverhead Books, 2008.

Van Kleeck, Mary. *Women in the Bookbinding Trade*. New York: Survey Associates, 1913.

Vinocour, Susan. *Nobody's Child: A Tragedy, a Trial, and a History of the Insanity Defense*. New York: W. W. Norton, 2020.

Wallace, Mike. *Greater Gotham: A History of New York City from 1898 to 1919*. New York: Oxford University Press, 2017.

Weinstein, James. *The Corporate Ideal in the Liberal State, 1900–1918*. Boston: Beacon Press, 1968.

Wesser, Robert F. *Charles Evans Hughes: Politics and Reform in New York, 1905–1910*. Ithaca, NY: Cornell University Press, 1967.

———. *A Response to Progressivism: The Democratic Party and New York Politics, 1902–1918*. New York: New York University Press, 1986.

White, G. Edward. *Law in American History, Volume II: From Reconstruction through the 1920s*. New York: Oxford University Press, 2016.

Willrich, Michael. *Pox: An American History*. New York: Penguin Press, 2011.

Winkler, Adam. *We the Corporations: How American Businesses Won Their Civil Rights*. New York: Liveright, 2018.

Woloch, Nancy. *A Class by Herself: Protective Laws for Women Workers, 1890s–1990s*. Princeton, NJ: Princeton University Press, 2015.

Yellowitz, Irwin. *Labor and the Progressive Movement in New York State, 1897–1916*. Ithaca, NY: Cornell University Press, 1965.

INDEX

Page numbers followed by *i* indicate illustrations.

Peckham, Rufus W., Jr, 55*i*, 18, 39, 56, 63, 66–73
People ex rel Nechamccus v. Warden, 106, 186, 189
People v. Adirondack Railway Company, 106–7
People v. Arensberg, 106
People v. Budd, 149
People v. Charles Schweinler Press, 199–211
People v. Gillson, 106
People v. Havnor, 19, 106
People v. Klinck Packing Company, 27
People v. Lochner, 24, 55–56, 68–69, 78–79, 107, 182–91, 208
People v. Marx, 18, 106
People v. Williams, 29, 176–93, 198–210, 227
Personal injury. *See* Worker compensation
Pitney, Mahlon, 251–52
The Police Power: Public Policy and Constitutional Rights (Freund), 100, 187
Pound, Cuthbert, 16, 20–22, 29–31, 220, 258
Pound, Roscoe, 20, 41, 155
Privacy: courts and, 37–39, 12–23; concept of, 44–45; freedom of speech, 43, 51; law and, 39–40; politics and, 52–53; right to, 40–41, 43–52; social changes and, 36–38, 48–49, 113
PSC. *See* Public Service Commission (PSC)
Public health, 192, 209–10, 232; legislature and, 102–5, 110–13; medical breakthrough and, 96–100; public policy and, 17–18, 26–27, 96–100; schools and, 100–7. *See also* Smallpox vaccinations, state responsibility

Public Service Commission (PSC), 138; courts and, 143–55, 165–73, 257; laws and, 145–51, 158–61
Pulitzer, Joseph, 38, 88

Queens, NY, 102–3, 150, 158

Reagan v. Farmers' Loan and Trust, 150
Rehnquist, William, 56, 72
Ritchie v. People of the State of Illinois, 180
"Right to Privacy," 40–41, 43–52
Roberson, Abigail, 29, 35–49, 64. *See also* Privacy
Roberson v. Rochester Folding Box Company and the Franklin Mills Company, 29, 36, 39
Roberts, Owen, 71
Roosevelt, Franklin, 70–72
Roosevelt, Theodore, 2, 29, 53, 65, 69–70, 76–83, 87–92, 160, 236
Russell Sage Foundation, 197, 215

Saratoga Gas and Electric Company, 137*i*, 142–54
Schuyler v. Curtis, 43
Schweinler, Charles, 199–211
Sherman Anti-Trust Act, 66
Sherman, Philemon Tecumseh, 178–81, 190–93
Sickles, Daniel, 119, 134
Smallpox vaccinations, 95*i*; courts and, 102–7; legislature and, 110–14; *Matter of Viemeister,* 102–10, 113–14; vaccinations and schools, 96–100
Smith, Alfred E., 14, 90, 197, 240
South Buffalo Railway Company, 29, 221–23, 225–33
Sperry & Hutchinson Company, 51–52
Stanchfield, John B., 129–33, 146, 154
Standard Oil, 89

State Board of Railroad
    Commissioners, 139, 149, 152, 160
Sulzer, William, 91–92, 110, 172,
    240–41, 245

Thaw, Harry K., 115*i*; appeals, 127–
    29; crime, 115–16; escape, 127–29;
    insanity defense; release, 129–34;
    temporary insanity, 124–27; trials,
    117–23, 129–36
A Treatise on the Law of Torts
    (Cooley), 40
Triangle Shirtwaist Factory Fire, 69,
    197, 199, 233, 239–40, 242, 245
Truax v. Raich, 252
Twain, Mark, 117–18

Unions, 28, 57, 60, 66, 69, 78, 93, 177,
    192, 196–98, 215, 219, 224, 239
U. S. Supreme Court, 16, 24–25,
    29–30, 255; *People v. Lochner*;
    privacy, 52; Public Service
    Commission and, 143–55, 165–66,
    252; rulings, 20–21, 180–83, 186,
    189. 192, 197, 204; vaccinations
    and, 108–14. See also *Lochner v.
    New York*; Women workers; Worker
    compensation

Vaccinations, 95*i. See also* Smallpox
    vaccinations
Van Kleeck, Mary, 175*i*, 197, 202, 206
Vann, Irving, 19, 25, 64, 105–9
Viemeister, Edmund C., 102–10,
    113–14
*Village of Saratoga Springs v. Saratoga
    Gas, etc. Co*, 142–54

Wages, 70, 100, 176, 180–81, 187–88,
    196, 242

Warren, Samuel D., 40–47
Werner, William, 24, 228–32, 248
West Coast Hotel Co. v. Parrish, 72
Wagner, Robert F., Sr., 14, 197, 207,
    240
Wainwright Commission, 217–23,
    226, 229–31, 251
Wainwright, Mayhew, 216, 236,
    244–46
White, Stanford, 116, 132
Whitman, Charles, 110, 199–201,
    205–7, 239, 245, 256
Williams Printing Company, 29,
    176–93, 198–210, 227
Women in Bookbinding Trade (Van
    Kleeck), 197
Women's Trade Union League, 196–
    98
Women workers: courts and, 181–93;
    discrimination and, 178–8; night
    work and, 78, 175–78; paternalism,
    177–83, 190; labor laws, 176–78
Workers' compensation, 255–57;
    accidents and, 214–15; challenges,
    225–29; claims, 221–23;
    Constitutionality of, 223–25, 236–
    39; courts and; 223–25, 246–50;
    due process and, 230–33, 247–52;
    injuries and, 221–23; laws, 216–21;
    politics and, 239–41; regulations
    and, 241–46; rulings, 229–33; U.S.
    Supreme Court and, 249–53
Workmen's Compensation. *See*
    Workers' compensation
Working hours: courts and, 182–89,
    200–7. See also *Lochner v. New
    York*, regulation of
Wright v. Hart, 24–26, 152, 227

Zucht v. King, 114

ABOUT THE AUTHOR

Bruce W. Dearstyne holds a BA in history from Hartwick College and a PhD in history from Syracuse University. He has taught history at SUNY Albany, SUNY Potsdam, and Russell Sage College.

Dearstyne has written dozens of articles on history, archives, libraries, and related topics. His books include *The Spirit of New York: Defining Events in the Empire State's History* (second edition, 2022); *Railroads and Railroad Regulation in New York State, 1903–1913* (1986); *New York: Yesterday, Today, and Tomorrow* (coauthored, 1990); and *Leading the Historical Enterprise: Strategic Creativity, Planning, and Advocacy for the Digital Age* (2015).

He served on the staff of the Office of State History from 1973 to 1976 and was a program director at the New York State Archives from 1976 to 1997. Dearstyne was associate professor, 1997–2000, and professor, 2000–2005, at the College of Information Studies, University of Maryland, where he still serves as an adjunct professor. He was interim dean of the college from 2001 to 2004 and also directed the university's joint history and library science (HiLS) graduate program from 1997 to 2005. Dearstyne has also written blog articles for *New York History* (now *New York Almanack*) and *History News Network* and opinion essays on history for the "Perspective" section of the Sunday Albany *Times Union*.